STUDY GUIDE

Foundations of Finance: The Logic and Practice of Financial Management

Arthur J. Keown
Virginia Polytechnic Institute and State University

John D. Martin
Baylor University

J. William Petty, II
Baylor University

David F. Scott, Jr.
University of Central Florida

AVP Executive Editor: Mark Pfaltzgraff
Assistant Editor: Mary Kate Murray
Production Editor: Melissa Feimer
Buyer: Michelle Klein

Pearson Prentice Hall[TM] **is a trademark of Pearson Education, Inc.**

10   9   8   7   6   5   4   3   2   1

ISBN-13: 978-0-13-233987-2
ISBN-10:   0-13-233987-0

CONTENTS

PREFACE   v

Chapter 1:   An Introduction to the Foundations of Financial
              Management - The Ties That Bind   1

Chapter 2:   The Financial Markets and Interest Rates   15

Chapter 3:   Understanding Financial Statements and Cash
              Flows   32

Chapter 4:   Evaluating A Firm's Financial Performance   46

Chapter 5:   The Time Value of Money   59

Chapter 6:   The Meaning and Measurement of Risk and Return   78

Chapter 7:   Valuation and Characteristics of Bonds   87

Chapter 8:   Valuation and Characteristics of Stock   99

Chapter 9:   Capital Budgeting Techniques and Practice   111

              Appendix 9A: Self-Teaching Supplement: Capital
              Budgeting Techniques   122

Chapter 10:   Cash Flows and Other Topics in Capital Budgeting   156

Chapter 11:   The Cost of Capital   166

Chapter 12:   Determining the Financial Mix   180

Chapter 13:   Dividend Policy and Internal Financing   208

Chapter 14:   Financial Forecasting, Planning, and Budgeting   227

Chapter 15:   Introduction to Working-Capital Management   235

Chapter 16:   Current Asset Management   250

Chapter 17:   International Business Finance   277

Supplementary Materials

Answers to Self Tests   292

Compound Sum and Present Value Interest Factors

    Computing Interest Factors Using a Financial Calculator   299

    Table Values   301

PREFACE

The objective of this *Study Guide* is to provide a student-oriented supplement to *Foundations of Finance*. There are several ways in which we have attempted to accomplish that end, these being:

1. <u>A condensation of each chapter in the form of a detailed sentence outline</u>. This overview of the key points of the chapter can serve both as a preview and quick survey of the chapter content and as a review.

2. <u>Problems (with detailed solutions) and self tests which can be used to aid in the preparation of outside assignments and in studying for examinations</u>. The problems were keyed to the end-of-chapter problems in the text in order to provide direct and meaningful student aid. Also, both multiple-choice and true-false questions are used to provide a self test over the descriptive chapter material.

3. <u>A tutorial on capital budgeting</u>. The tutorial helps the student work through this important topic on an individual basis at his or her own pace.

4. In addition to the tables giving compound sum and present value interest factors, we have tables showing how to compute the interest factors using a financial calculator.

The foregoing material provides what we believe is a valuable learning tool for the student of financial management. Best wishes in your study of finance.

CHAPTER 1

An Introduction to the Foundations of Financial Management—The Ties That Bind

Orientation: This chapter lays a foundation for what will follow. First, it focuses on the goal of the firm, followed by a review of the legal forms of business organization, and a discussion of the tax implications relating to financial decisions. Ten Principles that form the foundations of financial management then follow.

I. Goal of the firm

    A.   In this book, we will designate maximization of shareholder wealth, by which we mean maximization of the total market value of the firm's common stock, to be the goal of the firm. To understand this goal and its inclusive nature, it is first necessary to understand the difficulties involved with the frequently suggested goal of profit maximization.

    B.   While the goal of profit maximization stresses the efficient use of capital resources, it assumes away many of the complexities of the real world and for this reason is unacceptable.

        1.   One of the major criticisms of profit maximization is that it assumes away uncertainty of returns. That is, projects are compared by examining their expected values or weighted average profit.

        2.   Profit maximization is also criticized because it assumes away timing differences of returns.

    C.   Profit maximization is unacceptable, and a more realistic goal is needed.

II.   Maximization of shareholder wealth

    A.   We have chosen the goal of shareholder wealth maximization because the effects of all financial decisions are included in this goal.

    B.   In order to employ this goal, we need not consider every price change to be a market interpretation of the worth of our decisions. What we do focus on is the effect that our decision *should* have on the stock price if everything were held constant.

    C.   The agency problem is a result of the separation between the decision makers and the owners of the firm. As a result, managers may make decisions that are not in line with the goal of maximization of shareholder wealth.

III.   Legal forms of business organization

    A.   The significance of different legal forms

        1.   The predominant form of business organization in the United States in pure numbers is the sole proprietorship.

    B.   Sole proprietorship: A business owned by a single person and that has a minimum amount of legal structure.

        1.   Advantages

            a.   Easily established with few complications

            b.   Minimal organizational costs

            c.   Does not have to share profits or control with others

        2.   Disadvantages

            a.   Unlimited liability for the owner

            b.   Owner must absorb all losses

            c.   Equity capital limited to the owner's personal investment

            d.   Business terminates immediately upon death of owner

C. Partnership: An association of two or more individuals coming together as co-owners to operate a business for profit.

1. Two types of partnerships

    a. General partnership: Relationship between partners is dictated by the partnership agreement.

        (1) Advantages

            (a) Minimal organizational requirements
            (b) Negligible government regulations

        (2) Disadvantages

            (a) All partners have unlimited liability
            (b) Difficulty of raising large amounts of capital
            (c) Partnership dissolved by the death or withdrawal of general partner

    b. Limited partnership

        (1) Advantages

            (a) For the limited partners, liability limited to the amount of capital invested in the company
            (b) Withdrawal or death of a limited partner does not affect continuity of the business
            (c) Stronger inducement in raising capital

        (2) Disadvantages

            (a) There must be at least one general partner who has unlimited liability in the partnership.
            (b) Names of limited partners may not appear in the name of the firm.
            (c) Limited partners may not participate in the management of the business.
            (d) More expensive to organize than general partnership, as a written agreement is mandatory.

D. The corporation: An impersonal legal entity having the power to purchase, sell, and own assets and to incur liabilities while existing separately and apart from its owners.

1. Ownership is evidenced by shares of stock.

2. Advantages

    a. Limited liability of owners

    b. Ease of transferability of ownership, i.e., by the sale of one's shares of stock

    c. The death of an owner does not result in the discontinuity of the firm's life

    d. Ability to raise large amounts of capital is increased

3. Disadvantages

    a. Most difficult and expensive form of business to establish

    b. Control of corporation not guaranteed by partial ownership of stock

    c. Corporations also suffer from a double taxation on dividend. The firm first pays taxes on the income it earns, after taxes have been paid on this income it is returned to investors in the form of dividends. The investor then pays personal taxes on that dividend income.

4. S-Type Corporations and Limited Liability Companies (LLC)

    a. The S-type corporation provides limited liability while allowing the business owners to be taxed as if they were a partnership – that is, distributions back to the owners are not taxed twice as is the case with dividends in the corporate form.

    b. The limited liability company (LLC) is a cross between a partnership and a corporation. The LLC retains limited liability for its owners, but runs and is taxed like a partnership.

4

IV. Federal income taxation

    A.   Objectives of federal income taxation

        1.   Provide government revenues

        2.   Achieve socially desirable goals

        3.   Stabilize the economy

    B.   Income taxes for sole proprietorship

        1.   All income and expenses for the business are reported on the owner's personal income tax forms.

        2.   Taxation of the business income is the same as for the owner's personal income.

    C.   Income taxes for partnerships

        1.   Partnership tax return reports every transaction that has a tax consequence and allocates the transactions as specified by the partnership agreement.

        2.   The individual partners report their portions of the partnership income within their personal tax returns.

    D.   Income taxes for corporations

        1.   A tax return must be filed and the resulting taxes paid by the corporation.

        2.   Taxable income is basically determined as income less allowable exclusions and tax-deductible expenses.

        3.   At minimum, seventy percent of any dividends received from another corporation are tax-exempt.

        4.   Dividends paid by the corporation to its stockholders are not tax deductible.

5.   Corporate rate structure:

15%	$0	-	$50,000
25%	$50,001	-	$75,000
34%	$75,001	-	$10,000,000
35%	over		$10,000,000

There is an additional surtax of 5 percent for income between $100,000 and $335,000.

There is also an additional surtax of 3 percent on income between $15 million and $18.3 million.

6.   It may be that some of a firm's income originates in a foreign country. If so, the tax rates, and the method of taxing the firm, frequently vary. The financial manager would obviously want to minimize the firm's taxes by reporting as much income as possible in the low tax-rate countries and as little as possible in the high tax-rate countries. Of course, other factors, such as political risk, may discourage your efforts to minimize taxes across national borders.

7.   Depreciation

     a.   There are three basic depreciation methods that can be used.

         (1)   Straight-line
         (2)   Double-declining balance
         (3)   Accelerated Cost Recovery System (ACRS)

8.   Net operating loss: If a corporation has an operating loss in any year, the loss may be applied against the profits in the 2 prior years. If the loss has not been completely absorbed by the profits in these years, the loss may be carried forward to each of the 20 following years.

9.   If after deducting all capital gains and capital losses, the company has a net capital loss. Such losses may be carried back for three years and forward for five years to offset any capital gains occurring during these periods.

E. Implications of taxes in financial decision making

    1. Taxes and capital investment decisions

        a. When a plant or equipment acquisition is being considered, the returns from the investment should be measured on an after-tax basis using the marginal, not average, tax rate in the computations.

        b. The depreciation method will have an impact on the timing of taxes.

        c. The estimated salvage value also may have a tax impact; the greater the anticipated salvage value, the less the amount of annual depreciation charges.

    2. Taxes and the firm's capital structure: The tax deductibility of interest payments gives debt financing a definite cost advantage over preferred and common stock financing.

    3. Taxes and corporate dividend policies: The differential tax treatment for the firm's common stockholders might influence the firm's preference between stock price appreciation, i.e., capital gains for the investor, and dividends, i.e., ordinary income for the investor.

V. Ten Principles that form the foundations of financial management.

A. Principle 1: The risk-return tradeoff—we won't take additional risk unless we expect to be compensated with additional return. Almost all financial decisions involve some sort of risk-return tradeoff.

B. Principle 2: The time value of money—a dollar received today is worth more than a dollar received in the future.

C. Principle 3: Cash--not profits--is King. In measuring value, we will use cash flows rather than accounting profits because it is only cash flows that the firm receives and is able to reinvest.

D. Principle 4: Incremental cash flows—it's only what changes that counts. In making business decisions, we will concern our self only with what happens as a result of that decision.

E. Principle 5: The curse of competitive markets—why it's hard to find exceptionally profitable projects. In competitive markets, extremely large profits cannot exist for very long because of competition moving in to exploit those large profits. As a result, profitable projects can be found only if the market is made less competitive, either through product differentiation or by achieving a cost advantage.

F. Principle 6: Efficient capital markets—The markets are quick, and the prices are right.

G. Principle 7: The agency problem—managers won't work for the owners unless it's in their best interest. The agency problem is a result of the separation between the decision makers and the owners of the firm. As a result, managers may make decisions that are not in line with the goal of maximization of shareholder wealth.

H. Principle 8: Taxes bias business decisions.

I. Principle 9: All risk is not equal since, some risk can be diversified away, and some cannot. The process of diversification can reduce risk, and, as a result, measuring a project or an asset's risk is very difficult.

J. Principle 10: Ethical behavior is doing the right thing, and ethical dilemmas are everywhere in finance. Ethical behavior is important in financial management, just as it is important in everything we do. Unfortunately, precisely how we define what is and what is not ethical behavior is sometimes difficult. Nevertheless, we should not give up the quest.

Study Problems

1. A corporation had $145,000 in taxable earnings. What is the tax liability?

SOLUTION

Income		Marginal Tax Rate	Tax Liability
$ 50,000	x	15%	$ 7,500
25,000	x	25%	6,250
25,000	x	34%	8,500
45,000	x	39%	17,550
$145,000		Total tax liability =	$39,800

2. A corporation has earnings before interest and taxes of $86,000, dividend income of $8,000, and interest expenses of $9,000. Also, a contribution to a university was made in the amount of $1,000. What is the corporation's (a) taxable income and (b) tax liability?

SOLUTION

(a)

Operating income		$86,000
Dividend income	$8,000	
Dividend exclusion		
80% x $8,000	(6,400)	
Taxable dividend income		1,600
Interest expense		(9,000)
Contribution		(1,000)
Taxable income		$77,600

(b)

15%	x	$50,000	=	$ 7,500	
25%	x	25,000	=	6,250	
34%	x	2,600	=	884	
		$77,600		$14,634	= Tax liability

3. The M. M. Roscoe Corporation is a regional truck dealer. The firm sells new and used trucks and is actively involved in the parts business. During the most recent year, the company generated sales of $4 million. The combined cost of goods sold and the operating expenses were $3.2 million. Also, $300,000 in interest expense was paid during the year. The firm received $5,000 during the year in dividend income from 1,000 shares of common stock that had been purchased three years previously. However, the stock was sold toward the end of the year for $100 per share; its initial cost was $80 per share. The company also sold land that had been recently purchased and had been held for only four months. The selling price was $55,000; the cost was $45,000. Calculate the corporation's tax liability.

SOLUTION

M.M. Roscoe Corp.—Corporate Income Tax

Sales		$4,000,000
Cost of goods sold + operating expenses		(3,200,000)
Operating profits		$800,000
Dividend income	$5,000	
Less 70% exclusion	(3,500)	1,500
Interest expense		(300,000)
S-T capital gain		
Selling price	$55,000	
Cost	(45,000)	10,000
L-T capital gain		
Selling price		
(#shares)(price/share)		
1,000 x $100	$100,000	
Cost		
(#shares)(price/share)		
1,000 x $80	(80,000)	20,000
Taxable ordinary income		$531,500

Tax liability:

$50,000 x .15 =	$7,500
25,000 x .25 =	6,250
456,500 x .34 =	155,210
Surtax:	
$235,000 x .05 =	11,750
Total taxes due =	$180,710

10

4. The A.K.U. Corporation had sales of $5.5 million this past year. The cost of goods sold was $4.6 million, and operating expenses were $125,000. Dividend income totaled $5,000. The firm sold land for $150,000 that had cost $100,000 five months ago. The firm received $140 per share from the sale of 1,000 shares of stock. The stock was purchased for $100 per share three years ago. Determine the firm's tax liability.

SOLUTION

A.K.U. Corporation—Corporate Income Tax

Sales		$5,500,000
Cost of goods sold		(4,600,000)
Gross profits		$900,000
Operating expenses		(125,000)
Dividend income	$5,000	
Less 70% exclusion	(3,500)	1,500
Ordinary income		$776,500
Plus capital gains		
Land:		
Sales price	$150,000	
Selling price	(100,000)	50,000
Stock:		
Selling price		
(#shares)(price/share)		
1,000 x $140	$140,000	
Cost		
(#shares)(price/share)		
1,000 x $100	(100,000)	40,000
Taxable income		$866,500

Tax liability:

$50,000 x 0.15 =	$7,500
$25,000 x 0.25 =	6,250
$25,000 x 0.34 =	8,500
$235,000 x 0.39 =	91,650
$531,500 x 0.34 =	180,710
$866,500	$294,610

TRUE-FALSE

_____ 1. Profit maximization is considered to be a more appropriate goal than shareholder wealth maximization because it considers the timing of the expected returns of the firm.

_____ 2. Shareholder wealth maximization considers the effects of the riskiness of a prospective earnings stream.

_____ 3. Many businesses are formed as corporations because of the ease of establishment.

_____ 4. Two major criticisms of the profit maximization goal are that it does not deal adequately with the uncertainty and the timing of returns.

_____ 5. The income from a partnership is reported by the partners on their personal tax returns.

_____ 6. Interest and dividend payments made by a corporation are both tax deductible by the paying corporation.

_____ 7. In general, the less risk a firm is willing to assume, the higher the expected return will be from a given course of action.

_____ 8. Ethical considerations are not relevant in the financial management.

_____ 9. Product differentiation helps reduce competition and thereby allows for larger profits.

_____ 10. In order to employ the goal of shareholder wealth maximization, every stock price change should be considered to be a market interpretation of the worth of our financial decisions.

_____ 11. The agency problem is a result of a separation of management and the owners of the firm.

MULTIPLE CHOICE

1. The long-run goal of the firm is to

    a. hold large quantities of cash.
    b. increase sales regularly.
    c. maximize earnings per share.
    d. maximize shareholder wealth.

2. Maximizing shareholder wealth means maximizing the

    a. value of the firm's assets.
    b. value of the firm's cash.
    c. value of the firm's investments.
    d. value of the firm's profits.
    e. market value of the firm's common stock.

3. Advantages of the corporation include:

    a. transferability of ownership.
    b. unlimited liability.
    c. ability of the corporation to raise capital.
    d. double taxation of dividend income.
    e. a and c.
    f. a and b.

4. Disadvantages of the partnership are:

    a. expense of formation.
    b. lack of permanence.
    c. double taxation on income.
    d. unlimited liability.
    e. b and d.
    f. a and d.

5. Profit maximization is not the proper objective of a firm because

    a. it is not as inclusive a goal as the maximization of shareholder wealth.
    b. it does not consider the uncertainty of the return.
    c. it does not consider the timing of the returns.
    d. all of the above.
    e. none of the above.

6. The market price of a share of stock is determined by

 a. the New York Stock Exchange.
 b. the Federal Reserve.
 c. the company's management.
 d. individuals buying and selling the stock.

7. Which of the following forms of business organization is the largest in number?

 a. Corporation
 b. Partnership
 c. Sole proprietorship

8. The agency problem

 a. is associated with insuring the firm.
 b. is no longer important.
 c. invalidates the goal of maximization of shareholder wealth.
 d. is a result of the separation of the decision makers and the owners of the firm.
 e. is all of the above.

CHAPTER 2

The Financial Markets and Interest Rates

Orientation: This chapter considers the market environment in which long-term capital is raised. The underlying rationale for the existence of security markets is presented, investment banking services and procedures are detailed, private placements are discussed, and security market regulation is reviewed. Further discussions cover rates of return over long periods and recent periods, interest rate determinants, and theories of the term structure of interest rates.

I.   Components of the U.S. financial market system

    A.   *Public offerings* can be distinguished from *private placements*.

        1.   The public (financial) market is an impersonal market in which both individual and institutional investors have the opportunity to acquire securities.

            a.   A public offering takes place in the public market.

            b.   The security-issuing firm does not meet (face-to-face) the actual investors in the securities.

        2.   In a private placement of securities, only a limited number of investors have the opportunity to purchase a portion of the issue.

            a.   The market for private placements is more personal than its public counterpart.

            b.   The specific details of the issue may actually be developed on a face-to-face basis among the potential investors and the issuer.

B. Private placements and venture capital.

    1. Private placements can involve issuing both debt and equity, and "venture capitalists" can play an active role in both.

    2. For startup companies or companies in the early stages of business, as well as firms in "turnaround" situations, venture capital is a prime source of funds. The venture capitalist firm will frequently acquire a meaningful dollar state in the startup firm.

C. *Primary markets* can be distinguished from *secondary markets*.

    1. Securities are first offered for sale in a primary market. For example, the sale of a new bond issue, preferred stock issue, or common stock issue takes place in the primary market. These transactions increase the total stock of financial assets in existence in the economy.

    2. Trading in currently existing securities takes place in the secondary market. The total stock of financial assets is unaffected by such transactions.

D. The *money market* can be distinguished from the *capital market*.

    1. The money market consists of the institutions and procedures that provide for transactions in short-term debt instruments which are generally issued by borrowers who have very high credit ratings.

        a. "Short-term" means that the securities traded in the money market have maturity periods of not more than one year.

        b. Equity instruments are not traded in the money market.

        c. Typical examples of money market instruments are (1) U.S. Treasury bills, (2) federal agency securities, (3) bankers' acceptances, (4) negotiable certificates of deposit, and (5) commercial paper.

    2. The capital market consists of the institutions and procedures that provide for transactions in long-term financial instruments. This market encompasses those securities that have maturity periods extending beyond one year.

E. Spot markets can be distinguished from futures markets.

1. Cash markets are where something sells today, fight now, on the spot – in fact, cash markets are often referred to as "spot" markets.

2. Futures markets are where you can set a price to buy or sell something at some future date – in effect, you sign a contract that states what you're buying, how much of it you're buying, at what price you're buying it, and when you will actually make the purchase.

F. *Organized security exchanges* can be distinguished from *over-the-counter markets*.

1. Organized security exchanges are tangible entities whose activities are governed by a set of bylaws. Security exchanges physically occupy space, and financial instruments are traded on such premises.

    a. Major stock exchanges must comply with a strict set of reporting requirements established by the Securities and Exchange Commission (SEC). These exchanges are said to be *registered*.

    b. Organized security exchanges provide several benefits to both corporations and investors. They (1) provide a continuous market, (2) establish and publicize fair security prices, and (3) help businesses raise new financial capital.

    c. A corporation must take steps to have its securities *listed* on an exchange in order to directly receive the benefits noted above. Listing criteria differ from exchange to exchange.

2. Over-the-counter markets include all security markets except the organized exchanges. The money market is a prominent example. Most corporate bonds are traded over the counter.

II. Using an investment banker

A. The investment banker is a financial specialist who acts as an intermediary in the selling of securities. He or she works for an investment banking firm (house).

B. Three basic functions are provided by the investment banker:

1. He or she assumes the risk of selling a new security issue at a satisfactory (profitable) price. This is called *underwriting*. Typically, the investment banking house, along with the underwriting syndicate, actually buys the new issue from the corporation that is raising funds. The syndicate (group of investment banking firms) then sells the issue to the investing public at a higher price (hopefully) than it paid for it.

2. He or she provides for the *distribution* of the securities to the investing public.

3. He or she *advises* firms on the details of selling securities.

C. Several distribution methods are available for placing new securities into the hands of final investors. The investment banker's role is different in each case.

1. In a *negotiated purchase*, the firm in need of funds contacts an investment banker and begins the sequence of steps leading to the final distribution of the securities that will be offered. The price that the investment banker pays for the securities is "negotiated" with the issuing firm.

2. In a *competitive-bid purchase*, the investment banker and underwriting syndicate are selected by an auction process. The syndicate willing to pay the greatest dollar amount per new security to the issuing firm wins the competitive bid. This means that it will underwrite and distribute the issue. In this situation, the price paid to the issuer is not negotiated instead, it is determined by a sealed-bid process much on the order of construction bids.

3. In a *commission* (or *best-efforts*) offering, the investment banker does not act as an underwriter. He or she attempts to sell the issue in return for a fixed commission on each security that is actually sold. Unsold securities are simply returned to the firm hoping to raise funds.

4. In a *privileged subscription*, the new issue is not offered to the investing public. It is sold to a definite and limited group of investors. Current stockholders are often the privileged group.

5. In a <u>Dutch auction,</u> investors first put in bids giving the number of shares they would like to buy and the price they are willing to pay for them. Once the bids are in, they are ranked, and the selling price is calculated as the highest price that allows for all the stock to be sold.

6. In a *direct sale*, the issuing firm sells the securities to the investing public without involving an investment banker in the process. This is not a typical procedure.

D. The negotiated purchase is most likely to be the distribution method used by the private corporation. It consists of several steps.

1. The security-issuing firm selects an investment banker.

2. A series of pre-underwriting conferences takes place. Discussions center on: (1) the amount of capital to be raised; (2) the possible receptiveness of the capital markets to a specific mode of financing; and (3) the proposed use of the new funds. These conferences are consummated by the signing of a *tentative underwriting agreement*. The approximate price to be paid for each security is identified in this agreement.

3. An underwriting syndicate is formed. The syndicate is a temporary association of investment bankers formed to purchase the security issue from the corporation. The syndicate's objective is to resell the issue at a profit.

4. Most new public issues must be registered with the SEC before they can be sold to final investors. This involves filing a lengthy technical document called a *registration statement* with the SEC. This document aims to disclose relevant facts about the issuing

firm and the related security to potential investors. Another document, the *prospectus*, is also filed with the SEC for examination. It is a shortened version of the official registration statement. Once both documents are approved, the prospectus becomes the official advertising vehicle for the security offering.

5. A selling group is formed to distribute the new securities to final investors. Securities dealers who are part of the selling group are permitted to purchase a portion of the new issue at a price to the public. A *selling-group agreement* binds the syndicate and the members of the selling group.

6. A due-diligence meeting is held to finalize all details prior to taking the offering to the public. The price at which the issuing firm will sell the new securities to the syndicate is settled. Usually, the offering is made to the public on the day after this meeting.

7. The syndicate manager (from the investment banking house that generated the business) is permitted to mitigate downward price movements in the secondary market for the subject offering. This is accomplished by the syndicate managers placing buy orders for the security at the agreed-upon public offering price.

8. A contractual agreement among the syndicate members terminates the syndicate. In the most pleasant situations, this agreement is made when the issue is fully subscribed (sold).

III. Private placements

A. Each year, billions of dollars of new securities are privately (directly) placed with final investors. In a private placement, a small number of investors purchases the entire security offering. Most private placements involve debt instruments.

B. Large financial institutions are the major investors in private placements. These include (1) life insurance firms, (2) state and local retirement funds, and (3) private pension funds.

C.   The advantages and disadvantages of private placements as opposed to public offerings must be carefully evaluated by management.

        1.   The advantages include (1) greater speed than a public offering in actually obtaining the needed funds, (2) lower flotation costs than are associated with a public issue, and (3) increased flexibility in the financing contract.

        2.   The disadvantages include (1) higher interest costs than are ordinarily associated with a comparable public issue, (2) the imposition of several restrictive covenants in the financing contract, and (3) the possibility that the security may have to be registered some time in the future at the lender's option.

IV.   Flotation costs

A.   The firm raising long-term capital typically incurs two types of flotation costs: (1) the underwriter's spread and (2) issuing costs. The former is typically the larger.

        1.   The underwriter's spread is the difference between the gross and net proceeds from a specific security issue. This absolute dollar difference is usually expressed as a percent of the gross proceeds.

        2.   Many components comprise issue costs. The two most significant are (1) printing and engraving and (2) legal fees. For comparison purposes, these, too, are usually expressed as a percent of the issue's gross proceeds.

B.   SEC data reveal two relationships about flotation costs.

        1.   Issue costs (as a percent of gross proceeds) for common stock exceed those of preferred stock, which exceed those of bonds.

        2.   Total flotation costs per dollar raised decrease as the dollar size of the security issue increases.

V.   Regulation aimed at making the goal of the firm work

A.   Congress passed in July 2002 the Public Company Accounting Reform and Investor Protection Act. The short name for the act became the <u>Sarbanes-Oxley Act of 2002</u>.

1. The Sarbanes-Oxley Act was passed as the result of a large series of corporate indiscretions.

2. The act holds corporate advisors (like accountants, lawyers, company officers, and boards of directors) who have access to or influence company decisions strictly accountable in a legal sense for any instances of misconduct.

VI. An examination of observed rates of return in the financial markets yields the following historical findings:

   A. The average inflation rate (the "inflation-risk premium") has been about 3.2 percent annually.

   B. The default-risk premium for long-term corporate bonds over long-term government bonds has between about 1.0 percent annually.

   C. Large common stocks earned 5.5 percent more than the rate earned on long-term corporate bonds, and small firms earned 5.7 percent more than the average annual return on large firms.

VII. The effects of inflation on rates of return

   A. The real rate of interest is the difference in the nominal rate and the anticipated rate of inflation.

   B. The notion of a real rate of interest can be thought of as the "price for deferring consumption."

   C. Letting the nominal rate of interest be represented by k_{rf}, the anticipated rate of inflation by IRP, and the real rate of interest by k^*, we can express the result by the following equation:

   $$1 + k_{rf} = (1 + k^*)(1 + IRP)$$

   or $\quad k_{rf} = k^* + IRP + (IRP)(k^*)$

   For example, if the real rate, k^*, is 5 percent and the expected inflation rate, IRP, is 4 percent, the nominal rate, k_{rf}, would then be 9.2 percent, computed as follows:

   $$k_{rf} = .05 + .04 + (.05)(.04)$$
   $$= .092 \text{ or } 9.2\%$$

VIII.   The term structure of interest rates

    A.   The relationship between a debt security's rate of return and the length of time until the debt matures is known as the *term structure of interest rates*.

    B.   The term structure reflects observed rates or yields on similar securities, except for the length of time until maturity, at a particular moment in time.

    C.   Three theories have been suggested to explain the term structure of interest rates.

        1.   The *unbiased expectations theory* says that the term structure is determined by an investor's expectations about future interest rates.

        2.   The *liquidity preference theory* suggests that investors require liquidity premiums (addition returns) to compensate them for buying securities which expose them to a greater risk of fluctuating interest rates.

        3.   The *market segmentation theory* is built on the notion that legal restrictions and personal preferences limit investment choices to certain ranges of maturities, and, therefore, affect the rates of return required in each range.

IX.   Multinational firm and Intercountry Risk

    A.   Underdeveloped countries lack effective financial market systems.

    B.   Multinational firms cash to invest in foreign markets will not consider markets in which financial systems or political environments are uncertain or unstable.

Study Problem

1. If the expected inflation rate is 4%, and the real rate of interest is 8%, what is the nominal interest rate?

   SOLUTION

   $$\text{Nominal rate, } k_{rf} = \left(\begin{array}{c}\text{Real}\\\text{rate}\end{array}\right) + \left(\begin{array}{c}\text{Inflation}\\\text{rate}\end{array}\right) + \left(\begin{array}{c}\text{Real}\\\text{rate}\end{array}\right)\left(\begin{array}{c}\text{Inflation}\\\text{rate}\end{array}\right)$$

   $$= .08 + .04 + (.08)(.04)$$
   $$= .1232 = 12.32\%$$

Self Tests

TRUE-FALSE

_____ 1. A share of IBM common stock is a real asset.

_____ 2. Capital formation in underdeveloped countries might be assisted if those countries' financial market systems were more extensively developed.

_____ 3. General Motors is a typical example of a financial intermediary.

_____ 4. The Money Market is housed at 11 Wall Street, New York City.

_____ 5. Common stocks are money market instruments.

_____ 6. Price quotations on organized security exchanges have been facilitated by the existence of NASDAQ.

_____ 7. The cash market is also called the "spot" market.

_____ 8. In a negotiated purchase, the price the investment banker pays the security-issuing firm for the new issue is negotiated between these parties.

_____ 9. The futures market and the spot market are the same.

_____ 10. Life insurance companies are major purchasers of privately placed securities.

_____ 11. Secondary markets reduce the risk of investing in financial claims.

_____ 12. Equity instruments are traded in the money market.

_____ 13. The capital market includes those securities that have maturity periods extending beyond one year.

_____ 14. Trading in currently existing securities takes place in the primary market.

_____ 15. When new funds are being raised in a typical year, corporate equity markets are favored over corporate debt markets, in terms of dollar volume.

_____ 16. The U.S. tax system favors debt as a method of raising capital in comparison to equity instruments.

_____ 17. A life insurance company is an example of a financial intermediary.

_____ 18. "Market Segmentation Theory" refers to the use of debt versus the use of common stock to raise new funds.

_____ 19. Flotation costs for debt generally exceed those of common stock.

_____ 20. In general, the underwriter's spread component of flotation costs exceeds the issuing costs.

_____ 21. Inventories represent a category of financial assets.

_____ 22. Financial markets allocate savings in the economy to demanders of those funds.

_____ 23. Financial intermediaries issue their own financial claims called direct securities, and invest the money obtained in indirect securities, the financial claims of other economic units.

_____ 24. The U.S. government is the largest savings-surplus sector in the economy.

_____ 25. Financial markets provide a mechanism to facilitate the transfer of savings from those economic units that have a savings surplus to those that have a savings deficit.

_____ 26. The New York Stock Exchange, American Stock Exchange, and Midwest Stock Exchange are the only three <u>national</u> exchanges in the U.S.

_____ 27. There is an inverse relationship between the total flotation cost per dollar of funds raised and the amount of the security issue.

_____ 28. The primary objective of the Securities Act of 1933 is to provide potential investors with accurate and truthful disclosure about the firm and the new securities being sold.

_____ 29. Long-term corporate bonds are more risky than common stocks from the investor's point of view.

MULTIPLE CHOICE

1. Which of the following is *not* a benefit provided by the existence of organized security exchanges?

   a. A continuous market
   b. Helping business raise new capital
   c. Keeping long-term bond prices below 8 percent
   d. Establishing and publicizing fair security prices

2. What is it called when an investment banker agrees to sell only as many securities as he or she can at an established price?

   a. A private placement
   b. A direct placement
   c. A privileged subscription
   d. A best-efforts agreement
   e. An upset agreement

3. Which of the following security distribution methods is least profitable to the investment banker?

   a. Negotiated purchase
   b. Competitive-bid purchase
   c. Commission basis
   d. Privileged subscription
   e. Direct sale

4. A prospectus resembles most closely

   a. a registration statement.
   b. a red herring.
   c. a selling group agreement.
   d. a letter of credit.

5. The purpose of financial markets is to

   a. lower bond yields.
   b. allocate savings efficiently.
   c. raise stock prices.
   d. employ stock brokers.

6. The maturity boundary dividing the U.S. money and capital markets is

   a. an arbitrary classification system.
   b. set by the Federal Reserve Board.
   c. periodically reviewed and altered by the SEC.
   d. determined by the U.S. Treasury.

7. Flotation costs are highest on

   a. bonds.
   b. preferred stock.
   c. common stock.

8. The spot market is
   a. the same as the futures market.
   b. the same as the underwriting market.
   c. the same as the venture capital market.
   d. the same as the cash market.

9. Which of the following methods for the distribution of securities bypasses the use of an investment banker?

   a. Negotiated purchase
   b. Competitive-bid purchase
   c. Direct sales
   d. Best-efforts basis
   e. Privileged subscriptions

10. The difference between the gross and net proceeds from a given security issue expressed as a percent of the gross proceeds is known as

    a.   issue costs.
    b.   flotation costs.
    c.   underwriter's spread.
    d.   legal fees.

11. Which of the following is generally <u>not</u> an advantage of private placements?

    a.   Speed
    b.   Reduced flotation costs
    c.   Financing flexibility
    d.   Interest costs

12. Which of the following is <u>not</u> an example of a money market instrument?

    a.   U.S. Treasury bills
    b.   Common stock
    c.   Federal agency securities
    d.   Commercial paper

13. An agreement which obligates the investment banker to underwrite securities that are not accepted by privileged investors is known as a

    a.   privileged subscription.
    b.   standby agreement.
    c.   negotiated purchase.
    d.   best-efforts basis.

14. _____ is the interest rate paid on debt securities without adjusting for loss in purchasing power.

    a.   real risk-free interest rate
    b.   risk-free rate
    c.   nominal rate
    d.   risk premium
    e.   inflation rate

15. Insurance companies invest in the "long-end" of the securities market. In which of the following instruments would an insurance company be <u>least</u> likely to invest <u>most</u> of its funds in?

    a. Mortgages
    b. Corporate bonds
    c. Commercial paper
    d. Corporate stocks

16. Which of the following is/are NYSE listing requirements?

    a. Profitability
    b. Market value
    c. Public ownership
    d. All of the above
    e. None of the above

17. The indirect method of transferring savings in which securities are not transformed, but passed through to other purchasers, most frequently involves

    a. an established relationship between buyer and issuer.
    b. a finance company.
    c. a commercial bank.
    d. an investment banker.
    e. all of the above.

18. Which of the following does not describe an organized security exchange?

    a. It occupies physical space as opposed to being strictly communication links among traders.
    b. It is strictly regional in scope.
    c. It is regulated by the Securities and Exchange Commission.
    d. Its trades are conducted strictly by exchange members.

19. A seasoned equity offering or SEO is
    a. illegal in Canada.
    b. is also called an inverse IPO.
    c. is the same as an IPO.
    d. the sale of additional shares by a company whose shares are already publicly traded.

20. Primary markets are distinguished from secondary markets by the fact that

    a.   primary markets sell securities for corporations with assets over $2 million, while secondary markets sell securities for corporations with assets less than $2 million.

    b.   primary markets are more developed than the secondary markets.

    c.   primary markets trade new securities issues while secondary markets trade existing securities.

    d.   primary markets enjoy higher trading volume than the secondary markets.

21. How many registered stock exchanges are there in the United States?

    a.   4
    b.   5
    c.   more than 5
    d.   none

22. What is the correct <u>sequence</u> of steps for the negotiated purchase distribution method? The key steps follow each Roman numeral, below.

    I.   File a registration statement and prospectus with SEC.
    II.   Hold a due diligence meeting.
    III.   Form an underwriting syndicate.
    IV.   Form a contractual agreement among syndicate members to terminate the syndicate.
    V.   Form a selling group to distribute new securities.

    a.   I, II, III, IV, V
    b.   II, III, I, V, IV
    c.   III, I, V, II, IV
    d.   IV, I, II, III, V

23. Under a Dutch Auction

    a.   you know ahead of time how many shares you will get.
    b.   you know ahead of time what price you will get the shares at.
    c.   the final price set that fills the quota of shares to sell becomes the offering price to all successful bidders.
    d.   the shares must be sold in Holland.

24. In terms of risk, it is correct to say:

    a. Government securities are less risky than common stocks, but more risky than corporate bonds.
    b. Corporate bonds are less risky than common stocks.
    c. Long-term government securities are less risky than short-term government securities.
    d. Common stocks of large companies are more risky than the common stocks of small firms.

25. The term structure of interest rates refers to

    a. the different risk levels of interest rates.
    b. the different interest rates of securities with the same maturity dates.
    c. the different interest rates of securities with the same risk but with different maturity dates.
    d. the terms of agreement associated with a bond's interest payments.

CHAPTER 3

Understanding Financial Statements and Cash Flows

Orientation: In this chapter, we review the contents and meaning of a firm's income statement and balance sheet. We also look very carefully at how to compute a firm's cash flows from a finance perspective, rather than how the accountants calculate a company's cash flows. We will teach you how to compute what we call "free cash flows" and "financing cash flows".

I.   Basic Financial Statements

    A.   The Income Statement

        1.   The income statement reports the results from operating the business for a period of time, such as a year.

        2.   It is helpful to think of the income statement as comprising four types of activities:

            a.   Selling the product

            b.   The cost of producing or acquiring the goods or services sold

            c.   The expenses incurred in marketing and distributing the product or service to the customer, along with administrative operating expenses

            d.   The financing costs of doing business, for example, interest paid to creditors and dividend payments to the preferred stockholders

3.   An example of an income statement is provided in the *Foundations* textbook in Table 3-1 for the Starbucks Corporation.

B.   The Balance Sheet

    1.   The balance sheet provides a snapshot of the firm's financial position at a specific point in time, presenting its asset holdings, liabilities, and owner-supplied capital.

        a.   Assets represent the resources owned by the firm

            (1)   Current assets—consisting primarily of cash, marketable securities, accounts receivable, inventories, and prepaid expenses

            (2)   Fixed or long-term assets—comprising equipment, buildings, and land

            (3)   Other assets—all assets not otherwise included in the firm's current assets or fixed assets, such as patents, long-term investments in securities, and goodwill

        b.   The liabilities and owners' equity indicate how those resources are financed.

            (1)   The debt consists of such sources as credit extended from suppliers or a loan from a bank.

            (2)   The equity includes the stockholders' investment in the firm (common stock) and the cumulative profits retained in the business up to the date of the balance sheet (retained earnings).

    2.   The balance sheet is not intended to represent the current market value of the company, but rather reports the historical transactions recorded at their cost.

    3.   Balance sheets for the Starbucks Corporation are presented in the *Foundations* textbook in Table 3-2.

C.   Measuring Cash Flows

1.   While an income statement measures a company's profits, profits are not the same as cash flows; profits are calculated on an *accrual* basis rather than a *cash* basis.

2.   In measuring cash flows, we could use the conventional accountant's presentation called a *statement of cash flows*. However, we are more interested in considering cash flows from the perspective of the firm's shareholders and its investors, rather than from an accounting view. We will instead measure the cash flow that is free and available to be distributed to the firm's investors, both debt and equity investors or, what we will call *free cash flows*. We will then calculate the *financing cash flows*, which indicate exactly how the money was distributed or received from investors.

3.   The cash flows that are generated through a firm's operations less any investments in assets—free cash flows--will always equal its cash flows paid to—or received by--the company's investors—financing cash flows, where "investors" include both long-term creditors and stockholders).

4.   Free Cash Flows:

a.   A firm's *free cash flows* are the after-tax cash flows generated from operations less the firm's investments in assets. That is, a firm's free cash flows for a given period is equal to:

After-tax cash flow from operations
less
the investment in operating working capital for the period and
less
the investment in fixed assets and other long-term assets during the period.

b. After-tax cash flows from operations are calculated as follows:

Operating income
+   depreciation
-   income taxes
=   after-tax cash flows from operations

c. The increase or decrease in operating working capital is equal to the change in current assets (also called *gross working capital*) – the change in *non interest bearing* current liabilities.[i]

d. The change in *gross* fixed assets (and not *net* fixed assets) and any other assets that are on the balance sheet not already considered.

5. Financing Cash Flows

a. A firm's ***financing cash flows*** are equal to:

Interest and dividend payments to investors

+	increase in long-term debt
or	
-	decrease in debt

+	increase in equity
or	
-	decrease in equity

---

[i] Non interest bearing current liabilities are short-term liabilities that do not require the firm to pay interest for the use of the money, which primarily includes accounts payables and accrued operating expenses. Interest bearing current liabilities are short-term liabilities where the firm is charged interest, such as short-term loans from a bank—frequently shown as short-term notes.

6. To conclude, financing cash flows, if negative, are simply the net cash flows paid to the firm's investors, or if positive, the cash flows received from investors. In the second situation, the investors are putting money into the firm because the firm's free cash flows are negative, thereby requiring an infusion of capital by the investors.

Study Problems

1. Prepare a balance sheet for the A. R. Peterson Mfg. Co. from the scrambled list of items below. The owner's equity balance is not given but it can be determined as a balancing figure.

Building	$49,100	Office equipment	4,100
Accounts receivable	21,600	Land	22,000
Machinery	2,950	Notes payable	14,000
Cash	9,200	Owner's equity	
Accounts payable	16,500		

SOLUTION

A. R. Peterson Mfg. Co.
Balance Sheet

Cash	$ 9,200	Accounts payable	16,500
Accounts receivable	21,600	Notes payable	14,000
Land	22,000	Owner's equity	78,450
Building	49,100		
Machinery	2,950		
Office equipment	4,100	Total liabilities	
Total assets	$108,950	& owner's equity	$108,950

2. By studying the successive balance sheets for AMP, Inc. found below, determine what transactions have occurred. Prepare a list of the transactions and the corresponding balance-sheet dates. For example, on March 31, 2008, the firm's owners invested $200,000 in AMP, Inc. and started the business.

(a)

AMP, Inc.
Balance Sheet
March 31, 2008

Assets		Owner's Equity	
Cash	$200,000	Owner's equity	$200,000

(b)

AMP, Inc.
Balance Sheet
April 2, 2008

Assets		Owner's Equity	
Cash	$100,000	Owner's equity	$200,000
Land	100,000		
	$200,000		$200,000

(c)

AMP, Inc.
Balance Sheet
April 15, 2008

Assets		Owner's Equity	
Cash	$ 50,000	Owner's equity	$200,000
Building	50,000		
Land	100,000		
	$200,000		$200,000

(d)

AMP, Inc.
Balance Sheet
May 2, 2008

Assets		Liabilities & Owner's Equity	
Cash	$50,000	Accounts payable	$25,000
Inventories	25,000	Owner's equity	200,000
Building	50,000		
Land	100,000		
	$225,000		$225,000

(e)

AMP, Inc.
Balance Sheet
May 15, 2008

Assets		Liabilities & Owner's Equity	
Cash	$60,000	Accounts payable	$25,000
Inventories	25,000	Notes payable	25,000
Equipment	15,000	Owner's equity	200,000
Building	50,000		
Land	100,000		
	$250,000		$250,000

SOLUTION

(a) On March 31, 2008, the firm's owners invested $200,000 in AMP, Inc. and started the business.

(b) On April 2, 2008, $100,000 of the original investment by the owners was used to acquire land.

(c) On April 15, 2008, $50,000 of the original cash was used to acquire a building.

(d) On May 2, 2008, $25,000 of inventory was purchased on account (credit).

(e) On May 15, 2008, a $25,000 loan was obtained and $15,000 of the proceeds used to purchase equipment.

3. Burruss Inc. had the following condensed balance sheet at the end of operation for 2007:

Burruss, Inc.
Balance Sheet
December 31, 2007

Cash	$ 24,000	Accounts payable	$ 20,000
Accounts receivable	20,000	Short-term notes	10,000
Inventory	31,000	Long-term debt	73,000
Total current assets	$ 75,000	Common stock	150,000
Fixed assets(net)	125,000	Retained earnings	49,000
Land	62,000		
Investments	10,000		
	$302,000		$302,000

In the following year, 2008, the below activities occurred:

(a) Burruss, Inc. made investments of $ 10,000.

(b) Additional land for a plant expansion was purchased for $12,000.

(c) Long-term debt was reduced in the amount of $20,000.

(d) An additional $ 20,000 in common stock was issued.

(e) Dividends of $15,000 were paid to stockholders.

(f) Operating income for 2008 was $77,000 after allowing for $18,000 in depreciation.

(g) The firm paid $25,000 in income taxes

(h) Interest expense was $10,000.

(i) A second parcel of land was purchased for $18,000 through the issuance of long-term notes.

(j) Accounts receivable and inventory increased $10,000 and $15,000, respectively, while accounts payable increased $10,000.

(k) Short-term notes remained unchanged.

Required:

(a) Prepare a balance sheet for Burruss, Inc. at December 31, 2008.

(You will be able to determine all the items in the 2008 balance sheet except cash. But since it will be the only item not mentioned, it will simply be the amount that makes total assets equal to total debt and equity.).

(b) Compute the firm's free cash flows and its financing cash flows for 2008.

SOLUTION

Burruss, Inc.

Balance Sheet
December 31, 2008

Cash	$ 62,000	Accounts payable	$ 30,000
Accounts receivable	30,000	Short-term notes	10,000
Inventory	46,000	Total current liabilities	$40,000
Total Current Assets	$138,000	Long-term debt	71,000
Fixed assets (net)	107,000	Common stock	170,000
Land	92,000	Retained earnings	76,000
Investments	20,000		
Total	$357,000		$357,000

Burruss, Inc.
Free Cash Flows
For the Year Ended December 31, 2008

Operating income	$ 77,000
Plus depreciation	18,000
Less income taxes	(25,000)
After-tax cash flow from operations	$ 70,000
Change in current assets	($ 63,000)
Change in accounts payable	10,000
Change in operating working capital	($ 53,000)
Change in fixed assets	-
Change in land	(30,000)
Change in investments	(10,000)
Free cash flows	$ (23,000)

Financing free cash flows:

Interest	($	10,000)
Dividends		(15,000)
Increase in long-term notes		(2,000)
Increase in common stock		20,000
Financing free cash flows	($	7,000)

4. Financial statements are provided below for the Dalton Corporation. Compute the free cash flows and financing free cash flows for 2008.

ASSETS

	12/31/2007	12/31/2008
CURRENT ASSETS		
Cash	$ 19,607	$ 166,594
Accounts Receivable	138,021	186,829
TOTAL CURRENT ASSETS	$ 157,628	$ 353,423
FIXED ASSETS		
Trucks	$ 97,529	$ 124,949
Equipment	94,748	135,833
Accumulated Depreciation	(112,516)	(146,945)
TOTAL FIXED ASSETS	$ 79,760	$ 113,837
TOTAL ASSETS	$ 237,388	$ 467,261

LIABILITIES AND EQUITY

CURRENT LIABILITIES

	12/31/2007	12/31/2008
Accounts payable	$ 12,600	$ 14,300
Short-tern notes	49,810	119,282
Total current liabilities	$ 62,410	$ 133,582
EQUITY:		
Common stock	$ 146,944	$ 146,944
Retained earnings	28,034	186,735
TOTAL EQUITY	$ 174,978	$ 333,679
TOTAL LIABILITIES AND EQUITY	$ 237,388	$ 467,261

		12/31/2008
Sales		$ 1,824,568
Cost of goods sold		$ 649,214
Gross profit		$ 1,175,354
Operating expenses		
Selling, general & admin. expenses		861,816
Depreciation expense		34,429
Operating income		$ 279,109
Interest expense		8,205
Earnings before taxes		$ 270,904
Taxes		105,653
Net income		$ 165,252

SOLUTION

Free cash flows:

Operating income		$ 279,109
Plus depreciation		34,429
Less income taxes		105,653
After-tax cash flows from operations		$ 207,885
Change in current assets	($	195,795)
Change in accounts payable		1,700
Change in operating working capital	($	124,623)
Change in fixed assets		68,506
Free cash flows	($	54,716)

Financing Free Cash Flows:

Interest	($ 8,205)
Dividends	(6,551)
Increase in short-term notes	69,472
	$54,716

Self-Tests

TRUE-FALSE

_____ 1. The balance sheet is a statement of the firm's financial position over a specified time interval.

_____ 2. Non-current assets are those that are not expected to be converted into cash within the firm's operating cycle.

_____ 3. The income statement represents an attempt to measure the net results of the firm's operations on a given date.

_____ 4. The owner's equity represents the book value of the owner's investment in the assets of the firm.

_____ 5. A firm attempts to match sales from the period's operations with the expenses incurred in generating those revenues by compiling the income statement on an accrual basis.

_____ 6. Reported sales and expenses must represent actual cash flows for the period when the income statement is prepared on an accrual basis.

_____ 7. Investments in securities are always considered to be current assets.

_____ 8. Payments on loans is a component of a firm's financing free cash flows.

_____ 9. In determining the operating working capital, all of a firm's liabilities are considered.

_____ 10. A firm's free cash flows and financing cash flows are always equal, except for the signs.

_____ 11. Cash flows from operations are equal to a firm's operating income plus depreciation and amortization.

_____ 12. Current liabilities include accounts payables and accruals.

_____ 13. Depreciation expense is added back to operating income when computing after-tax cash flows from operations because it is a non-cash expense.

_____ 14. Interest expense is an operating expense.

_____ 15. Retained earnings change is affected by a firm's net income and common stock dividends paid.

MULTIPLE CHOICE

1. Which of the following is generally considered to be the most important for judging the economic well being of a firm?

    a.   Income statement.
    b.   Assets and liabilities
    c.   Cash flows.
    d.   All of the above.
    e.   None of the above.

2. Which Income Statement activity is not found above the Operating Profit line?

    a.   Financing
    b.   Operating Expenses
    c.   Revenue
    d.   Cost of acquiring the product or service.

3. Which type of income may be distributed to the company's owners or reinvested in the company?

    a.   Gross Profit
    b.   Net Income
    c.   Operating Income
    d.   Earnings before preferred dividends

4. The balance sheet provides us with

    a.   How the company's resources are financed.
    b.   The results from operating the business for a period of time,
    c.   The result of all financial transactions since the company began its operations.
    d.   Both a and c

5. Which item is not considered to be a liability?

    a.   Credit extended by suppliers to a firm for the purchase of inventory
    b.   Interest payable
    c.   Accrued taxes
    d.   Prepaid rent

6. Common Stockholder's Equity equals:

   a. Common stock issued, plus treasury stock, plus retained earnings.
   b. Common stock issued, minus common stock repurchased, plus cumulative net income over the firm's life, minus taxes and total dividends paid over the firm's life.
   c. Preferred stock issued plus common stock issued, minus treasury stock, plus retained earnings.
   d. Common stock issued, minus common stock repurchased, plus retained earnings.

7. Which item below is not considered a difference between accrual-basis and cash-basis accounting?

   a. Depreciation expense.
   b. The accounting treatment of employees' salaries that are paid on a bi-weekly basis.
   c. Credit purchases of inventory
   d. Cash sales, as opposed to credit.

8. Which item listed below is not part of the calculation of operating working capital for computing free cash flows?

   a. Long-term notes payable
   b. Accounts payable
   c. Accounts receivable
   d. Prepaid expenses

9. Select the statement that reflects the relationship between free cash flows and financing free cash flows?

   a. Negative operating cash flows allow for positive cash flows to be received by the investors.
   b. Infusion of capital by the investors of the firm is required as the result of positive cash flows from operations.
   c. Positive free cash flows distributed to the firm's investors (both debt and equity).
   d. None of the above.

10. Which of the following is not considered to be a financing activity?

   a. Dividend payments
   b. Issuing stock
   c. Purchase of a Capital Asset
   d. Interest payments

CHAPTER 4

Evaluating a Firm's Financial Performance

Orientation: Financial analysis can be defined as the process of assessing the financial condition of a firm. The principal analytical tool of the financial analyst is the financial ratio. In this chapter, we provide a set of key financial ratios and a discussion of their effective use.

I   Financial ratios help us identify some of the financial strengths and weaknesses of a company.

II.   The ratios give us a way of making meaningful comparisons of a firm's financial data at different points in time and with other firms.

III.   We could use ratios to answer the following important questions about a firm's operations.

   A.   Question 1: How liquid is the firm?

        1.   The liquidity of a business is defined as its ability to meet maturing debt obligations. That is—does or will the firm have the resources to pay the creditors when the debt comes due?

        2.   There are two ways to approach the liquidity question.

             a.   We can look at the firm's assets that are relatively liquid in nature and compare them to the amount of the debt coming due in the near term.

             b.   We can look at how quickly the firm's liquid assets are being converted into cash.

B. Question 2: Is management generating adequate operating profits on the firm's assets?

   1. We want to know if the profits are sufficient relative to the assets being invested.

   2. We have several choices as to how we measure profits: gross profits, operating profits, or net income. Gross profits are not acceptable because it overlooks important information such as marketing and distribution expenses. Net income includes the unwanted effects of the firm's financing policies. This leaves operating profits as our best choice in measuring the firm's operating profitability. Thus, the appropriate measure is the operating return on assets (OROA):

   $$\text{OROA} = \frac{\text{operating profits}}{\text{total assets}}$$

C. Question 3: How is the firm financing its assets?

   Here we are concerned with the mix of debt and equity capital the firm is using. Two primary ratios used to answer this question are the debt ratio and times interest earned. The debt ratio is the proportion of total debt to total assets. Times interest earned compares operating profits to interest expense for a crude measure of the firm's capacity to service its debt.

D. Question 4: Are the owners (stockholders) receiving an adequate return on their investment?

   1. We want to know if the earnings available to the firm's owners or common equity investors are attractive when compared to the returns of owners of similar companies in the same industry.

   2. Return on equity (ROE) $= \dfrac{\text{net income}}{\text{common equity}}$

   3. The effect of using debt on net income: This example shows how, through the use of debt, firms can affect their return on equity.

4. Return on equity is a function of:

    (1) the operating return on assets less the interest rate paid, and

    (2) the amount of debt used in the capital structure relative to the equity.

E. Question 5: Is the management team creating shareholder value?

1. We want to know if management is creating or destroying shareholder value.

2. We use two approaches to answer this question.

    a. We examine the market-value ratios: Price/Earnings (PE) and Price/Book ratios.

    b. We estimate the value being created for shareholders using the Economic Value Added (EVA^{TM}).

IV. Limitations of Ratio Analysis

This list warns of the potential pitfalls that may be encountered in computing and interpreting financial ratios. Ratio users should be aware of these concerns prior to making decisions based solely on ratio analysis.

Study Problems

1. Balance sheets for Marion Mfg. Co. and the Sterlington Corp. are found below. Both firms are involved in the manufacture of electrical components used in small electronic calculators and digital wristwatches. Since both firms are less than three years old, their book values are reasonably close to actual market value.

Marion Mfg. Co.
Balance Sheet
November 30, 2008

Assets		Liabilities & Equity	
Cash	$ 50,000	Notes payable	$ 520,000
Accounts receivable	90,000	(due in 30 days)	
Building	225,000	Accounts payable	420,000
Machinery	350,000	Owner's equity	150,000
Land	375,000		
	$1,090,000		$1,090,000

Sterlington Co.
Balance Sheet
November 30, 2008

Assets		Liabilities & Equity	
Cash	$ 50,000	Notes payable	$120,000
Accounts receivable	200,000	(due in 30 days)	
Land	10,000	Accounts payable	150,000
Machinery	350,000	Owner's equity	640,000
Building	300,000		
	$910,000		$910,000

    (a)   Assume the role of a commercial banker who has been approached by both of the previous firms with a request for a 90-day loan for $200,000. For which of the firms are you most likely to approve the loan? Why?

(b)   If you were considering the purchase of one of these firms and assuming the liabilities of each, for which one would you be willing to pay the higher price? (Obviously, you would want more information in order to make a complete analysis, but make your evaluation based on the balance sheets above.)

SOLUTION

(a)   Sterlington Corp. In reviewing requests for short-term loans, the commercial loan officer is most interested in the liquidity of the subject firm. The current ratio of Marion Mfg. Co. is a very weak 0.15 while Sterlington Corp.'s current ratio is .93. In addition, a quick glance at the balance sheet of Marion Mfg. shows that a very substantial note of $520,000 comes due in 30 days which the company may have difficulty paying.

(b)   Sterlington Corp. If it is assumed that book values are reasonably close to actual market values, the difference between Sterlington's total assets and assumed debt is $640,000, as opposed to Marion's net difference of $150,000.

2.   The financial manager of Sudhop, Inc. has just hired you (a recent finance graduate). Now he wishes to test your familiarity with financial ratios and your overall ability to work with financial statements. He gives you the following incomplete year-end balance sheet:

Sudhop, Inc.
Balance Sheet
December 31, 2008

Cash	$	Accounts payable	$
Accounts receivable		Long-term debt	
Inventory	_____	Total Debt	$
Total current assets	$	Common stock	125,000
Fixed assets	400,000	Retained earnings	275,000
	$		$

He then gives you the following additional information and asks you to complete the above balance sheet.

Average collection period (assume a 360-day year)	30 days
Interest paid on long-term debt (10% rate)	$5,000
Debt-to-equity ratio	75%
Sales to total assets	2.0 times
Quick ratio	1.1
Current ratio	1.2

SOLUTION

Sudhop, Inc.
Balance Sheet
December 31, 2008

Cash	$225,000	Accounts payable	$250,000
Accounts receivable	50,000	Long-term debt	50,000
Inventory	25,000	Total Debt	$300,000
Total current assets	$300,000	Common stock	125,000
Fixed assets	400,000	Retained earnings	275,000
Total assets	$ 700,000	Total debt and equity	$700,000

Computations:

(a) Since debt to equity is 0.75, than debt must be $300,000 (0.75 x $400,000 equity).

(b) Debt plus equity equals total debt and equity and total assets, which comes to $700,000.

(c) Current assets equal total assets less fixed assets ($700,000 - $400,000).

(d) Since current assets ÷ current liabilities equals 1.20, then current liabilities equal $250,000 ($300,000 ÷ current liabilities = 1.2).

(e) Sales ÷ total assets = 2.0; so, sales ÷ $700 = 2.0; and sales = $1,400

(f) Accounts receivable may be determined to be $50,000 as follows:

$$\text{Average collection period} = \frac{\text{accounts receivable}}{\text{daily credit sales}}$$

From what we already know and assuming all sales are on credit,

$$30 = \frac{\text{accounts receivable}}{\$1,400 \div 360}$$

(g) Given a quick ratio of 1.1, then inventory must be $25,000:

$$\frac{\$300,000 - \text{inventories}}{\$250,000} = 1.1$$

(h) Cash equals current assets minus accounts receivable and inventory.

3. The balance sheet and income statement for Miller Company are given for the year 2008 in addition to various financial ratios for the industry in which Miller operates.

Miller Company
Balance Sheet
December 31, 2008
(000's)

Cash	$ 230	Notes payable	$ 1,015
Accounts receivable	9,380	Accounts payable	3,545
Inventories	7,515	Accrued taxes	225
Current assets	17,125	Current liabilities	4,785
Fixed assets (net)	34,125	Long-term debt	18,035
Total Assets	$51,250	Deferred income taxes	2,840
		Total Debt	$20,875
		Common stock-par	575
		Paid in capital	7,945
		Retained earnings	17,070
		Common equity	25,590
		Total liabilities & net worth	$51,250

Miller Company
Income Statement
Year Ended December 31, 2008

Net sales (credit)	$46,235
Cost of sales	33,167
Gross profit	13,068
General and administrative expense	9,590
Operating income	3,478
Interest changes	1,120
Net income before taxes	2,358
Income taxes	1,130
Net income	$ 1,228

Industry Ratios

	Industry
Current ratio	4.02
Acid-test ratio	3.00
Inventory turnover	7.50
Average collection period	63.1
Operating profit margin	6.0%
Total asset turnover	2.0
Fixed asset turnover	3.0
Debt ratio	38.0%
Times interest earned	3.90
Return on equity	4.0%

Required:

Evaluate Miller's financial performance, using the "four-question approach" presented in Chapter 3 of the text.

SOLUTION

(a)

	Industry	Miller
Current ratio	4.02	3.58
Acid-test ratio	3.00	2.01
Inventory turnover	7.50	4.41
Average collection period	63.1	74.1
Operating profit margin	6.0%	7.5
Total asset turnover	2.0	0.9
Fixed asset turnover	3.0	1.4
Debt ratio	38.0%	50.1%
Times interest earned	3.90	3.11
Return on equity	4.0%	4.8%

(b) Miller's liquidity ratios are well below the industry averages. The most serious problem is with inventory turnover which is almost one-half the industry norm.

The operating return on assets, OROA, for Miller and the industry are determined as follows:

Since OROA = operating profit margin X total asset turnover

then:

Miller: 7.5%   X   0.9   =   6.8%

Industry: 6.0%   X   2.0   =   12%

Thus, Miller's management is not generating satisfactory operating profits on the firm's assets. However, Miller's operating profit margin exceeds the industry, which suggests that they are better than the average firm at some combination of the following:

1. Receive above-average prices for their products.

2. Sell more units of their products.

3. Lower cost of goods sold.

4. Lower operating expenses (general and administrative and marketing).

However, the firm is clearly not using its assets efficiently, as suggested by all the turnover ratios and collection period, to generate sales.

The net effect of the operating profit margin and the asset turnovers is a low OROA.

The firm uses more debt to finance its assets, as reflected by the higher debt ratio and the lower times interest earned. The low times interest earned is also due to the lower OROA, which affects the numerator of the ratio.

Miller's stockholders received an above-average return on their investment (return on equity), but it was accomplished by using more debt, which exposes the investors to greater financial risk.

4. Seward, Inc.'s, balance sheet shows a stockholders' book equity value of $300.000. The firm's earnings per share was $2, resulting in a price/earnings ratio of 8. There are 25,000 shares of common stock outstanding. What is the price/book ratio?

SOLUTION:

To calculate the price to book ratio, we need to determine the market price per share as well as the balance sheet book value per share. The market price is derived as follows:

$$\text{Earnings per share} = \frac{\text{Earnings}}{25,000 \text{ shares}} = \$2; \quad \text{Earnings} = \$50,000$$

$$\text{Price/Earnings} = \frac{\text{Price}}{\$2} = 8,; \quad \text{Market price per share} = \mathbf{\$16}$$

$$\text{Book values per share} = \frac{\text{Equity Book Value}}{\text{Number of shares}} = \frac{\$300,000}{25,000 \text{ shares}} = \mathbf{\$12}$$

$$\frac{\text{Price}}{\text{Book}} = \frac{\$16}{\$12} = 1.33$$

5. During the past year, Winand, Inc. earned an operating income return on investment of 14 percent, compared to an industry norm of 10 percent. It has been estimated that the firm's investors have a required rate of return of 15 percent. The firm's total assets for the year were $400 million. Compute the amount of economic value created or destroyed by the firm.

SOLUTION

$$\text{EVA} = (14\% - 15\%) \times \$400 \text{ million} = (\$4 \text{ million})$$

TRUE-FALSE

_____ 1. Accounts receivable turnover gives us the same information as the average collection period.

_____ 2. Operating return on assets is affected by the firm's operating profit margin and its debt ratio.

_____ 3. The operating profit margin is a measure of asset efficiency.

_____ 4. Return on equity is partly a function of operating return on assets

_____ 5. Times interest earned is equal to net income divided by interest expense.

_____ 6. Operating return on assets is equal to operating profit margin times total asset turnover.

_____ 7. Operating profit margin measures how well management is managing the firm's income statement.

_____ 8. Liquidity is measured by the times interest earned ratio.

_____ 9. Total asset turnover tells us how efficiently management is using the firm's assets.

_____ 10. Financial ratios help us identify financial strengths and weaknesses of firms by way of being able to make meaningful comparisons of firm's financial data at different points in time and with other firms.

_____ 11. A firm's cash account is not considered in determining its liquidity.

_____ 12. The current ratio is more conservative than the acid-test ratio.

_____ 13. Inventory turnover and the average collection period may be used to measure the same thing—operating profitability.

_____ 14. Return on equity measures the dividends investors received in the current year.

_____ 15. The Economic Value Added (EVA^{TM}) is used to estimate a firm's liquidity and financing decisions.

MULTIPLE CHOICE

1. Which ratio does not help answer the question of adequate operating profitability generated by the firm's assets?

    a. Operating return on assets
    b. Return on common equity
    c. Total asset turnover
    d. Operating Profit margin

2. Which ratio is used in both measuring a firm's liquidity and generating adequate operating profitability?

    a. Average collection period
    b. Operating profit margin
    c. Acid-test ratio
    d. Inventory turnover
    e. a and d

3. Which of the following is not used to evaluate how management is doing at creating shareholder value?

    a. Price/Earnings ratio
    b. Price/Book ratio.
    c. Operating profit margin.
    d. Economic Value Added (EVA^{TM}).

4. Current assets minus inventories over current liabilities is

    a. Acid-test ratio
    b. Current ratio
    c. Average collection period
    d. Current asset turnover

5. Return on Common equity is affected by which of the following

    a. Sales
    b. Total asset turnover
    c. Equity ratio
    d. Net profit margin
    e. All of the above

6. The difference between the current ratio and the quick ratio is

    a. inventories.
    b. inventories is subtracted from the numerator.
    c. inventories is subtracted from the denominator.
    d. the current ratio is more conservative.

7. The ratio of total debt over total assets is

    a. the current ratio.
    b. the debt ratio.
    c. a measure of a firm's liquidity.
    d. referred to as the quick ratio because it is so easily determined.

8. Robert Morris Associates and other published industry averages are

    a. offered for every industry.
    b. scientifically determined averages.
    c. only approximations.
    d. good for many years.

9. An industry average is best used as

    a. a desirable target or norm for the firm
    b. a guide to the financial position of the average firm in the industry.
    c. a scientifically determined average of the ratios of a representative sample of firms within an industry.
    d. a point or rule with which to measure profitability.

10. Operating return on assets is affected by

    a. depreciation expense
    b. interest expense
    c. income tax
    d. all of the above

CHAPTER 5

The Time Value of Money

Orientation: In this chapter, the concept of a time value of money is introduced; that is, a dollar today is worth more than a dollar received a year from now. Thus, if we are to logically compare projects and financial strategies, we must move all dollar flows either back to the present or out to some common future date.

I. Compound interest results when the interest paid on the investment during the first period is added to the principal and, during the second period, the interest is earned on the original principal plus the interest earned during the first period.

    A. Mathematically, the future value of an investment if compounded annually at a rate of i for n years will be:

$$FV_n \quad = \quad PV \, (1 + i)^n$$

        where n = the number of years during which the compounding occurs,

        i = the annual interest (or discount) rate,

        PV = the present value or original amount invested at the beginning of the first year,

        FV_n = the future value of the investment at the end of n years.

        1. The future value of an investment can be increased either by increasing the number of years we let it compound or by compounding it at a higher rate.

59

2. If the compounded period is less than one year, the future value of an investment can be determined as follows:

$$FV_n = PV \left(1 + \frac{i}{m}\right)^{mn}$$

where m = the number of times compounding occurs during the year.

II. Determining the present value, that is, the value in today's dollars of a sum of money to be received in the future, involves nothing other than inverse compounding. The differences in these techniques come about merely from the investor's point of view.

A. Mathematically, the present value of a sum of money to be received in the future can be determined with the following equation:

$$PV = FV_n \left(\frac{1}{(1+i)^n}\right)$$

where n = the number of years until payment will be received,

i = the annual interest (or discount) rate,

PV = the present value of the future sum of money,

FV_n = the future value of the investment at the end of n years

1. The present value of a future sum of money is inversely related to both the number of years until the payment will be received and the opportunity rate.

III. An annuity is a series of equal dollar payments for a specified number of years. Because annuities occur frequently in finance, for example, bond interest payments, we treat them specially.

A. A compound annuity involves depositing or investing an equal sum of money at the end of each year for a certain number of years and allowing it to grow.

1. This can be done by using our compounding equation and compounding each one of the individual deposits to the future or by using the following compound annuity equation:

$$FV_n \quad = \quad PMT \left(\sum_{t=0}^{n-1} (1+i)^t \right)$$

where PMT = the annuity payment deposited or received at the end of each year,

i = the annual interest (or discount) rate,

n = the number of years for which the annuity will last,

FV_n = the future value of the annuity at the end of the nth year.

B. Pension funds, insurance obligation, and interest received from bonds all involve annuities. To compare these financial instruments, we would like to know the present value of each of these annuities.

1. This can be done by using our present value equation and discounting each one of the individual cash flows back to the present or by using the following present value of an annuity equation:

$$PV \quad = \quad PMT \left(\sum_{t=1}^{n} \frac{1}{(t+i)^t} \right)$$

where PMT = the annuity payment deposited or received at the end of each year,

i = the annual interest (or discount) rate,

PV = the present value of the future annuity,

n = the number of years for which the annuity will last.

C.   This procedure of solving for PMT, the annuity value when i, n, and PV are known, is also the procedure used to determine what payments are associated with paying off a loan in equal installments. Loans paid off in this way, in periodic payments, are called amortized loans.

1.   Here again, we know three of the four values in the annuity equation and are solving for a value of PMT, the annual annuity.

2.   For example: Suppose a firm borrows $5,000 to be repaid in five equal payments at the end of each of the next 5 years to purchase some machinery and the interest rate that is paid to the lender is 15 percent on the outstanding portion of the loan. Using the annuity equation to solve, we get

$$\$5,000 \;=\; PMT \left(\sum_{t=1}^{5} \frac{1}{(1+.15)^t} \right)$$

$$\$5,000 \;=\; PMT(3.352)$$

$$PMT \;=\; \$1,491.65$$

IV.   A perpetuity is an annuity that continues forever; that is, every year from now on this investment pays the same dollar amount.

A.   An example of a perpetuity is preferred stock which yields a constant dollar dividend infinitely.

B.   The following equation can be used to determine the present value of a perpetuity:

$$PV \;=\; \frac{PP}{i}$$

where   PV   =   the present value of the perpetuity,

PP   =   the constant dollar amount provided by the perpetuity,

i   =   the annual interest or discount rate.

V.   To aid in the calculations of present and future values, tables are provided at the back of *Foundations of Finance (FOF)*.

A.   To aid in determining the value of FV_n in the compounding formula

$$FV_n = PV (1 + i)^n = PV (FVIF_{i,n})$$

tables have been compiled for values of $FVIF_{i,n}$ or $(i + 1)^n$ in Appendix B, "Compound Sum of $1," in *FOF*.

B.   Thus, to determine the value of:

$$FV_{10} = \$1,000(1 + 0.08)^{10}$$

we need merely to look up the value of $FVIF_{8\%, 10 \text{ yr.}}$ in Appendix B and substitute it in. The table value given in the $n = 10$ row and 8% column of Appendix B is 2.159. Substituting this in the equation, we get

$$FV_{10} = \$1,000(2.159)$$

$$FV_{10} = \$2,159$$

C.   To aid in the computation of present values

$$PV = FV_n \frac{1}{(1 + i)^n} = FV_n (PVIF_{i,n})$$

tables have been compiled for values of

$$\frac{1}{(1 + i)^n} \quad \text{or} \quad PVIF_{i,n}$$

and appear in Appendix C in the back of *FOF*.

D. Because of the time-consuming nature of compounding an annuity,

$$FV_n = PMT \sum_{t=0}^{n}(1 + i)^t = PMT\ (FVIFA_{i,n})$$

tables are provided in Appendix D of *FOF* for

$$\sum_{t=0}^{n-1}(1+i)^t \quad or \quad FVIFA_{i,n}$$

for various combinations of n and i.

E. To simplify the process of determining the present value of an annuity

$$PV = PMT \sum_{t=0}^{n}(1+i)^t = PMT\ (PVIFA_{i,n})$$

tables are provided in Appendix E of *FOF* for various combinations of n and i for the value

$$\sum_{t=0}^{n}\frac{1}{(1+i)^t} \quad or \quad PVIFA_{i,n}$$

Study Problems

1. What will $1,000 invested for 10 years at 10% compounded annually accumulate to?

SOLUTION

Substituting into the compound value formula, we get:

$$FV_n = PV(1+i)^n$$

$$FV_{10} = \$1,000(1 + 0.10)^{10}$$

$$FV_{10} = \$1,000(2.594)$$

$$FV_{10} = \$2,594$$

Or:

N	=	10
I/Y	=	10
PV	=	-1,000
PMT	=	0
CPT FV =		**$2,594**

2. How many years will it take $500 to grow to $1,586 if it is invested at 8% compounded annually?

SOLUTION

From the compound value formula we know:

$$FV_n = PV (1 + i)^n$$

Substituting in the values that we know, we get:

$$\$1,586 = \$500 (1 + 0.08)^n$$

or using table values, we get:

$$\$1,586 = \$500 (FVIF_{8\%, n\,yr.})$$

Dividing both sides by $500, we get:

$$3.172 = FVIF_{8\%, n\,yr}$$

Looking in the 8% column, we find a value of 3.172 in the 15-year row. Thus, it will take 15 years.

Or:

CPT N =		**15**
I/Y	=	8
PV	=	-500
PMT	=	0
FV	=	$1,586

3. At what annual rate would \$1,000 have to be invested in order to grow to \$4,046 in 10 years?

SOLUTION

From the compound value formula, we know:

$$FV_n = PV(1+i)^n = PV(FVIF_{i,n})$$

Substituting the table value given in Appendix B of *FOF* for $(1+i)^n$, we get:

$$FV_n = PV(FVIF_{i,n})$$

Substituting in the given values, we get:

$$\$4,046 = \$1,000(FVIF_{i,\ 10\ yr.})$$

$$4.046 = FVIF_{i,\ 10\ yr.}$$

Thus, we are looking for a table value of 4.046 in the 10-year row of Appendix B. This appears in the 15% column; thus, 15% is the annual rate we are looking for.

Or:

N	=	10
CPT I/Y =		**15**
PV	=	-1,000
PMT	=	0
FV	=	\$4,046

4. What is the present value of \$1,000 to be received 8 years from now discounted back to present at 10%?

SOLUTION

Substituting in the present value formula, we get:

$$PV = FV_n\left(\frac{1}{(1+i)^n}\right) = FV_n(PVIF_{i,n})$$

$$PV = \$1{,}000 \left(\frac{1}{(1+0.10)^8} \right)$$

$$PV = \$1{,}000[0.467]$$

$$PV = \$467$$

Or:

N	=	8
I/Y	=	10
CPT PV =		**467**
PMT	=	0
FV	=	$1,000

5. What is the accumulated sum of the following streams of payments, $1,000 per year for 5 years compounded annually at 5%?

SOLUTION

Substituting into the compound annuity formula, we get:

$$FV_n = PMT \sum_{t=0}^{n-1} (1+t)^t = PMT(FVIFA_{i,n})$$

$$FV_5 = \$1{,}000 \sum_{t=0}^{5-1} (1+0.05)^t$$

$$FV_5 = \$1{,}000(5.526)$$

$$FV_5 = \$5{,}526$$

Or:

N	=	5
I/Y	=	5
PV	=	0
PMT	=	-1,000
CPT FV =		**$5,526**

6. What is the present value of $100 a year for 15 years discounted back to the present at 15%?

SOLUTION

Substituting into the present value of an annuity formula:

$$PV = PMT \left(\sum_{t=1}^{n} \frac{1}{(1+t)^t} \right) = PMT \, (PVIFA_{i,n})$$

$$PV = \$100 \left(\sum_{t=1}^{15} \frac{1}{(1+0.15)^t} \right)$$

$$PV = \$100(5.847)$$

$$PV = \$584.70$$

Or:

N	=	15
I/Y	=	15
CPT PV =		**584.74**
PMT	=	-100
FV	=	0

7. If you receive a 9% $100,000 loan that has annual payments of $14,695.08, how many loan payments must you make in order to pay off the loan?

SOLUTION

Substituting into the present value of an annuity formula:

$$PV = PMT \left(\sum_{t=1}^{n} \frac{1}{(1+t)^t} \right)$$

$$\$100,000 = \$14,695.08 \; PVIFA_{9\%, \, n \, yr.}$$

$$6.805 = PVIFA_{9\%, n \, yr.}$$

Looking down the 9% column of Appendix E, we find a value of 6.805 in the 11-year row. Thus, in 11 years, the loan will be paid off.

Or:

$$
\begin{array}{lll}
\textbf{CPT N =} & & \textbf{11} \\
\text{I/Y} & = & 9 \\
\text{PV} & = & -100,000 \\
\text{PMT} & = & 14,695.08 \\
\text{FV} & = & 0
\end{array}
$$

8. At what annual rate would the following have to be invested?

   (a) $550 to grow to $1,898.60 in 13 years

   (b) $275 to grow to $406.18 in 8 years

   (c) $60 to grow to $279.66 in 20 years

   (d) $180 to grow to $486.00 in 6 years

SOLUTION

   (a) $FV_n = PV (1 + i)^n$

   $\$1,898.60 = \$550 (1 + i)^{13}$

   $3.452 = FVIF_{i\%,\ 13\ yr.}$

   Thus, i = 10% (because the Appendix B value of 3.452 occurs in the 12-year row in the 10% column)

Or:

$$
\begin{array}{lll}
\text{N} & = & 13 \\
\textbf{CPT I/Y =} & & \textbf{10} \\
\text{PV} & = & -550 \\
\text{PMT} & = & 0 \\
\text{FV} & = & \$1,898.60
\end{array}
$$

(b) FV^n $=$ $PV (1 + i)^n$

406.18 $=$ $275 \ (1 + i)^8$

1.477 $=$ $FVIF_{i\%, \ 8 \ yr.}$

Thus, i $=$ 5%

Or:

N $=$ 8
CPT I/Y =   **5**
PV $=$ -275
PMT $=$ 0
FV $=$ $406.18

(c) FV_n $=$ $PV (1 + i)^n$

279.66 $=$ $60 \ (1 + i)^{20}$

4.661 $=$ $FVIF_{i\%, \ 20 \ yr.}$

Thus, i $=$ 8%

Or:

N $=$ 20
CPT I/Y =   **8**
PV $=$ -60
PMT $=$ 0
FV $=$ $279.66

(d) FV_n $=$ $PV (1 + i)^n$

486.00 $=$ $180 (1 + i)^6$

2.700 $=$ $FVIF_{i\%, \ 6 \ yr.}$

Thus, i $=$ 18%

Or:

N $=$ 6
CPT I/Y =   **18**
PV $=$ -180
PMT $=$ 0
FV $=$ $486

9.   What is the accumulated sum of each of the following streams of payments?

  (a) $500 a year for 10 years compounded annually at 6%

  (b) $150 a year for 5 years compounded annually at 11%

  (c) $35 a year for 8 years compounded annually at 7%

  (d) $25 a year for 3 years compounded annually at 2%

SOLUTION

  (a) $FV_n = PMT \left(\sum_{t=0}^{n-1} (1+i)^t \right)$

         $FV_{10} = \$500 \left(\sum_{t=0}^{10-1} (1+0.06)^t \right)$

         $FV_{10} = \$500 \,(13.181)$

         $FV_{10} = \$6{,}590.50$

Or:

         $N = 10$
         $I/Y = 6$
         $PV = 0$
         $PMT = -500$
         CPT FV = $6,590.40

  (b) $FV_n = PMT \left(\sum_{t=0}^{n-1} (1+i)^t \right)$

         $FV_5 = \$150 \left(\sum_{t=0}^{5-1} (1+0.11)^t \right)$

         $FV_5 = \$150 \,(6.228)$

         $FV_5 = \$934.20$

<u>**Or:**</u>

N	=	5
I/Y	=	11
PV	=	0
PMT	=	-150
CPT FV =		**$934**

(c) $\quad FV_n \quad = \quad PMT \left(\sum_{t=0}^{n-1} (1+i)^t \right)$

$\quad FV_7 \quad = \quad \$35 \left(\sum_{t=0}^{8-1} (1+0.07)^t \right)$

$\quad FV_7 \quad = \quad \$35 \,(10.260)$

$\quad FV_7 \quad = \quad \$359.10$

<u>**Or:**</u>

N	=	8
I/Y	=	7
PV	=	0
PMT	=	-35
CPT FV =		**$359**

(d) $\quad FV_n \quad = \quad PMT \left(\sum_{t=0}^{n-1} (1+i)^t \right)$

$\quad FV_3 \quad = \quad \$25 \left(\sum_{t=0}^{3-1} (1+0.02)^t \right)$

$\quad FV_3 \quad = \quad \$25 \,(3.060)$

$\quad FV_3 \quad = \quad \$76.50$

<u>**Or:**</u>

N	=	3
I/Y	=	2
PV	=	0
PMT	=	-25
CPT FV =		**$76.51**

10. Hanna purchased a new house for $150,000. She paid $30,000 down and agreed to pay the rest over the next 25 years in 25 equal annual payments that include principal payments plus 10% compound interest on the unpaid balance. What will these equal payments be?

SOLUTION

$$PV = PMT \left(\sum_{t=1}^{n} \frac{1}{(1+t)^t} \right)$$

$$\$120,000 = PMT \left(\sum_{t=1}^{25} \frac{1}{(1+0.1)^t} \right)$$

$$\$120,000 = PMT(9.077)$$

Thus, PMT = $13.220.23 per year for 25 years

Or:

N = 25
I/Y = 10
PV = -120,000
CPT PMT = 13,220
FV = 0

11. How much do you have to deposit today so that beginning 11 years from now you can withdraw $10,000 a year for the next 5 years (periods 11 through 15) plus an *additional* amount of $15,000 in that last year (period 15)? Assume an interest rate of 7%.

SOLUTION

Step 1: First, discount the annuity back to the beginning of year 11, which is the end of year 10. Then, discount this equivalent sum to present.

$$PV = PMT\left(\sum_{t=1}^{n} \frac{1}{(1 + i)^t}\right)$$

$$= \$10,000\left(\sum_{t=1}^{5} \frac{1}{(1 + .07)^t}\right)$$

$$= \$10,000(4.100)$$

$$= \$41,000 \text{ — then discount the equivalent sum}$$

back to present.

Step 2: Then discount the $41,000 back to present (it is now at the end of year 10):

$$PV = FV_n\left(\frac{1}{(1 + i)^n}\right)$$

$$PV = \$41,000\left(\frac{1}{(1 + .07)^{10}}\right)$$

$$PV = \$41,000 (.508)$$

$$PV = \$20,828$$

Then add the present value of the $15,000 withdrawal at the end of year 15 to this amount:

$$PV = FV_{15}\left(\frac{1}{(1 + .07)^{15}}\right)$$

$$= \$15,000(.362)$$

$$= \$5,430$$

Thus, you would have to deposit $20,828 + $5,430 or $26,258 today.

<u>Or:</u>

Step 1 (First, discount the annuity back to the beginning of year 11, which is the end of year 10.):

    N =   5
    I/Y = 7
    CPT PV = -41,002
    PMT =   10,000
    FV = 0

Step 2 (Then, discount this equivalent sum to present.):

    N =   10
    I/Y = 7
    CPT PV = 23,473
    PMT =   0
    FV = -20,843

Step 3 (Then, determine the present value of the $15,000 withdrawal at the end of year 15):

    N   =   15
    I/Y = 7
    CPT PV = 5,437
    PMT =   0
    FV = -15,000

Step 4: (Add the present values together):

Thus, you would have to deposit $20,843 + $5,437 or $26,280 today.

TRUE-FALSE

_____ 1. The fact that there is an opportunity cost to money brings on the concept of the time value of money.

_____ 2. The higher the rate used to compound a given sum, the larger it will be at some future date.

_____ 3. The future value of an investment can be increased by reducing the number of years we let it compound.

_____ 4. There is an inverse relationship between the present value of a future cash flow and the discount rate.

_____ 5. Daily, as opposed to annual, compounding takes on importance because it allows interest to be earned on interest more frequently.

_____ 6. Determining present value is merely the inverse of compounding.

_____ 7. A compound annuity involves depositing or investing an equal sum of money at the end of each year for a certain number of years and allowing it to grow.

_____ 8. A perpetuity is an annuity that continues for 30 years or more.

_____ 9. The present value of an annuity increases as the discount rate decreases.

_____ 10. An example of perpetuity is the interest received on long-term bonds.

MULTIPLE CHOICE

1. To determine the present value of a future sum, we need only multiply it by,

    a. $\dfrac{1}{(1+i)^n}$

    b. $\dfrac{1}{(1+n)^1}$

    c. $(1 + n)^i$

    d. $(1 + i)^n$

2. The present value of a $100 perpetuity discounted back to present at 6% is

    a. $6,000.00.
    b. $6,666.66.
    c. $1,666.67.
    d. $1,200.00.

3. If we place $100 in a savings account that yields 6% compounded semiannually, what will our investment grow to at the end of 5 years?

    a. $133.80
    b. $130.00
    c. $125.00
    d. $134.40

4. A bond maturing in 10 years pays $80 each year and $1,000 upon maturity. Assuming 10% to be the appropriate discount rate, the present value of the bond is

    a. $1,010.84.
    b. $925.74.
    c. $877.60.
    d. $1,000.00.

5. The Fuller Company has received a $50,000 loan. The annual payments are $6,202.70. If the Fuller Company is paying 9% interest per year, how many loan payments must the company make?

    a. 15
    b. 13
    c. 12
    d. 19

CHAPTER 6

The Meaning and Measurement of Risk and Return

Orientation: In this chapter, we examine the factors that determine rates of return (discount rates) in the capital markets. We are particularly interested in the relationship between risk and rates of return. We look at risk both in terms of the riskiness of an individual security and that of a portfolio of securities.

I. Expected Return Defined and Measured

    A. The expected benefits or returns to be received from an investment come in the form of the cash flows the investment generates.

    B. Conventionally, we measure the expected cash flow, $\bar{X}$, as follows:

$$\bar{X} \quad = \quad P(X_1)X_1 + P(X_2)X_2 + \cdots + P(Xn)Xn$$

    where n =   the number of possible states of the economy

                 X_i =   the cash flow in the *ith* state of the economy

             $P(X_i)$ =   the probability of the *ith* cash flow

II. Risk Defined and Measured

    A. Risk can be defined as the possible variation in cash flow about an expected cash flow.

    B. Statistically, risk may be measured by the standard deviation about the expected cash flow.

III. Rates of Return: The Investors' Experience

    A.   Data have been compiled by Ibbotson and Associates on the actual returns for various portfolios of securities from 1926-2003.

    B.   The following portfolios were studied:

        1.   Common stocks of large firms
        2.   Common stocks for small firms
        3.   Long-term corporate bonds
        4.   Long-term U.S. government bonds
        5.   Intermediate U.S. government bonds
        6.   U.S. Treasury bills

    C.   Investors historically have received greater returns for greater risk-taking with the exception of the long-term U.S. government bonds.

    D.   The only portfolio with returns consistently exceeding the inflation rate has been common stocks.

IV. Risk and Diversification

    A.   The market rewards diversification. We can lower risk without sacrificing expected return, and/or we can increase expected return without having to assume more risk.

    B.   Diversifying among different kinds of assets is called asset allocation. Compared to diversification within the different asset classes, the benefits received are far greater through effective asset allocation.

    C.   Total variability can be divided into:

        a.   The variability of returns unique to the security (diversifiable or unsystematic risk)
        b.   The risk related to market movements (nondiversifiable or systematic risk)

    D.   By diversifying, the investor can eliminate the "unique" security risk. The systematic risk, however, cannot be diversified away.

E. Measuring Market Risk

    1. The **characteristic line** tells us the average movement in a firm's stock price in response to a movement in the general market, such as the S&P 500 Index. The slope of the characteristic line, which has come to be called **beta**, is a measure of a stock's systematic or market risk. The slope of the line is merely the ratio of the "rise" of the line relative to the "run" of the line.

    2. If a security's beta equals one, a 10 percent increase (decrease) in market returns will produce on average a 10 percent increase (decrease) in security returns.

    3. A security having a higher beta is more volatile and thus more risky than a security having a lower beta value.

F. A portfolio's beta is equal to the average of the betas of the stocks in the portfolio.

G. Risk and diversification can be demonstrated by a comparison of three portfolios consisting of short-term government securities, long-term government bonds, and large-company stocks.

V. The Investor's Required Rate of Return

A. The required rate of return is the minimum rate necessary to compensate an investor for accepting the risk he or she associates with the purchase and ownership of an asset.

B. Two factors determine the required rate of return for the investor:

    1. The risk-free rate of interest which recognizes the time value of money.

    2. The risk premium which considers the riskiness (variability of returns) of the asset and the investor's attitude toward risk.

C. Capital asset pricing model--CAPM

   1. The required rate of return for a given security can be expressed as

$$\begin{array}{c} \text{Required} \\ \text{rate} \end{array} = \begin{array}{c} \text{risk} - \text{free} \\ \text{rate} \end{array} + \text{beta} \times \left(\begin{array}{c} \text{market} \\ \text{return} \end{array} - \begin{array}{c} \text{risk} - \text{free} \\ \text{rate} \end{array} \right)$$

   or

$$k_j = k_{rf} + \beta_j \ (k_m - k_{rf})$$

   2. Security market line

      a. Graphically illustrates the CAPM.

      b. Designates the risk-return trade-off existing in the market, where risk is defined in terms of beta according to the CAPM equation.

Study Problems

   1. Phillips, Inc. is considering an investment in one of two common stocks. Given the information below, which investment is better, based on risk and return?

Common Stock A		Common Stock B	
Probability	*Return*	*Probability*	*Return*
0.10	-10%	0.30	5%
0.20	6	0.20	12
0.40	15	0.40	10
0.30	9	0.10	20

SOLUTION

Common Stock A

Expected Return

$$= 0.1(-10\%) + 0.2(6\%) + 0.4(15\%) + 0.3(9\%)$$
$$= -1\% + 1.2\% + 6\% + 2.7\% = 8.9\%$$

Standard Deviation

$$= [(-10\% - 8.9\%)^2(0.10) + (6\% - 8.9\%)^2(0.2)$$
$$+ (15\% - 8.9\%)^2 (0.4) + (9\% - 8.9\%)^2(0.30)]^{1/2}$$
$$= (35.721\% + 1.682\% + 14.884\% + 0.003\%)^{1/2} = .23\%$$

Common Stock B

Expected Return

$$= 0.3(5\%) + 0.2(12\%) + 0.4(10\%) + 0.10(20\%)$$
$$= 1.5\% + 2.4\% + 4\% + 2\% = 9.9\%$$

Standard Deviation

$$= [(5\% - 9.9\%)^2(0.3) + (12\% - 9.9\%)^2(0.2)$$
$$+ (10\% - 9.9\%)^2(0.4) + (20\% - 9.9\%)^2(0.1)]^{1/2}$$
$$= (7.203\% + 0.882\% + 0.004\% + 10.201\%)^{1/2} = 4.28\%$$

Common stock B has both a higher expected return and a smaller standard deviation (less risk). Hence, B is better.

2. Compute the annual holding-period return for the following stock.

Year	Stock Price
2007	$98
2008	105
2009	115
2010	100
2011	120

SOLUTION

Year	Return
2007	
2008	7.1%
2009	9.5%
2010	-13.0%
2011	20.0%

3.   From the graph below, estimate Archie's beta.

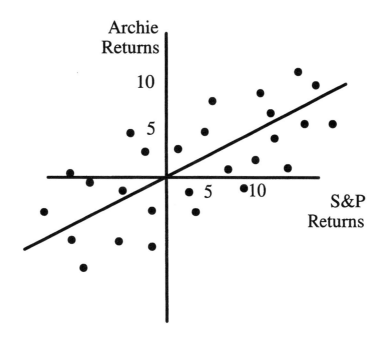

SOLUTION

Archie's beta is about 0.50, since Archie's returns change about 5% while the market's returns change 10%. Thus, $5 \div 10 = 0.50$.

4.   BC Incorporated, has a beta of 0.65. If the expected market return is 10% and the risk-free rate is 5%, what is the appropriate expected return of BC Incorporated?

SOLUTION

Expected return of BC Incorporated

$$= \text{risk-free rate} + \text{Beta} \left(\begin{array}{c} \text{expected risk} \\ \text{market} - \text{free} \\ \text{return rate} \end{array} \right)$$

$= 5\% + 0.65(10\%\text{-}5\%)$

$= 5\% + 3.25\% = 8.25\%$

TRUE-FALSE

_____ 1. The investor's required rate of return is the minimum rate necessary to attract an investor to purchase or hold a security.

_____ 2. Risk, as defined in this chapter, is the variation in returns about an expected value.

_____ 3. Time value of money can be represented by a risk-free rate of return only for risk-free securities.

_____ 4. A proxy for the risk-free rate is the Corporate AA Bond rate.

_____ 5. An investor's required rate of return is always greater than the expected rate of return.

_____ 6. By proper diversification, an investor can eliminate the market-related (systematic) risk.

_____ 7. A security having a beta of 1 will move up (or down) on average with the market by the same percentage.

_____ 8. The addition of a security with a beta of 0 provides no additional risk to a well-diversified portfolio.

_____ 9. The annual return on common stock historically has been greater than that of U.S. Treasury bills.

_____ 10. A security with an expected return of 15.9% and a standard deviation of 9.8% is obviously better than a Treasury bill earning 8%.

_____ 11. The real average annual rate of return is the nominal return minus the risk-free rate of return.

_____ 12. Corporate bonds are always more risky than Treasury bills and long-term government bonds.

MULTIPLE CHOICE

1.   Under the capital-asset pricing model, the relevant risk is

       a.   diversifiable risk.
       b.   systematic risk.
       c.   financial risk.
       d.   standard deviation.

2.   If the required return for a security is 15% and the risk-free rate is 6%, the risk premium is

       a.   0%.
       b.   6%.
       c.   10%.
       d.   9%.
       e.   15%.

3.   In terms of the security market line, a security with a beta of 1.5 should provide a risk premium _____ times the risk premium existing for the market as a whole.

       a.   0
       b.   1
       c.   1.5
       d.   2.5
       e.   0.5

4.   The beta for a portfolio is determined by

       a.   calculating the standard deviation of the betas of the individual stocks in the portfolio.
       b.   computing the unweighted average of the individual betas.
       c.   calculating a weighted average of the individual stock betas, where the weights equal the individual stocks' expected returns.
       d.   calculating a weighted average of the individual stock betas, where the weights equal the percentage invested in each stock.

5. A stock's holding period return represents

   a. the dividend received each period.
   b. the rate of return that would be earned on a stock if bought at the beginning of the period and sold at the end of the period.
   c. the return received from diversifying one's portfolio.
   d. the return from a stock relative to the return of the portfolio.

6. An investor's required rate of return should be a function of

   a. the riskiness of the investment being made without regard for the riskiness of other investments.
   b. the risk-free rate of return less the inflation rate.
   c. the risk-free rate of return plus the inflation rate.
   d. the risk-free rate of return plus a risk premium for the stock's systematic risk.

7. You should expect a higher rate of return from

   a. long-term corporate bonds than from common stocks.
   b. small company stocks than from common stocks of large firms.
   c. U.S. Treasury bills than from long-term government securities.
   d. none of the above.

8. Market risk can also be called

   a. unsystematic risk
   b. non-diversifiable risk
   c. diversifiable risk
   d. firm-specific risk
   e. company-unique risk

9. _____ is the only risk that matters to investors with broadly diversified portfolios.

   a. Systematic risk
   b. Unsystematic risk
   c. Firm-specific risk
   d. Diversifiable risk

CHAPTER 7

Valuation and Characteristics of Bonds

Orientation: This chapter introduces the concepts that underlie asset valuation. We are specifically concerned with bonds. We also look at the concept of the bondholder's expected rate of return on an investment.

I. Types of bonds

    A. Debentures: unsecured long-term debt.

    B. Subordinated debentures: bonds that have a lower claim on assets in the event of liquidation than do other senior debtholders.

    C. Mortgage bonds: bonds secured by a lien on specific assets of the firm, such as real estate.

    D. Eurobonds: bonds issued in a country different from the one in whose currency the bond is denominated; for instance, a bond issued in Europe or Asia that pays interest and principal in U.S. dollars.

    E. Zero and low coupon bonds allow the issuing firm to issue bonds at a substantial discount from their $1,000 face value with a zero or very low coupon.

        1. The disadvantages are, when the bond matures, the issuing firm will face an extremely large nondeductible cash outflow much greater than the cash inflow they experienced when the bonds were first issued.

        2. Discount bonds are not callable and can be retired only at maturity.

3. On the other hand, annual cash outflows associated with interest payments do not occur with zero coupon bonds.

F. Junk bonds: bonds rated BB or below.

II. Terminology and characteristics of bonds

A. A bond is a long-term promissory note that promises to pay the bondholder a predetermined, fixed amount of interest each year until maturity. At maturity, the principal will be paid to the bondholder.

B. In the case of a firm's insolvency, a bondholder has a priority of claim to the firm's assets before the preferred and common stockholders. Also, bondholders must be paid interest due them before dividends can be distributed to the stockholders.

C. A bond's par value is the amount that will be repaid by the firm when the bond matures, usually $1,000.

D. The contractual agreement of the bond specifies a coupon interest rate that is expressed either as a percent of the par value or as a flat amount of interest which the borrowing firm promises to pay the bondholder each year. For example: A $1,000 par value bond specifying a coupon interest rate of nine percent is equivalent to an annual interest payment of $90.

E. The bond has a maturity date, at which time the borrowing firm is committed to repay the loan principal.

F. A convertible bond allows the investor to exchange the bond for a predetermined number of the firm's shares of common stock.

G. A bond is callable or redeemable when it provides the firm with the right to pay off the bond at some time before its maturity date. These bonds frequently have a call protection period which prevents the firm from calling the bond for a pre-specified time period.

H. An indenture (or trust deed) is the legal agreement between the firm issuing the bonds and the bond trustee who represents the bondholders. It provides the specific terms of the bond agreement such as the rights and responsibilities of both parties.

I. The current yield on a bond refers to the ratio of annual interest payment to the bond's market price.

J.   Bond ratings

    1.   Bond ratings are simply judgments about the future risk potential of the bond in question. Bond ratings are extremely important in that a firm's bond rating tells much about the cost of funds and the firm's access to the debt market.

    2.   Three primary rating agencies exist—Moody's, Standard & Poor's, and Fitch Investor Services.

    3.   The different ratings and their implications are described.

III.   Definitions of value

    A.   Book value is the value of an asset shown on a firm's balance sheet which is determined by its historical cost rather than its current worth.

    B.   Liquidation value is the amount that could be realized if an asset is sold individually and not as part of a going concern.

    C.   Market value is the observed value of an asset in the marketplace where buyers and sellers negotiate an acceptable price for the asset.

    D.   Intrinsic value is the value based upon the expected cash flows from the investment, the riskiness of the asset, and the investor's required rate of return. It is the value in the eyes of the investor and is the same as the present value of expected future cash flows to be received from the investment.

IV.   Valuation: An Overview

    A.   Value is a function of three elements:

        1.   The amount and timing of the assets' expected cash flows

        2.   The riskiness of these cash flows

        3.   The investors' required rate of return for undertaking the investment

    B.   Expected cash flows are used in measuring the returns from an investment.

V. Valuation: The Basic Process

The value of an asset is found by computing the present value of all the future cash flows expected to be received from the asset. Expressed as a general present value equation, the value of an asset is found as follows:

$$V = \frac{\$C_1}{(1+k)^1} + \frac{\$C_2}{(1+k)^2} + \cdots + \frac{\$C_n}{(1+k)^n}$$

where C_t = the cash flow to be received at time t

V = the intrinsic value or present value of an asset producing expected future cash flows, C_t, in years 1 through N

k = the investor's required rate of return

N = the number of periods

VI. Bond Valuation

A. The value of a bond is simply the present value of the future interest payments and maturity value discounted at the bondholder's required rate of return. This may be expressed as:

$$V_b = \frac{\$I_1}{(1+k_b)^1} + \frac{\$I_2}{(1+k_b)^2} + \cdots + \frac{\$I_n}{(1+k_b)^n} + \frac{\$M}{(1+k_b)^n}$$

where I_t = the dollar interest to be received in each payment

M = the par value of the bond at maturity

k_b = the required rate of return for the bondholder

N = the number of periods to maturity

In other words, we are discounting the expected future cash flows to the present at the appropriate discount rate (required rate of return).

B. If interest payments are received semiannually (as with most bonds) the valuation equation becomes:

$$V_b = \frac{\$I_1/2}{\left(1+\dfrac{k_b}{2}\right)^1} + \frac{\$I_2/2}{\left(1+\dfrac{k_b}{2}\right)^2} + \cdots + \frac{\$I_{2n}/2}{\left(1+\dfrac{k_b}{2}\right)^{2n}} + \frac{\$M}{\left(1+\dfrac{k_b}{2}\right)^{2n}}$$

VII.   Yield to Maturity

    A.   The bondholder's expected rate of return is the rate the investor will earn if the bond is held to maturity, provided of course that the company issuing the bond does not default on the payments. This rate is also known as the yield to maturity.

    B.   We compute the bondholder's expected rate of return by finding the discount rate that gets the present value of the future interest payments and principal payment just equal to the bond's current market price.

VIII.   Bond Value: Three Important Relationships

    A.   First relationship

        A decrease in interest rates (required rates of return) will cause the value of a bond to increase; an interest rate increase will cause a decrease in value. The change in value caused by changing interest rates is called interest rate risk.

    B.   Second relationship

        1.   If the bondholder's required rate of return (current interest rate) equals the coupon interest rate, the bond will sell at par, or maturity value.

        2.   If the current interest rate exceeds the bond's coupon rate, the bond will sell below par value, or at a "discount."

        3.   If the current interest rate is less than the bond's coupon rate, the bond will sell above par value, or at a "premium."

    C.   Third relationship

        A bondholder owning a long-term bond is exposed to greater interest rate risk than when owning a short-term bond.

Study Problems

1. Gents Clothiers, Inc. has bonds maturing in 6 years and pays 6% interest semiannually on a $1000 face value.

    a. If your required rate of return is 10%, what is the value of the bond?

    b. How would your answer change if the interest were paid annually?

SOLUTION

    a. Value of bond if interest is paid semiannually:

       (1) Present value of interest payments:

$$= \$30 \ (PVIFA_{12,5\%}) = \$30 \ (8.863)$$

$$= \$265.89$$

       (2) Present value of principal:

$$= \$1,000 \ (PVIFA_{12,5\%}) = \$1,000(0.557)$$

$$= \$557$$

       (3) Present value of the interest and principal

Present value of the interest	$265.89
Present value of the principal	557.00
Value of the bond	$822.89

    b. Value of bond if interest is paid annually:

       (1) Present value of the interest payments:

$$= \$60 \ (PVIFA_{6,10\%}) = \$60(4.355)$$

$$= \$261.30$$

       (2) Present value of the principal:

$$= \$1,000 \ (PVIFA_{6,10\%}) = \$1,000(0.564)$$

$$= \$564$$

       (3) Present value of the interest and principal

Present value of the interest	$261.30
Present value of the principal	564.00
Value of the bond	$825.30

2. Edge Manufacturing Corporation's bonds are selling in the market for $1,193.96. These 15-year bonds pay 8% interest (annually) on a $1,000 par value. If they are purchased at the market price, what is the expected rate of return?

SOLUTION

Expected Rate of Return:

$$\$1,193.96 = \$80 \, (PVIFA_{15, k_b}) + \$1,000 \, (PVIFA_{15, k_b})$$

where k_b is the expected rate of return to be solved for by trial and error. Try a 6% rate of return. At 6% the present value of the interest and principal is equal to

$$\$80(9.712) + \$1,000(0.417) = \$1,193.96$$

The expected rate of return is 6%.

(Note: With a financial calculator, there is no need to guess as to the rate. The rate may be determined by the calculator.)

3. The market price is $865.60 for a 5-year, 12% bond ($1,000 face value) that pays interest semiannually. What is the expected rate of return?

SOLUTION

$$\$865.60 = \$60 \, (PVIFA_{10, k_b}) + \$1,000 \, (PVIF_{10, k_b})$$

where k_b is the expected rate of return (to be solved by trial and error).

Try 8%:

$$\$60(6.710) + \$1,000(0.463) = \$865.60$$

The required rate of return is 8% (on a semiannual basis) or 16% (on an annual basis).

TRUE-FALSE

_____ 1. The par value of a bond is essentially independent of the market value of a bond.

_____ 2. The only variable that can cause the value of a bond to increase or decrease is a change in the bondholder's required rate of return.

_____ 3. In an efficient marketplace, the intrinsic value of a security will equal its market value.

_____ 4. If the market price of a security is larger than the value assigned to the security by an investor, then the expected rate is greater than the required rate of return.

_____ 5. Bond ratings indicate the chance that the bondholder will experience interest rate risk with a given bond.

_____ 6. The intrinsic value of an asset can be defined as the present value of the asset's expected future cash flows.

_____ 7. The yield to maturity of a bond is the current value of the bond.

_____ 8. The three items that directly affect the cash flows from owning a bond are the bond's par value, maturity date, and the coupon rate of interest.

_____ 9. The expected rate of return is equal to the required rate of return of bondholders who are willing to pay the present market price for the bonds.

_____ 10. An increase in interest rates will cause the value of a bond to increase.

_____ 11. An increase in interest automatically drives bonds' stated rates up.

_____ 12. Changes in interest rates have a greater impact on the value of short-term bonds as opposed to the value of long-term bonds.

_____ 13. The stated coupon rate of interest has no effect on the market price of a bond.

_____ 14. Investors are attracted to zero coupon bonds by their high periodic interest payments.

_____ 15. In the case of insolvency, bondholders are honored before common stock but after preferred stock.

_____ 16. A bond denominated by yen, issued in Japan, and not registered with the SEC, could not be classified as a Eurobond.

_____ 17. Junk bonds differ from high-yield bonds in that junk bonds will almost always carry a lower rating than high-yield bonds.

_____ 18. In an efficient marketplace, the intrinsic value of a security will equal its market value.

MULTIPLE CHOICE

1. For a $1,000 par-value bond carrying an 8% coupon (interest paid quarterly) and having a 10% yield to maturity, the quarterly interest payments would be

   a. $20.
   b. $30.
   c. $25.
   d. $50.
   e. $10.

2. The value of a security may be expressed as a function of

   a. expected cash flows.
   b. riskiness of cash flows.
   c. the investor's required rate of return.
   d. a and b only.
   e. a, b, and c.

3. If the market is in equilibrium, the expected rate of return and the required rate of return

   a. will be the same.
   b. will be different.
   c. have no relationship to each other.

4. If everything else is assumed to be constant, as the investor's required rate of return decreases, the value of a security

    a.   stays the same.
    b.   increases.
    c.   decreases.
    d.   has no relationship to the investor's required rate of return.

5. In the basic security valuation model

$$V = \frac{\$C_1}{(1+k)^1} + \frac{\$C_2}{(1+k)^2} + \cdots + \frac{\$C_n}{(1+k)^n}$$

C_1 stands for

    a.   the investor's required rate of return.
    b.   cash flow to be received in year 1.
    c.   the intrinsic value of an asset producing expected future cash flows.
    d.   none of the above.

6. The _____ of an asset is the observed value for the asset in the marketplace.

    a.   intrinsic value
    b.   liquidation value
    c.   market value
    d.   none of the above

7. The _____ is the legal agreement that provides the specific terms of the loan agreement.

    a.   mortgage
    b.   debenture
    c.   indenture
    d.   prospectus

8. A(n) _____ is a bond secured by a lien on real property.

    a.   mortgage bond
    b.   subordinated debenture
    c.   Eurobond
    d.   coupon bond

9. Junk bonds have all the following characteristics except

   a. rated BB or lower.
   b. low rates of return.
   c. highly speculative.
   d. no security.

10. Bond valuation depends on all but

    a. the amount of cash flows to be received.
    b. the maturity date of the loan.
    c. the investor's required rate of return.
    d. when the loan was issued.

11. When a bond is worth more than its face value, it is said to sell

    a. at a discount.
    b. at a premium.
    c. at its maturity value.
    d. above its market return.

12. When the market interest rate rises above the stated interest rate of a bond, the bond

    a. will sell at a discount.
    b. will sell at a premium.
    c. will sell at its par or stated value.
    d. will not sell because investors can receive a better return from the market.

13. The risk of changing bond values due to the variability of future interest rates is

    a. time value of money.
    b. interest-rate risk.
    c. timing risk.
    d. investment risk.

14. The current yield on a bond refers to

  a.   the interest payments due within the next year.
  b.   the ratio of the annual interest payment to the bond's market price.
  c.   the interest earned in the current period.
  d.   the coupon rate of interest.

15. Bond ratings are favorably affected by all except

  a.   profitable operations.
  b.   large firm size.
  c.   low variability in past earnings.
  d.   taking more advantage of financial leverage.

16. When bond prices are quoted, they are generally expressed at

  a.   par value.
  b.   face value.
  c.   a percentage of par value.
  d.   current yield.

17. The current interest rate can also be called

  a.   the yield to maturity.
  b.   the coupon interest rate.
  c.   the expected rate of return.
  d.   the risk premium.
  e.   a and c

CHAPTER 8
Valuation and Characteristics of Stock

Orientation: This chapter continues the introduction of concepts underlying asset valuation began in Chapter 7. We are specifically concerned with valuing preferred stock and common stock. We also look at the concept of a stockholder's expected rate of return on an investment.

I. Preferred Stock

    A. Features of preferred stock

        1. Owners of preferred stock receive dividends instead of interest.

        2. Most preferred stocks are perpetuities (non-maturing).

        3. Multiple series, each having different characteristics, can be issued.

        4. Preferred stock has priority over common stock with regard to claims on assets in the care of bankruptcy.

        5. Most preferred stock carries a cumulative feature that requires all past unpaid preferred stock dividends to be paid before any common stock dividends are declared.

        6. Preferred stock may contain other protective provisions.

        7. Preferred stock may contain provisions to convert to a predetermined number of shares of common stock.

8. Retirement features for preferred stock are frequently included.

   a. Callable preferred refers to a feature which allows preferred stock to be called or retired, like a bond.

   b. A sinking fund provision requires the firm periodically to set aside an amount of money for the retirement of its preferred stock.

B. Valuation of preferred stock (V_{ps}):

The value of a preferred stock equals the present value of all future dividends. If the stock is nonmaturing, where dividends are expected in equal amount each year in perpetuity, the value may be calculated as follows:

$$V_{ps} = \frac{\text{annual dividend}}{\text{required rate of return}} = \frac{D}{k_{ps}}$$

II. Common Stock

A. Features of Common Stock

   1. As owners of the corporation, common shareholders have the right to the residual income and assets after bondholders and preferred stockholders have been paid.

   2. Common stock shareholders are generally the only security holders with the right to elect the board of directors.

   3. Preemptive rights entitles the common shareholder to maintain a proportionate share of ownership in the firm.

   4. Common stock shareholders liability as owners of the corporation is limited to the amount of their investment.

   5. Common stock's value is equal to the present value of all future cash flows expected to be received by the stockholder.

B. Valuing common stock

   1. Company growth occurs either by:

      a. The infusion of new capital.

b. The retention of earnings, which we call internal growth. The internal growth rate of a firm equals:

$$\text{Return on equity} \times \left(\begin{array}{c} \text{Percentage of earnings} \\ \text{retained within the firm} \end{array} \right)$$

2. The earnings growth of a firm should be reflected in a higher price for the firm's stock.

3. The present value of future dividends approach is one method of valuing common stock.

a. Common stock dividends are not pre-determined, but are based on the profitability of the firm.

b. In finding the value of a common stock (V_{cs}), we should discount all future expected dividends (D_1, D_2, D_3, ..., D_∞) to the present at the required rate of return for the stockholder (k_c). That is:

$$V_{cs} = \frac{D_1}{(1+k_{cs})^1} + \frac{D_2}{(1+k_{cs})^2} + ... + \frac{D_\infty}{(1+k_{cs})^\infty}$$

c. If we assume that the amount of dividend is increasing by a constant growth rate each year,

$$D_t \quad = \quad D^0 (1+g)^t$$

where g = the growth rate

D_0 = the most recent dividend payment

If the growth rate, g, is the same each year and is less than the required rate of return, K_{cs}, the valuation equation for common stock can be reduced to

$$V_{cs} \quad = \quad \frac{D_1}{k_{cs} - g} = \frac{D_0(1+g)}{k_{cs} - g}$$

4. The second approach to valuing common stock is by determining the present value of free cash flows.

    a. This method determines free cash flows for a "competitive advantage period," and then continues with an estimation of free cash flows for the "post-competitive advantage period" based on a constant growth rate.

    b. We calculate the present value of free cash flows during the competitive-advantage period discounted at the cost of capital

$$\text{Present Value Competitive Advantage Period} = \frac{FCF_1}{(1+k)^1} + \frac{FCF_2}{(1+k)^2} + \ldots \frac{FCF_T}{(1+k)^T}$$

    c. Next we assume that the free cash flows will grow at a constant rate, and we calculate the residual value as:

$$RV_T = \frac{FCF_{T+1}}{k - g}$$

And the present value of the residual value is:

$$\text{Present value of the Residual} = \frac{\text{Residual value year T}}{(1 + k)^T}$$

    d. The firm value is then determined by adding the present value of the competitive advantage period to the present value of the residual value. To arrive at shareholder value, debt is subtracted by firm value, and then divided by shares outstanding to arrive at the value per share.

III. Shareholder's Expected Rate of Return

    A. The shareholder's expected rate of return is of great interest to financial mangers because it tells about the investor's expectations.

    B. Preferred stockholder's expected rate of return.

    If we know the market price of a preferred stock and the amount of the dividends to be received, the expected rate of return from the investment can be determined as follows:

$$\text{expected rate of return} = \frac{\text{annual dividend}}{\text{market price of the stock}}$$

or

$$\overline{k}_{ps} = \frac{D}{P_{ps}}$$

C. Common stockholder's expected rate of return

1. The expected rate of return for common stock can be calculated from the valuation equations discussed earlier.

2. Assuming that dividends are increasing at a constant annual growth rate (g), we can show that the expected rate of return for common stock, $\overline{k}_{cs}$ is

$$\overline{k}_{cs} = \left(\frac{\text{dividend in year1}}{\text{market price}}\right) + \begin{pmatrix} \text{annual} \\ \text{growth} \\ \text{rate} \end{pmatrix}$$

$$= \frac{D_1}{P_{cs}} + g$$

Since dividend ÷ price is the "dividend yield," the

$$\text{Expected rate of return} = \begin{pmatrix} \text{dividend} \\ \text{yield} \end{pmatrix} + \begin{pmatrix} \text{annual} \\ \text{growth} \\ \text{rate} \end{pmatrix}$$

1. The preferred stock of Craft Company pays a $3 dividend. What is the value of the stock if your required rate of return is 8%?

SOLUTION

$$\text{Value of preferred stock} = \frac{\text{dividend}}{\text{required rate of return}}$$

$$P_{ps} = \frac{\$3}{0.08} = \$37.50$$

2. Universal Machines' common stock paid $1.50 in dividends *last year*, and dividends are expected to grow indefinitely at an annual 6% rate. What is the value of the stock if you require a 12% return?

SOLUTION

$$\text{Value } (P_{cs}) = \frac{\text{dividend in year 1}}{\text{required rate - growth rate}} = \frac{D_1}{k_{cs} - g}$$

$$\text{where } D_1 = D_0(1+g) = \$1.50(1 + 0.06) = \$1.59$$

Then,

$$P_{cs} = \frac{\$1.59}{0.12 - 0.06} = \$26.50$$

3. Texas Mining Company's common stock is selling for $35. The stock paid dividends of $2.50 last year and has a projected growth rate of 10%. If you buy the stock at the market price, what is the expected rate of return?

SOLUTION

Expected rate of return (k_{cs}):

$$\overline{k}_{cs} = \frac{\text{dividend in year 1}}{\text{price}} + \frac{\text{growth}}{\text{rate}} = \frac{D_1}{P_{cs}} + g$$

where D_1 = $D_0 (1+g) = \$2.50\,(1+0.10) = \$2.75$

P_0 = $35

$\overline{k}_{cs} = \dfrac{\$2.75}{\$35.00} + 0.10 = 0.1785$

= 17.85%

4. Idalou Power Company's preferred stock is selling for $25 in the market and pays $2.50 in dividends.

   a.   What is the expected rate of return on the stock?

   b.   If your required rate of return is 12%, what is the fair value of the stock for you?

   c.   Should you acquire the stock?

SOLUTION

   a.   Expected rate of return = $\dfrac{\$2.50}{\$25.00}$ = 10%

   b.   Value of the stock to you = $\dfrac{\$2.50}{0.12}$ = $20.83

   c.   Since your required rate of return is higher than the expected rate of return, you should not acquire it.

5. The market price of International Electric Corporation is $40. The price at the end of one year is expected to be $45. Dividends for next year should be $2.50. What is the expected rate of return for a single holding period of one year?

SOLUTION

$$\text{current price } (P_{cs}) = \frac{\text{dividend in year 1}}{1 + \text{expected rate of return}} + \frac{\text{price in year 1}}{1 + \text{expected rate of return}}$$

$$\frac{\text{expected}}{\text{return}} = \frac{\text{dividend in year 1} + \text{price in year 1}}{\text{current price}} - 1$$

$$\frac{\text{expected}}{\text{return}} = \frac{\$2.50 + \$45.00}{\$40.00} - 1 = 18.75\%$$

TRUE-FALSE

_____ 1. An assumption necessary in the model for common stock valuation

$$P_{cs} = \frac{D_1}{k_{cs} - g}$$

is that the amount of the dividend increases by a constant percent each year.

_____ 2. Protective provisions can allow preferred stockholders a voting right in the event of nonpayment of dividends.

_____ 3. If the market price of a security is larger than the value assigned to the security by an investor, then the expected rate is greater than the required rate of return.

_____ 4. The term "growth" when used in the context of a valuation model includes growth from reinvesting profits and from issuing stock.

_____ 5. The value of a preferred stock is the future value of the stock at maturity.

_____ 6. The constant growth common stock valuation model is defined as:

$$\text{common stock value} = \frac{\text{required rate of return}}{\text{dividend in year 1}}$$

assuming the dividends grow each year at a constant rate.

_____ 7. Valuation does not support the financial officer's objective of maximizing the value of the firm's common stock.

_____ 8. The option involved in convertible preferred stock belongs to the corporations issuing the shares.

_____ 9. A sinking-fund provision requires the firm to pay all unpaid preferred stock dividends before any common stock dividends are declared.

_____ 10. A cumulative feature requires the firm to set aside an amount of money for the retirement of its preferred stock.

_____ 11. The preemptive right entitles current shareholders to get the first opportunity to purchase new stock issues.

_____ 12. Preferred stockholders have a stronger voice in company operations than common stockholders.

_____ 13. An advantage of preferred stock over common stock is the regular interest payments that must be paid before dividends can be paid to common stockholders.

_____ 14. A majority voting feature pertains to the margin by which elections must be won.

_____ 15. A proxy allows a designated party to temporarily vote for someone else.

MULTIPLE CHOICE

1.   The most recent dividend paid by Xeron on its common stock was $1.50 (annual). The required rate of return for the security is 6%. Growth is anticipated to be at 4% annually. The market price of the stock should be

      a. $78.
      b. $100.
      c. $50.
      d. $150.
      e. $75.

2.   The income received by the holder of a preferred stock is similar to the income received from which other financial asset in terms of it being a constant amount each year?

      a.   Common stocks
      b.   Bonds
      c.   Both a and b
      d.   None of the above

3. What is the expected rate of return for a stock with a current market price of $44, if the expected dividend at the conclusion of this year is $2.20, and earnings are growing at a 10% annual rate? (Assume that the dividends are anticipated to grow at the same rate.)

    a. 25%
    b. 10%
    c. 5%
    d. 15%

4. Which of the following is not a common trait of preferred stock?

    a. Convertibility
    b. Cumulative dividends
    c. Voting rights
    d. Preferred claim on assets and income over common stock

5. _____ allows the preferred stockholder to be paid beyond the payment of the stated dividend.

    a. A carry-back feature
    b. A cumulative feature
    c. A stock premium
    d. A preemptive right

6. _____ allows the issuing corporation to retire the stock.

    a. A preemptive right
    b. Convertibility
    c. Callable preferred
    d. PIK preferred

7. Common stock involves _____ the corporation.

    a. ownership in
    b. personally managing
    c. being a creditor of
    d. the maturity of

8. _____ allows a designated party the temporary power of attorney to vote for the signee at the corporation's annual meeting.

    a.   Majority voting
    b.   A proxy
    c.   Absentee voting
    d.   Protective provisions

9. _____ gives the shareholder one vote for each share of stock, and each board position is voted on separately.

    a.   Cumulative voting
    b.   A proxy
    c.   Majority voting
    d.   Preemptive right

10. Which of the following does not affect the value of a stock?

    a.   Expected cash inflow
    b.   Riskiness of the stock
    c.   The investor's required rate of return
    d.   The stock's par or stated value

11. Common stock dividends must be _____ before issued.

    a.   approved by common stockholders
    b.   registered with the SEC
    c.   approved by preferred stockholders
    d.   declared by the firm's board of directors

12. Common stock dividends are

    a.   limited to twice the amount received by preferred stockholders
    b.   unlimited
    c.   always paid on a monthly basis
    d.   recognized before preferred stock dividends

CHAPTER 9
Capital-Budgeting Techniques and Practice

<u>Orientation</u>: Capital budgeting involves the decision-making process with respect to investment in fixed assets; specifically, it involves measuring the incremental cash flows associated with investment proposals and evaluating the attractiveness of these cash flows relative to the project's costs. This chapter focuses on the various decision criteria. It also examines how to deal with complications in the capital-budgeting process including mutually exclusive projects and capital rationing.

I.   Methods for evaluating projects

      A.   The payback period method

            1.   The payback period of an investment tells the number of years required to recover the initial investment. The payback period is calculated by adding the cash flows up until they are equal to the initial fixed investment.

            2.   Although this measure does, in fact, deal with cash flows and is easy to calculate and understand, it ignores any cash flows that occur after the payback period and does not consider the time value of money within the payback period.

      B.   Present-value methods

            1.   The net present value of an investment project is the present value of the cash inflows less the present value of the cash outflows. By assigning negative values to cash outflows, it becomes

$$NPV = \sum_{t=1}^{n} \frac{FCF_t}{(1 + k)^t} - IO$$

where FCF_t =   the annual free cash flow in time period t (this can take on either positive or negative values)

         k =   the required rate of return or appropriate discount rate or cost of capital

         IO =   the initial cash outlay

         n =   the project's expected life

a.   The acceptance criteria are

accept if NPV $\geq$ 0

reject if NPV $<$ 0

b.   The advantage of this approach is that it takes the time value of money into consideration in addition to dealing with cash flows.

2.   The profitability index is the ratio of the present value of the expected future net cash flows to the initial cash outlay, or

$$\text{profitability index} = \frac{\sum_{t-1}^{n} \frac{FCF_t}{(1+k)^t}}{IO}$$

a.   The acceptance criteria are

accept if PI $\geq$ 1.0

reject if PI $<$ 1.0

b.   The advantages of this method are the same as those for the net present value.

c.   Either of these present-value methods will give the same accept/reject decisions to a project.

C.   The internal rate of return is the discount rate that equates the present value of the project's future net cash flows with the project's initial outlay. Thus the internal rate of return is represented by IRR in the equation below:

$$IO = \sum_{t=1}^{n} \frac{FCF_t}{(1 + IRR)^t}$$

1.   The acceptance-rejection criteria are:

accept if IRR $\geq$ required rate of return

reject if IRR $<$ required rate of return

The required rate of return is often taken to be the firm's cost of capital.

2.   The advantages of this method are that it deals with cash flows and recognizes the time value of money; however, the procedure is rather complicated and time-consuming.

D.   The MIRR is similar to the IRR except it relies on the assumption that all free cash flows over the life of the project are reinvested at the required rate of return until the termination of the project. Thus, to calculate the *MIRR*, we:

Step 1: Determine the present value of the project's free cash *out*flows. We do this by discounting all the free cash *out*flows, back to the present at the required rate of return. If the initial outlay is the only free cash *out*flow, then the initial outlay is the present value of the free cash *out*flows.

Step 2: Determine the present value of the project's free cash inflows. Take all the annual free cash *in*flows and find their future value at the end of the project's life, compounded forward at the required rate of return. We will call this the project's *terminal value*, or *TV*.

Step 3: Calculate the MIRR. The MIRR is the discount rate that equates the present value of the free cash outflows with the present value of the project's terminal value.

1.   The modified internal rate of return is defined as the value of MIRR in the following equation:

$$PV_{outflows} = \frac{TV_{inflows}}{(1 + MIRR)^n} \qquad (9\text{-}4)$$

Where $PV_{outflows}$ = the present value of the project's free cash outflows

$TV_{inflows}$ = the project's terminal value, calculated by taking all the annual free cash *in*flows and find their future value at the end of the project's life, compounded forward at the required rate of return

n = the project's expected life

MIRR = the project's modified internal rate of return

II.   Mutually exclusive projects: Although the IRR and the present-value methods will, in general, give consistent accept-reject decisions, they may not rank projects identically. This becomes important in the case of mutually exclusive projects.

   A.   A project is mutually exclusive if acceptance of it precludes the acceptance of one or more projects. Then, in this case, the project's relative ranking becomes important.

   B.   Ranking conflicts come as a result of the different assumptions on the reinvestment rate on funds released from the proposals. The MIRR method can take care of this problem.

   C.   Thus, when conflicting ranking of mutually exclusive projects results from the different reinvestment assumptions, the decision boils down to which assumption is best.

   D.   In general, the net present value method is considered to be theoretically superior.

III.   Capital rationing is the situation in which a budget ceiling or constraint is placed upon the amount of funds that can be invested during a time period.

   A.   Theoretically, a firm should never reject a project that yields more than the required rate of return. Although there are circumstances that may create complicated situations in general, an investment policy limited by capital rationing is less than optimal.

Study Problems

1. The cost of new machinery for a given investment project will be $100,000. Incremental cash flows after taxes will be $40,000 in years 1 and 2 and will be $60,000 in year 3. What is the payback period for this project, and if acceptable projects must recover the initial investment in 2.5 years, should this project be accepted or rejected?

SOLUTION

After 2 years they will have recovered $80,000 of the $100,000 outlay and they expect to recover an additional $60,000 in the third year. Thus, the payback period becomes

$$2 \text{ years} + \frac{\$20,000}{\$60,000} = 2.33 \text{ years}$$

2.33 years < 2.5 years. Therefore, accept the project.

2. A given investment project will cost $50,000. Incremental annual cash flows after taxes are expected to be $10,000 per year for the life of the investment, which is 5 years. There will be no salvage value at the end of the 5 years. The required rate of return is 14%. On the basis of the profitability index method, should the investment be accepted?

SOLUTION

PV of cash flow = $10,000(3.433) = $34,330

PV of cash outlay = $50,000

$$PI = \frac{\$34,330}{\$50,000} = 0.6866 < 1$$

Therefore, the project should be rejected.

3. Determine the internal rate of return on the following projects:

(a) An initial outlay of $10,000 resulting in a cash flow of $2,146 at the end of each year for the next 10 years

(b) An initial outlay of $10,000 resulting in a cash flow of $1,960 at the end of each year for the next 20 years

(c) An initial outlay of $10,000 resulting in a cash flow of $1,396 at the end of each year for the next 12 years

(d) An initial outlay of $10,000 resulting in a cash flow of $3,197 at the end of each year for the next 5 years

SOLUTION

(a) $IO = FCF_t [PVIFA_{IRR\%, t\ yrs.}]$

$\$10,000 = \$2,146 [PVIFA_{IRR\%, 10\ yrs.}]$

$4.659 = PVIFA_{IRR\%, 10\ yrs.}$

Thus, IRR = 17%

(b) $\$10,000 = \$1,960 [PVIFA_{IRR\%, 20\ yrs.}]$

$5.102 = PVIFA_{IRR\%, 20\ yrs}$

Thus, IRR = 19%

(c) $\$10,000 = \$1,396 [PVIFA_{IRR\%, 12\ yrs.}]$

$7.163 = PVIFA_{IRR\%, 12\ yrs.}$

Thus, IRR = 9%

(d) $\$10,000 = \$3,197 [PVIFA_{IRR\%, 5\ yrs.}]$

$3.128 = PVIFA_{IRR\%, 5\ yrs.}$

Thus, IRR = 18%

4. The Battling Bishops Corporation is considering two mutually exclusive pieces of machinery that perform the same task. The two alternatives available provide the following set of after-tax net cash flows:

Year	Equipment A	Equipment B
0	-$20,000	-$20,000
1	13,000	6,500
2	13,000	6,500
3	13,000	6,500
4		6,500
5		6,500
6		6,500
7		6,500
8		6,500
9		6,500

Equipment A has an expected life of 3 years, whereas equipment B has an expected life of 9 years. Assume a required rate of return of 14%.

(a) Calculate each project's payback period.

(b) Calculate each project's net present value.

(c) Calculate each project's internal rate of return.

(d) Are these projects comparable?

(e) Compare these projects using replacement chains and EAAs. Which project should be selected? Support your recommendation.

SOLUTION

(a) Payback A   =   1.5385 years

 Payback B   =   3.0769 years

(b) NPV_A = $\displaystyle\sum_{t=1}^{3} \frac{\$13,000}{(1 + 0.14)^t} - \$20,000$

 = $13,000 (2.322) - $20,000

 = $30,186 - $20,000

 = $10,186

117

$$NPV_B = \sum_{t=1}^{9} \frac{\$6,500}{(1 + 0.14)^t} - \$20,000$$

$$= \$6,500 \, (4.946) - \$20,000$$

$$= \$32,149 - \$20,000$$

$$= \$12,149$$

(c) $\$20,000 = \$13,000 \, [PVIFA_{IRR_A \%, 3 \, yrs}]$

Thus, IRR_A = over 40% (42.75%)

$\$20,000 = \$6,500 \, [PVIFA_{IRR_B \%, 9 \, yrs}]$

Thus, IRR_B = 29%

(d)   These projects are not comparable because future profitable investment proposals are affected by the decision currently being made. If project A is taken, at its termination the firm could replace the machine and receive additional benefits, while acceptance of project B would exclude this possibility.

(e)   Using 3 replacement chains, project A's cash flows would become:

Year	Cash flow
0	-$20,000
1	13,000
2	13,000
3	- 7,000
4	13,000
5	13,000
6	- 7,000
7	13,000
8	13,000
9	13,000

$$NPV_A = \sum_{t=1}^{9} \frac{\$13,000}{(1 + 0.14)^t} - \$20,000 - \frac{\$20,000}{(1+0.14)^3} - \frac{\$20,000}{(1+0.14)^6}$$

$$= \$13,000(4.946) - \$20,000 - \$20,000 \, (0.675)$$
$$- \$20,000 \, (0.456)$$

$$= \$64,298 - \$20,000 - \$13,500 - \$9,120$$

$$= \$21,678$$

The replacement chain analysis indicated that project A should be selected, as the replacement chain associated with it has a larger NPV than project B.

Project A's EAA:

Step 1: Calculate the project's NPV (from part b):

$$NPV_A = \$10,186$$

Step 2: Calculate the EAA:

$$EAA_A = NPV / PVIFA_{14\%, \, 3 \, yr.}$$

$$= \$10,186 / 2.322$$

$$= \$4,387$$

Project B's EAA:

Step 1: Calculate the project's NPV (from part b):

$$NPV_B = \$12,149$$

Step 2: Calculate the EAA:

$$EAA_B = NPV / PVIFA_{14\%, \, 9 \, yr.}$$

$$= \$12,149 / 4.946$$

$$= \$2,256$$

Project B should be selected because it has a higher EAA.

TRUE-FALSE

_____ 1. Capital rationing occurs because profitable projects must be rejected based on a lack of capital.

_____ 2. The net present value of a project decreases as the required rate of return increases.

_____ 3. The higher the discount rate, the more valued is the proposal with the early cash flows, all else being equal.

_____ 4. The net present value of a project will equal zero whenever the profitability index equals 1.0.

_____ 5. The net present value of a project will equal zero whenever the payback period of a project equals the firm's required payback period.

_____ 6. Capital rationing is not an optimal capital-budgeting strategy.

_____ 7. The profitability index provides the same accept/reject decision result as the net present value method.

_____ 8. If two projects are mutually exclusive, the one with the highest expected value should always be chosen, even if it is riskier.

_____ 9. One difference between the NPV and IRR approaches is the reinvestment rate assumption.

_____ 10. The NPV approach is preferred over the profitability index for mutually exclusive projects because it measures worth in absolute terms while the PI measures worth in relative terms.

MULTIPLE CHOICE

1. Which of the following considers the time value of money?

   a. Payback method
   b. Return on investment
   c. Profitability index
   d. None of the above

2. Which of the following is a non-discounted cash flow approach?

   a. Payback period
   b. Profitability index
   c. Internal rate of return
   d. Net present value

3. If the internal rate of return is greater than the required rate of return,

   a. the present value of all the cash flows will be less than the initial outlay.
   b. the payback will be less than the life of the investment.
   c. the project should be accepted.
   d. a and c.

4. If the cash flow pattern for a project has two sign reversals, then there can be as many as _____ positive IRRs.

   a. 1
   b. 2
   c. 3
   d. 4

APPENDIX 9A

Self-Teaching Supplement: Capital-Budgeting Techniques

I. Net Present Value and Profitability Index Methods

In making investment decisions regarding fixed assets, the analyst compares the benefits of projects with their associated costs. Unfortunately, this comparison is complicated by the fact that the benefits and costs accruing from a given project usually do not occur in the same time period and, thus, are not directly comparable. This incomparability is a result of the time value of money (i.e., a dollar received today is worth more than a dollar received in the future). This comes about because a dollar today can be put into the bank and earn interest, resulting in a larger sum in the future. In economic terms, we refer to the time value of money as its opportunity cost.

A. Using the net present value and profitability index

In this section, we compare the present value of a project's benefits with the present value of its cost. The difference in these present values is referred to as the net present value, and the ratio of benefits to cost is called the profitability index. Definitionally, then

$$\text{net present value} = \left(\begin{array}{c}\text{present value of}\\\text{future net cash flows}\end{array}\right) - \left(\begin{array}{c}\text{initial}\\\text{cash outlay}\end{array}\right)$$

$$\text{profitability index} = \frac{\left(\begin{array}{c}\text{present value of}\\\text{future net cash flows}\end{array}\right)}{\left(\begin{array}{c}\text{initial}\\\text{cash outlay}\end{array}\right)}$$

Although both capital-budgeting techniques provide us with the same accept/reject decision, they may rank two or more projects differently. This difference results because the net-present-value criterion measures the total dollar value of a project, while the profitability index measures its value relative to project cost. The decision criteria used in applying these decision tools are:

	NPV	PI
Accept	≥ 0	≥ 1
Reject	< 0	< 1

SOLVED PROBLEMS

EXERCISE 1

The initial cash outlay of a project is $100; the present value of the cash flows is $75. Compute the project's net present value and its profitability index. Should it be accepted?

SOLUTION

$$\text{net present value} = \left(\begin{array}{c}\text{present value of}\\\text{future net cash flows}\end{array}\right) - \left(\begin{array}{c}\text{initial}\\\text{cash outlay}\end{array}\right)$$

$$= \$75 - \$100 = -\$25$$

$$\text{profitability index} = \frac{\left(\begin{array}{c}\text{present value of}\\\text{future net cash flows}\end{array}\right)}{\left(\begin{array}{c}\text{initial}\\\text{cash outlay}\end{array}\right)}$$

$$= \frac{\$75}{\$100} = 0.75$$

Thus, the project should be rejected because its net present value is negative and its profitability index is less than 1.

123

EXERCISE 2

The present value of a project's future net cash flow is $580, and the initial cash outlay is $500. What is the project's net present value, and what is its profitability index? Should the project be accepted?

SOLUTION

$$\text{NPV} = \$580 - \$500 = \$80$$

$$\text{PI} = \frac{\$580}{\$500} = 1.16$$

This project should be accepted because the project's net present value is positive and its profitability index is greater than 1.0.

EXERCISE 3

A project's net present value is $300; the initial outlay is $500. What is the present value of the project's net cash flows?

SOLUTION

NPV = PV of project's net cash flows - initial outlay

$300 = PV of project's net cash flows - $500

$800 = PV of project's net cash flows

EXERCISE 4

A project's profitability index is 1.5, and the present value of its net cash flows is $450. What is the project's initial cash outlay?

SOLUTION

$$\text{PI} = \frac{\left(\begin{array}{c}\text{present value of}\\\text{future net cash flows}\end{array}\right)}{\left(\begin{array}{c}\text{initial}\\\text{cash outlay}\end{array}\right)}$$

$$1.5 = \frac{\$450}{\text{X}}$$

$$\text{X} = \$300$$

124

EXERCISE 5

If either the net-present-value criterion or the profitability index gives an accept signal, will the other criteria give a similar signal?

SOLUTION

Yes. The net-present-value and profitability index will always give similar accept/reject signals. Any time the present value of future net cash flows is greater than the initial outlay, the net-present-value criterion will be positive, signaling accept, and the profitability index will be greater than 1.0, signaling accept. However, because of size differences in projects, a small project, which is relatively more profitable than a project requiring a larger initial outlay, may have a smaller net present value. In this case, unless there is a limit on the amount of funds that is allocated, the net-present-value criterion should be used.

B. Compounding and Discounting: Single Cash Flows

To determine the present value of future cash flows, it is necessary to discount those cash flows back to the present. As demonstrated in Chapter 7 of the text, discounting cash flows back to the present is merely the reverse of compounding. For example, if we put $100 (P) in the bank, earning a rate of 10% (i) annually, at the end of 1 year (n) we would have $110 ($FV_1$):

$$FV_1 = PV(1+i)$$

$$\$110 = \$100(1+0.10)$$

Correspondingly, at the end of 3 years we would have $133.10:

$$\$133.10 = \$100(1+0.10)^3$$

On the other hand, with an opportunity rate of 10%, the present value (PV) of $110 to be received in 1 year can be found as follows:

$$\$110 = \$100(1+0.10)$$

$$PV = \$110\left(\frac{1}{(1+0.10)}\right)$$

$$= \$100$$

125

The present value of $133.10 to be received in 3 years is found similarly:

$$\$100 = \$133.10 \left(\frac{1}{(1+0.10)^3} \right)$$

SOLVED PROBLEMS

EXERCISE 1

What is the present value of $300 to be received in 3 years discounted at:

(a) 10% per annum?

(b) 5% per annum?

(c) 100% per annum?

SOLUTION

(a) $\text{PV} = \text{FV}_n \left(\dfrac{1}{(1+i)^n} \right)$

$\qquad = \$300 \left(\dfrac{1}{(1+0.10)^3} \right)$

$\qquad = \dfrac{\$300}{1.331} = \$225.39$

(b) $\text{PV} = \$300 \left(\dfrac{1}{(1+0.05)^3} \right)$

$\qquad = \dfrac{\$300}{1.157625} = \$259.15$

(c) $\text{PV} = \$300 \left(\dfrac{1}{(1+01.0)^3} \right)$

$\qquad = \dfrac{\$300}{8} = \$37.50$

EXERCISE 2

If the appropriate discount rate is 8%, what is the present value of $300 to be received in:

(a) 5 years?

(b) 10 years?

(c) 25 years?

SOLUTION

(a) $PV = FV_n \left(\dfrac{1}{(1+i)^n} \right)$

$= \$300 \left(\dfrac{1}{(1+0.08)^5} \right)$

$= \dfrac{\$300}{1.4693} = \$204.18$

(b) $PV = \$300 \left(\dfrac{1}{(1+0.08)^{10}} \right)$

$= \dfrac{\$300}{2.15189} = \$138.96$

(c) $PV = \$300 \left(\dfrac{1}{(1+0.08)^{25}} \right)$

$= \dfrac{\$300}{6.8485} = \$43.81$

Fortunately, it is not necessary to do the individual calculation for

$1/(1 + i)^n$ because, in the table in Appendix C (hereafter referred to as Table C with the table values being referred to as $PVIF_{i,n}$) of the text, the results of these calculations are presented for a large number of combinations of i and n. Thus, in order to determine the value of 1/(1

$+ 0.08)^5$, we need only look in the row of Table C corresponding to the fifth period and the 8% column to find an appropriate value of 0.681. Similarly, in Appendix B, a table is provided (hereafter referred to as Table B with the table values being referred to as $FVIF_{i,n}$) which gives the value of $(1 + i)^n$ for various combinations of i and n. This table can be used in compounding.

SELF TEST 1

1. What is the present value of $250 to be received in 10 years if the appropriate discount rate is 8%?

2. How much must I put in the bank compounded annually at 6% to have $5,000 at the end of 10 years?

3. If a new machine costs $5,000 and will return $3,000 the first year, $4,000 the second year, $2,000 the third year, and my opportunity rate on money is 8%, what is the project's profitability index?

4. What is the NPV for the project in question 3? Should it be accepted?

5. If a new tractor costs $10,000 and will return $3,000 the first year, $5,000 the second year, and $4,000 the third year, calculate the net present value and profitability index using a 10% discount rate. Should the project be accepted?

6. Calculate the net present value and profitability index for the following. Assume a 12% discount rate:

Year	Benefit (+) or Cost (-)
0	$-8,000
1	+3,000
2	+6,000
3	+2,000
4	+1,000
5	-1,000

7. What is the net present value of a bond that pays $100 per year in interest at the end of each year for 10 years, and additionally at the end of 10 years will pay the $1,000 par value if the appropriate discount rate is 8% and the bond costs $1,093?

C. Compounding and Discounting: Annuities

Problem 7 of Self Test 1 was actually an annuity problem. An annuity is simply a series of fixed payments for a specified number of years. This situation comes up frequently in finance, and in order to make the calculation of the present value of an annuity easier, you are provided with the present value of an annuity table (hereafter referred to as Table E with the table values being referred to as $PVIFA_{i,n}$) in Appendix E of the text, which gives present-value factors for an annuity. In addition, a compound annuity or sum of an annuity of $1 for n periods table (hereafter referred to as Table D with the table values referred to as $FVIFA_{i,n}$) is provided in Appendix D of the text. Now, in order to determine the present value of $1,000 received at the end of each year for 5 years, discounted back to present at 7%, you have two alternatives. You could use Table C and discount each one of the five $1,000 flows individually as follows:

$$FV_n \left(\frac{1}{(1+0.07)^1} \right) \quad = \quad \$1,000\ (0.935) \quad = \quad \$935.00$$

$$FV_n \left(\frac{1}{(1+0.07)^2} \right) \quad = \quad \$1,000\ (0.873) \quad = \quad \$873.00$$

$$FV_n \left(\frac{1}{(1+0.07)^3} \right) \quad = \quad \$1,000\ (0.816) \quad = \quad \$816.00$$

$$FV_n \left(\frac{1}{(1+0.07)^4} \right) \quad = \quad \$1,000\ (0.763) \quad = \quad \$763.00$$

$$FV_n \left(\frac{1}{(1+0.07)^5} \right) \quad = \quad \$1,000\ (0.713) \quad = \quad \underline{\$713.00}$$

$$\underline{\$4,100.00}$$

Alternatively, you could look up the annuity discount factor in Table E. The annuity factor for 5 years at 7% is 4.100; multiplying this times $1,000 gives $4,100—the same answer you obtained using Table C. This is because you really have only one table, Table C, the values of which have been summed to form Table E. Thus, the annuity discount factor for 5 years at 7% in Table E is equal to the sum of the discount factors for years 1 through 5 at 7% as found in Table C. Therefore, the annuity table value for n years at i% is equal to:

$$PVIFA_{i,n} = \left(\sum_{t=1}^{n} \frac{1}{(1+t)^t} \right) = \sum_{t=1}^{n} (PVIF_{i,n})$$

SOLVED PROBLEMS

EXERCISE 1

Pick any number in Table E; note the number of years (call it n) and the discount rate (call it i). Now look in Table C and add up the table values in the i discount rate column for the first n years. What do you find?

SOLUTION

The value found in Table E is equal (except perhaps for minor rounding errors) to the value found from summing the values in Table C.

EXERCISE 2

What is the present value of $50 to be received each year for 5 years if the appropriate discount rate is 8%? Solve this problem by using Table C.

SOLUTION

Present value

= $50 (PVIF_{8\%, 1 \text{ yr.}}) + $50 (PVIF_{8\%, 2 \text{ yr.}})

+ $50 (PVIF_{8\%, 3 \text{ yr.}}) + $50 (PVIF_{8\%, 4 \text{ yr.}})

+ $50 (PVIF_{8\%, 5 \text{ yr.}})

= $50(0.926) + $50(0.857) + $50(0.794) + $50(0.735)

+ $50(0.681)

130

$$= \$46.30 + \$42.85 + \$39.70 + \$36.75 + \$34.05$$

$$= \$199.65$$

EXERCISE 3

Solve Exercise 2 using Table E.

SOLUTION

$$\text{Present value} = \$50(\text{PVIFA}_{8\%,\ 5\ \text{yr.}}) = \$50\ (3.993)$$

$$= \$199.65$$

EXERCISE 4

What is the NPV of a bond that yields $80 per year in interest at the end of each year for the next 15 years and matures in 15 years, at which time it pays an additional $1,000; it is currently selling for $800 and your discount rate is 10%?

SOLUTION

$$\text{NPV} = \$\text{-}800 + \$80(\text{PVIFA}_{10\%,\ 15\ \text{yr.}})$$

$$+ \$1,000(\text{PVIF}_{10\%,\ 15\ \text{yr.}})$$

$$= \$\text{-}800 + \$80(7.606) + \$1,000(0.239)$$

$$= \$\text{-}800 + \$608.48 + \$239.00$$

$$= \$47.48$$

EXERCISE 5

What is the profitability index for the bond described in Exercise 4?

SOLUTION

$$\text{PI} = \frac{\$847.48}{\$800} = 1.059$$

131

EXERCISE 6

Given the following cash flows:

Year	Cash Flow
0	$-10,000
1	+ 5,000
2	+ 5,000
3	+ 5,000
4	+ 5,000
5	+ 5,000
6	+ 5,000
7	+10,000

What is the NPV of this project given an appropriate discount rate of

(a) 5%?

(b) 10%?

(c) 30%?

SOLUTION

(a) NPV $= \$-10,000 + \$5,000(\text{PVIFA}_{5\%, \, 6 \text{ yr.}})$

$+ \$10,000(\text{PVIF}_{5\%, \, 7 \text{ yr.}})$

$= \$-10,000 + \$5,000(5.076) + \$10,000(0.711)$

$= \$-10,000 + \$25,380 + \$7,110$

$= \$22,490$

(b) NPV $= \$-10,000 + \$5,000(\text{PVIFA}_{10\%, \, 6 \text{ yr.}})$

$+ \$10,000(\text{PVIF}_{10\%, \, 7 \text{ yr.}})$

$= \$-10,000 + \$5,000(4.355) + \$10,000(0.513)$

$= \$-10,000 + \$21,775 + \$5,130$

$= \$16,905$

(c) NPV = \$-10,000 + \$5,000(\text{PVIFA}_{30\%, 6\text{ yr.}})

+\$10,000(\text{PVIF}_{30\%, 7\text{ yr.}})

= \$-10,000 + \$5,000(2.643) + \$10,000(0.159)

= \$-10,000 + \$13,215 + \$1,590

= \$4,805

SELF TEST 2

1. What is the NPV of the following cash flows if the appropriate discount rate is 20%?

Year	Cash Flow
0	\$-15,000
1	+ 2,000
2	+ 2,000
3	+ 4,000
4	+ 5,000
5	+ 6,000

What is the profitability index? Should the project be accepted?

2. For how many years must \$1,000 compound at 8% to accumulate to \$2,000?

3. At what rate must \$1,000 compound to accumulate to \$3,000 in 7 years?

4. How much must you put in the bank compounded annually at 8% to accumulate to \$3,000 at the end of 10 years?

5. What is the present value of \$100 to be received at the end of each of the next 10 years discounted back to the present at

(a) 5%?

(b) 10%?

(c) 20%?

(d) 30%?

133

6. How much is $50 worth if it is to be received at the end of 4 years if the appropriate discount rate is

    (a) 10%?

    (b) 20%?

    (c) 0%?

    (d) 100%?

7. What is the future value of $100 if it is placed in the bank for 5 years and compounded at 16%?

    (a) Annually?

    (b) Semiannually?

    (c) Quarterly?

8. A company is examining a new machine to replace an existing machine that currently has a book value of $5,000 and can be sold for $2,000. The old machine has 5 years of expected life left, is being depreciated on a simplified straight-line basis, and will have a salvage value of zero in 5 years. The new machine will perform the same task but more efficiently, resulting in cash benefits before depreciation and taxes of $10,000. The expected life of the new machine is 5 years; it costs $20,000 and has no salvage value at the end of the fifth year. Assuming simplified straight-line depreciation, a 40% tax rate, and an appropriate discount rate of 14%, find the NPV and profitability index of the project.

II. The Internal-Rate-of-Return Method

In the previous section, we made capital-budgeting decisions through the use of the profitability index and net present-value criteria, by comparing the present value of the benefits of the project with the present value of its costs either through division (determining the profitability index) or subtraction (determining a net present value). In each case, you were supplied with an appropriate discount rate or cost of capital with which to determine the present value of future flows. You will now examine a method of evaluating projects that does not rely on an input discount rate but determines the discount rate that would make the project's NPV = 0, or, alternatively, makes its profitability index = 1.0. With the PI and NPV criteria, we have a measure of the relative profitability and absolute profitability of the project, with all flows adjusted for the time value of money. The next criterion we examine, the internal rate of return, can be thought of as a rate of return or yield on the project. The decision rules on this criterion can be stated as follows: If the IRR is greater than or equal to the required rate of return or hurdle rate, the project should be accepted; otherwise, the project should be rejected. Although this seems quite straightforward and easy to understand, one finds that the solution process is often complex and time-consuming.

A.   The Internal Rate of Return: The Case of a Single Cash Inflow

The internal rate of return is defined as that rate, IRR, which equates the present value of a project's anticipated cash inflows with the present value of the relevant cash outflows. Where ACF_t is the cash flow for period t, whether it be positive (an inflow) or negative (an outflow), and n is the last period in which any cash flow is expected, the internal rate of return is represented by IRR in equation (A.l):

$$\sum_{t=0}^{n} \frac{ACF_t}{(1+IRR)^t} \ = \ 0 \qquad\qquad (A.l)$$

A solution to this problem becomes quite simple in the case in which the only outlay occurs in time period 0 (the initial outlay, IO) and *only one* cash inflow occurs, say in time period t:

$$IO \ = \ \frac{ACF_t}{(1 + IRR)^t}$$

Since you can determine a numerical value for IO/ACF_t and you know that Table C in the text gives you values for $1/(1 + IRR)$, we can easily solve for IRR. All we have to do is look in Table C in the nth row (corresponding to the number of years until the cash inflow) until we find the value IO/ACF_t; the column that gives this value indicates the appropriate value of IRR.

135

EXERCISE 1

What is the internal rate of return on a project with an initial outlay of $6,000 which in the ninth year will produce one cash inflow of $18,000?

SOLUTION

$$\$6,000 = \frac{\$18,000}{(1+IRR)^9}$$

$$\frac{\$6,000}{\$18,000} = \frac{1}{(1+IRR)^9}$$

$$0.333 = \frac{1}{(1+IRR)^9}$$

The value of 0.333 is found in the 9-year row of Table C in the 13% column; thus, 13% is the project's internal rate of return.

EXERCISE 2

Given the following cash flows, what is the project's internal rate of return?

Year	Cash Flow
0	$-10,000
5	+40,000

SOLUTION

$$\frac{\$10,000}{\$40,000} = \frac{1}{(1+IRR)^5}$$

$$0.25 = \frac{1}{(1+IRR)^5}$$

Looking in Table C, IRR = 32%

EXERCISE 3

If a project requires an initial outlay of $6,000 and will return $10,000 in year 13, what is its internal rate of return?

SOLUTION

$$\frac{\$6,000}{\$10,000} = \frac{1}{(1+IRR)^{13}}$$

$$0.6 = \frac{1}{(1+IRR)^{13}}$$

Looking in Table C, IRR = 4%

The accept/reject criteria for the internal-rate-of-return method states that if the project's internal rate of return is greater than the required rate of return or hurdle rate, the project should be accepted; otherwise, the project should be rejected. In other words,

IRR $\geq$ required rate of return,   Accept

IRR $<$ required rate of return,   Reject

Thus, if the required rate of return in Exercises 1 through 3 were 10%, the projects examined in Exercises 1 and 2 would be accepted, and the project in Exercise 3 would be rejected.

B.   The Internal Rate of Return: Multiple and Equal Cash Inflows

In the case in which there is more than one cash inflow resulting from a project's acceptance, and the cash inflows form an annuity, a similar approach to that just outlined but using Table E instead of Table C will result in a correct solution. In this case, the simplification proceeds as follows:

$$IO = \sum_{t=0}^{T} \frac{ACF_t}{(1+IRR)^t}$$

If all the ACF values are equal and occur periodically (e.g., annually), we have an annuity. The value of the annuity discount factor, $\sum_{t=0}^{T} 1/(1 + IRR)^t$, can be found in Table E. Since we know the term of the annuity, n years, when solving for IRR we need merely look in the T-year row until we find the value IO/ACF_t; then looking to the column heading yields the internal rate of return.

SOLVED PROBLEMS

EXERCISE 1

What is the internal rate of return on a project with an initial outlay of $24,000 which will produce cash inflows of $6,000 for each of the next 15 years?

SOLUTION

$$\$24,000 = \sum_{t=0}^{15} \frac{\$6,000}{(1 + IRR)^t}$$

$$4.0 = \sum_{t=0}^{15} \frac{1}{(1 + IRR)^t}$$

Looking in Table E, IRR = 24%.

EXERCISE 2

What is the internal rate of return on a project with an initial outlay of $18,000 which will produce cash inflows of $3,000 for each year for the next 9 years?

SOLUTION

$$\$18,000 = \sum_{t=0}^{9} \frac{\$3,000}{(1 + IRR)^t}$$

$$6.0 = \sum_{t=0}^{9} \frac{1}{(1 + IRR)^t}$$

Looking in Table E, IRR = 9%.

EXERCISE 3

Given the following cash flows, what is this project's internal rate of return?

Year	Cash Flow
0	$20,000
1	5,000
2	5,000
3	5,000
4	5,000
5	5,000

SOLUTION

$$\$20,000 = \sum_{t=0}^{5} \frac{\$5,000}{(1 + IRR)^t}$$

$$4.0 = \sum_{t=0}^{5} \frac{1}{(1 + IRR)^t}$$

Looking in Table E, IRR = 8%.

For Exercises 1 through 3, if the required rate of return were 10%, the project in Exercise 1 would be accepted and the projects in Exercises 2 and 3 would be rejected.

C.   The Internal Rate of Return: Multiple and Unequal Cash Flows

The solution using the internal-rate-of-return criterion becomes more complex when there are unequal cash inflows resulting from a project's acceptance. In this case, the solution can be found only by trial and error, or with the use of a good financial calculator, or even a not-so-good calculator. Without the calculator, we first arbitrarily pick a return and solve the problem; then, depending on the result, raise or lower that rate until the present value of the inflows equals the present value of the outflows.

SOLVED PROBLEMS

EXERCISE 1

What is the internal rate of return on a project that costs $20,000 and returns $3,000 per year for the first 4 years and $5,000 per year in years 5 through 8?

SOLUTION

$$\$20,000 \ = \ \sum_{t=1}^{4} \frac{\$3,000}{(1 + .IRR)^t} \ + \ \sum_{t=5}^{8} \frac{\$5,000}{(1 + IRR)^t}$$

First, solve the problem using a discount rate picked arbitrarily. Try 20%. In this case, this equation reduces to

$\$20,000 \ = \ \$3,000(2.589) + \$7,000(3.837 - 2.589)$

$= \ \$7,767 + \$8,736$

$\neq \ \$16,503$

Thus, 20% is not this project's internal rate of return. If it were the internal rate of return, the present value of the inflows would equal the present value of the outflows; but the present value of the inflows is much less than the present value of the outflows. Since all the inflows occur in the future, the present value of these flows will increase as the discount rate is lowered, so here you should try a lower discount rate. If you try 13%, this equation becomes

$\$20,000 \ = \ \$3,000(2.974) + \$7,000(4.799 - 2.974)$

$= \ \$8,922 \ + \ \$21,775$

$\neq \ \$21,697$

This time, the present value of the inflows is less than the present value of the outflows. In order to raise the present value of the inflows, the discount rate must be lowered. This time, try 15%.

$$\$20,000 = \$3,000(2.855) + \$7,000(4.487 - 2.855)$$

$$= \$8,565 + \$11,424$$

$$\neq \$19,989$$

Now, the present value of the inflows is approximately equal to the present value of the outflows using a discount rate of 15%; the project's internal rate of return is very close to 15%.

EXERCISE 2

Given the following cash flows, what is the project's IRR?

Year	Cash Flow
0	$-12,000
1	+ 4,000
2	+ 4,000
3	+ 4,000
4	+ 4,000
5	+ 4,000
6	+ 2,000

SOLUTION

First, try 30%:

$$\$12,000 = \$4,000(2.436) + \$2,000(0.207)$$

$$= \$9,744 + \$414$$

$$\neq \$10,158$$

Since the present value of the cash inflows is too low, you must lower the discount rate and try again. This time, try 23%:

$$\$12,000 = \$4,000(2.689) + \$2,000(0.262)$$

$$= \$10,756 + \$524$$

$$\neq \$11,280$$

Again, the present value of the cash inflows is too low. Therefore, the discount rate is lowered and the problem is tried again. Next, try 20%:

$$\$12,000 = \$4,000(2.991) + \$2,000(0.335)$$

$$= \$11,964 + \$670$$

$$\neq \$12,634$$

Since the present value of the cash inflows is too high, the discount rate must be raised. We arbitrarily raise it to 23%:

$$\$12,000 \;=\; \$4,000(2.803) + \$2,000(0.289)$$

$$= \$11,212 + \$578$$

$$\neq \$11,790$$

This time, the present value of the inflows is too low; thus, the discount rate is lowered. We now try 22%:

$$\$12,000 \;=\; \$4,000(2.864) + \$2,000(0.303)$$

$$= \$11,456 + \$606$$

$$\neq \$12,062$$

Thus, the IRR for this problem is between 22% and 23%, and closer to 22%.

EXERCISE 3

What is the IRR associated with this project?

Year	Cash Flow
0	$-10,000
1	+ 3,000
2	+ 6,000
3	+ 9,000

SOLUTION

Try 20%:

$$\$10,000 = \$3,000(0.833) + \$6,000(0.694) + \$9,000\,(0.579)$$

$$= \$2,499 + \$4,164 + \$5,211$$

$$\neq \$11,874$$

The present value of the cash inflows is too large; therefore, the discount rate must be raised. Try 30%:

$$\$10,000 = \$3,000(0.769) + \$6,000(0.592) + \$9,000(0.455)$$

$$= \$2,307 + \$3,552 + \$4,095$$

$$\neq \$9,954$$

Now, it is too small; so try 29%:

$$\$10,000 = \$3,000(0.775) + \$6,000(0.601) + \$9,000(0.466)$$

$$= \$2,325 + \$3,606 + \$4,194$$

$$\neq \$10,125$$

Thus, this project's IRR is just under 30%.

As you can see by now, calculating the IRR can become quite time-consuming when a trial-and-error search is necessitated. If it is necessary, remember the following guidelines:

1. Always try a larger discount rate (or trial IRR) when the present value of the cash inflows is larger than the initial outlay.

2. Always try a smaller discount rate (or trial IRR) when the present value of the cash inflows is smaller than the initial cash outlay.

SELF TEST 3

1. What is the internal rate of return on a project that requires an initial outlay of $10,000 and returns $14,000 at the end of the fifth year?

2. What is the internal rate of return on a project that requires an initial outlay of $700 and returns $1,857 at the end of the twentieth year?

3. What is the internal rate of return on a project that requires a $30,000 outlay and returns $6,000 at the end of each of the next 10 years?

4. What is the internal rate of return on a project that requires an initial outlay of $20,000 and returns $3,928 at the end of each year for the next 15 years?

5. Given the following cash flows, determine an internal rate of return.

Year	Cash Flow
0	$-40,000
1	+10,000
2	+10,000
3	+10,000
4	+10,000
5	+10,000
6	+15,000

6. Given the following cash flows, determine an internal rate of return.

Year	Cash Flow
0	$-61,630
1	+10,000
2	+10,000
3	+10,000
4	+10,000
5	+10,000
6	+10,000
7	+70,000

7. Given the following cash flows, determine an internal rate of return.

Year	Cash Flow
0	$-2,992
1	+700
2	+1,400
3	+3,000

8. Given the following cash flows, determine an internal rate of return.

Year	Cash Flow
0	$5,492
1	2,000
2	2,000
3	4,000
4	3,000

9. What is the internal rate of return on a project that requires an initial outlay of $1,000 and returns $4,000 at the end of the second year?

APPENDIX A

SELF TEST 1

1. $250(PVIF_{8\%, 10\ yr.})$

   $250(0.463) = \$115.75$

2. $P = FV_{10}(PVIF_{6\%, 10\ yr.})$

   $= \$5,000(.558)$

   $= \$2,790$

3. Profitability index $= \dfrac{\left(\begin{array}{c}\text{present value of}\\ \text{future net cash flows}\end{array}\right)}{\left(\begin{array}{c}\text{initial}\\ \text{cash outlay}\end{array}\right)}$

   Present value of future net cash flows

   $= \$3,000\ (PVIF_{8\%, 1\ yr.}) + \$4,000(PVIF_{8\%, 2\ yr.})$
   $\quad + \$2,000(PVIF_{8\%, 3\ yr.})$

   $= \$3,000(0.926) + \$4,000(0.857) + \$2,000(0.794)$

   $= \$2,778 + \$3,428 + \$1,588$

   $= \$7,794$

   Profitability index

   $= \dfrac{\$7,794}{\$5,000} = 1.5588$

4. NPV $=$ PV inflows - PV outflows

   $= \$7,794 - \$5,000$

   $= \$2,794$

   Accept the project, because its NPV is positive and its PI is greater than 1.0.

5. $\text{NPV} = \$-10,000 + \$3,000(\text{PVIF}_{10\%, 1 \text{ yr.}})$
$+ \$5,000(\text{PVIF}_{10\%, 2 \text{ yr.}})$
$+ \$4,000(\text{PVIF}_{10\%, 3 \text{ yr.}})$

$= \$-10,000 + \$3,000(0.909) + \$5,000(0.826)$
$+ \$4,000(0.751)$

$= \$-10,000 + \$2,727 + \$4,130 + \$3,004$

$= \$-139$

$\text{PI} \quad = \dfrac{\$9,861}{\$10,000} = 0.9861$

Reject the project, because the NPV is negative and the PI is less than 1.0.

6. $\text{NPV} = \$-8,000 + \$3,000 (\text{PVIF}_{12\%, 1 \text{ yr.}})$
$+ \$6,000 (\text{PVIF}_{12\%, 2 \text{ yr.}})$
$+ \$2,000 (\text{PVIF}_{12\%, 3 \text{ yr.}})$
$+ \$1,000 (\text{PVIF}_{12\%, 4 \text{ yr.}})$
$- \$1,000 (\text{PVIF}_{12\%, 5 \text{ yr.}})$

$= \$-8,000 + \$3,000(0.893) + \$6,000(0.797)$
$+ \$2,000(0.712) + \$1,000(0.636) - \$1,000(0.567)$

$= \$-8,000 + \$2,679 + \$4,782 + \$1,424 + \$636 - \$567$

$= \$954$

$\text{PI} \quad = \dfrac{\$8,954}{\$8,000} = 1.1192$

7. $\text{NPV} = \$-1,093.00 + \$100(\text{PVIF}_{8\%, 1 \text{ yr.}}) + \$100(\text{PVIF}_{8\%, 2 \text{ yr.}})$
$+ \$100(\text{PVIF}_{8\%, 3 \text{ yr.}}) + \$100(\text{PVIF}_{8\%, 4 \text{ yr.}})$
$+ \$100(\text{PVIF}_{8\%, 5 \text{ yr.}}) + \$100(\text{PVIF}_{8\%, 6 \text{ yr.}})$
$+ \$100(\text{PVIF}_{8\%, 7 \text{ yr.}}) + \$100(\text{PVIF}_{8\%, 8 \text{ yr.}})$
$+ \$100(\text{PVIF}_{8\%, 9 \text{ yr.}}) + \$1,100(\text{PVIF}_{8\%, 10 \text{ yr.}})$

$$\begin{aligned}
\text{NPV} &= \$-1{,}093.00 + \$100(0.926) + \$100(0.857) + \$100(0.794) \\
&\quad + \$100(0.735) + \$100(0.681) + \$100(0.630) \\
&\quad + \$100(0.583) \ + \$100(0.540) + \$100(0.500) \\
&\quad + \$1{,}100(0.463) \\
&= \$-1{,}093.00 + \$92.60 + \$85.70 + \$79.48 + \$73.50 \\
&\quad + \$68.10 + \$63.00 + \$58.30 + \$54.00 + \$50.00 \\
&\quad + \$509.30 \\
&= \$40.90
\end{aligned}$$

SELF TEST 2

1. $$\begin{aligned}
\text{NPV} &= \$-15{,}000 + \$2{,}000(\text{PVIFA}_{20\%,\,2\,\text{yr.}}) \ + \ \$4{,}000(\text{PVIF}_{20\%,\,3\,\text{yr.}}) \\
&\quad + \$5{,}000\,(\text{PVIF}_{20\%,\,4\,\text{yr.}}) + \$6{,}000\,(\text{PVIF}_{20\%,\,5\,\text{yr.}}) \\[4pt]
&= \$-15{,}000 + \$2{,}000(1.528) + \$4{,}000(0.579) \\
&\quad + \$5{,}000(0.482) + \$6{,}000(0.402) \\[4pt]
&= \$-15{,}000 + \$3{,}056 + \$2{,}316 + \$2{,}410 + \$2{,}412 \\[4pt]
&= \$-4{,}806
\end{aligned}$$

$$\text{PI} \quad = \frac{\$10{,}194}{\$15{,}000} = 0.6796$$

The project should be rejected, because its NPV is negative and the PI is less than 1.0.

2. $\$1{,}000 \ = \$2{,}000(\text{PVIF}_{8\%,\,?\,\text{yr.}})$

   $0.500 \ = (\text{PVIF}_{8\%,\,?\,\text{yr.}})$

   The table value in the 8% column comes closest to 0.500 in the 9-year row. Thus, it will take 9 years for \$1,000 to accumulate to \$2,000 if it is compounded at 8%.

3. $\$1{,}000 \ = \$3{,}000\,(\text{PVIF}_{?\%,\,7\,\text{yr.}})$

   $0.333 \ = (\text{PVIF}_{?\%,\,7\,\text{yrs.}})$

   The table value in the 7-year row comes closest to 0.333 in the 17% column. Thus, it is necessary to compound \$1,000 at 17% for 7 years in order to accumulate \$3,000.

4.   P   = $3,000 (PVIF$_{8\%, 10 \text{ yr.}}$)

              = $3,000 (0.463)

              = $1,389

5.   a.   P   = $100 (PVIFA$_{8\%, 10 \text{ yr.}}$)

              = $100 (7.722)

              = $772.20

    b.   P   = $100 (PVIFA$_{10\%, 10 \text{ yr.}}$)

              = $100(6.145)

              = $614. 50

    c.   P = $100 (PVIFA$_{20\%, 10 \text{ yr.}}$)

              = $100(4.192)

              = $419.20

    d.   P = $100 (PVIFA$_{20\%, 10 \text{ yr.}}$)

              = $100(3.092)

              = $309.20

6.   a.   P = $50 (PVIF$_{10\%, 4 \text{ yr.}}$)

              = $50 (0.683)

              = $34.15

    b.   P = $50 (PVIF$_{20\%, 4 \text{ yr.}}$)

              = $50(0.482)

              = $24.10

    c.   P $= \$50 \dfrac{1}{(1+0)^4}$

            $= \$50 \left(\dfrac{1}{1}\right)$

            = $50

d. $P = \$50 \dfrac{1}{(1+1.0)^4}$

$\qquad = \$50 \left(\dfrac{1}{16}\right)$

$\qquad = \$3.125$

7. a. $FV_5 = \$100 \,(FVIF_{16\%,\,5\,yr.})$

$\qquad = \$100 \,(2.100)$

$\qquad = \$210.00$

b. $FV_{10} = \$100 \,(FVIF_{8\%,\,10\,yr.})$

$\qquad = \$100 \,(2.159)$

$\qquad = \$215.90$

c. $FV_{20} = \$100 \,(FVIF_{4\%,\,20\,yr.})$

$\qquad = \$100 \,(2.191)$

$\qquad = \$219.10$

8. a. Initial Outlay

New machine	$-20,000
Sale of old machine	+ 2,000
Tax gain	
($5,000 - $2,000) 0.4	+ 1,200
	$-16,800

b. Annual cash flows

	Book Method	Cash Method
Savings	$10,000	$ 10,000
Change in depreciation	(4,000 - 1,000)	
Taxable increase	7,000	
Taxes	2,800	2,800
Annual net cash flow		$ 7,200

c. Terminal flow:
    Annual cash flow   7,200

d. Cash flow diagram

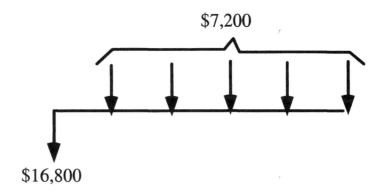

$7,200

$16,800

e. NPV = -$16, 800 + $7,200 (PVIFA$_{14\%, 5\,yr.}$)

       = -$16,800 + $7,200 (3.433)

       = -$16,800 + $24,717.60

       = $7,917.60

    PI   = $\dfrac{\$24,717.60}{\$16,800}$ = = 1.47

SELF TEST 3

1. $10,000   = $\dfrac{\$14,000}{(1+IRR)^5}$

    0.714   = $\dfrac{1}{(1+IRR)^5}$

Therefore, IRR = 7% because the Table C value for 5 years closest to 0.714 occurs in the 7% column (0. 713).

2. $\$700 \quad = \dfrac{\$1,857}{(1+\text{IRR})^{20}}$

      $0.377 \quad = \dfrac{1}{(1+\text{IRR})^{20}}$

In Table C, we see that IRR = 5%

3. $\$30,000 \quad = \$6,000 \displaystyle\sum_{t=0}^{10} \dfrac{1}{(1+\text{IRR})^{t}}$

      $5.0 \quad = \displaystyle\sum_{t=0}^{10} \dfrac{1}{(1+\text{IRR})^{t}}$

From Table E, IRR = approximately 15%.

4. $\$20,000 \quad = \$3,928 \displaystyle\sum_{t=0}^{15} \dfrac{1}{(1+\text{IRR})^{t}}$

      $5.092 \quad = \displaystyle\sum_{t=0}^{15} \dfrac{1}{(1+\text{IRR})^{t}}$

From Table E, IRR = 18%.

5. $\$40,000 \quad = \$10,000 \displaystyle\sum_{t=1}^{5} \dfrac{\$1}{(1+.\text{IRR})^{t}} + \$15,000 \dfrac{1}{(1+\text{IRR})^{6}}$

Try 20%

$\$40,000 \quad = \$10,000(2.991) + \$15,000(0.335)$

           $= \$29,910 + \$5,025$

           $\neq \$34,935$

Try 15%:

$$\$40,000 \quad = \$10,000(3.352) + \$15,000(0.432)$$
$$= \$33,520 + \$6,480$$
$$= \$40,000$$

Thus, 15% is the approximate IRR.

6. $$\$61,630 \quad = \$10,000 \sum_{t=1}^{6} \frac{\$1}{(1+.IRR)^t} + \$70,000 \frac{1}{(1+IRR)^7}$$

Try 20%:

$$\$61,630 \quad = \$10,000(3.326) + \$70,000(0.279)$$
$$= \$33,260 + \$19,530$$
$$\neq \$52,790$$

Try 15%:

$$\$61,630 \quad = \$10,000(3.784) + \$70,000(0.376)$$
$$= \$37,840 + \$26,320$$
$$\neq \$64,160$$

Try 16%:

$$\$61,630 \quad = \$100,000(3.685) + \$70,000(0.354)$$
$$= \$36,850 + \$24,780$$
$$= \$61,630$$

Therefore, IRR = 16%.

7. $$\$2,992 \quad = \$700 \frac{\$1}{(1+.IRR)} + \$1,400 \frac{1}{(1+IRR)^2}$$
$$+ \$3,000 \frac{1}{(1+IRR)^3}$$

153

Try 20%:

$2,992 = \$700(0.833) + \$1,400(0.694) + \$3,000(0.579)$

$\qquad = \$583.10 + \$971.60 + \$1,737.00$

$\qquad \neq \$3,291.70$

Try 25%:

$2,992 = \$700(0.800) + \$1,400(0.640) + \$3,000(0.512)$

$\qquad = \$560 + \$896 + \$1,536$

$\qquad = \$2,992$

Thus, the IRR = 25%.

8. $\$5,492 = \$2,000 \sum_{t=1}^{2} \dfrac{\$1}{(1+.IRR)} + \$4,000 \dfrac{1}{(1+IRR)^3}$

$\qquad\qquad + \$3,000 \dfrac{1}{(1+IRR)^4}$

Try 20%:

$\$5,492 = \$2,000(1.528) + \$4,000(0.579) + \$3,000(0.482)$

$\qquad = \$3,056 + \$2,316 + \$1,446$

$\qquad \neq \$6,818$

Try 30%

$\$5,492 = \$2,000(1.361) + \$4,000(0.455) + \$3,000(0.350)$

$\qquad = \$2,722 + \$1,820 + \$1,050$

$\qquad \neq \$5,592$

Try 31%

$$\$5,492 = \$2,000(1.346) + \$4,000(0.445) + \$3,000(0.340)$$
$$= \$2,692 + \$1,780 + \$1,020$$
$$= \$5,492$$

Thus, 31% is this project's IRR.

9.

$$\$1,000 = \$4,000 \frac{1}{(1+IRR)^2}$$

$$(1+IRR)^2 = 4.0$$

$$1+IRR = \sqrt{4.0}$$

$$1+IRR = 2.0$$

$$IRR = 1.0, \text{ or } IRR = 100\%$$

CHAPTER 10

Cash Flows and Other Topics in Capital Budgeting

Orientation: Capital budgeting involves the decision-making process with respect to investment in fixed assets; specifically, it involves measuring the incremental cash flows associated with investment proposals and evaluating the attractiveness of these cash flows relative to the project's costs. This chapter focuses on the estimation of those cash flows based on various decision criteria, and how to adjust for the riskiness of a given project or combination of projects.

I.   What criteria should we use in the evaluation of alternative investment proposals?

     A.   Use cash flows rather than accounting profits because cash flows allow us to correctly analyze the time element of the flows.

     B.   Examine cash flows on an after-tax basis because they are the flows available to shareholders.

     C.   Include only the incremental cash flows resulting from the investment decision. Ignore all other flows.

II.   Measuring free cash flows. We are interested in measuring the incremental after-tax cash flows, or free cash flows, resulting from the investment proposal. In general, there will be three major sources of cash flows: initial outlays, differential cash flows over the project's life, and terminal cash flows.

     A.   Initial outlays include whatever cash flows are necessary to get the project in running order, for example:

          1.   The installed cost of the asset

2. In the case of a replacement proposal, the selling price of the old machine plus (or minus) any tax gain (or loss) offsetting the initial outlay

3. Any expense items (for example, training) necessary for the operation of the proposal

4. Any other non-expense cash outlays required, such as increased working-capital needs

B. Differential cash flows over the project's life include the incremental after-tax flows over the life of the project, for example:

1. Added revenue (less added selling expenses) for the proposal

2. Any labor and/or material savings incurred

3. Increases in overhead incurred

4. Changes in taxes.

5. Change in net working capital.

6. Change in capital spending.

7. Make sure calculations reflect the fact that while depreciation is an expense, it does not involve any cash flows.

8. A word of warning not to include financing charges (such as interest or preferred stock dividends), for they are implicitly taken care of in the discounting process.

C. Terminal cash flows include any incremental cash flows that result at the termination of the project; for example:

1. The project's salvage value plus (or minus) any taxable gains or losses associated with the project

2. Any terminal cash flow needed, perhaps disposal of obsolete equipment

3. Recovery of any non-expense cash outlays associated with the project, such as recovery of increased working-capital needs associated with the proposal.

III. Measuring the cash flows.

    A. A project's free cash flows =

        project's change in operating cash flows

        - change in net working capital

        - change in capital spending

    B If we rewrite this, inserting the calculations for the project's change in operating cash flows, we get:

        A project's free cash flows =

        Change in earnings before interest and taxes

        - change in taxes

        + change in depreciation

        - change in net working capital

        - change in capital spending

IV. Risk and the investment decision

    A. Up to this point, we have treated the expected cash flows resulting from an investment proposal as being known with perfect certainty. We will now introduce risk.

    B. The riskiness of an investment project is defined as the variability of its cash flows from the expected cash flow.

V. Incorporating risk into capital budgeting

    A. The use of the risk-adjusted discount rate is based on the concept that investors demand higher returns for more risky projects.

        1. If the risk associated with the investment is greater than the risk involved in a typical endeavor, then the discount rate is adjusted upward to compensate for this risk.

2. The expected cash flows are then discounted back to present at the risk-adjusted discount rate. Then, the normal capital budgeting criteria are applied, except in the case of the internal rate of return, in which case the hurdle rate to which the project's internal rate of return is compared now becomes the risk-adjusted discount rate.

3. Expressed mathematically the net present value using the risk-adjusted discount rate becomes

$$NPV = \sum_{t=1}^{n} \frac{FCF_t}{(1+i^*)^t} - IO$$

where FCF_t = the annual after-tax free cash flow in time period t

IO = the initial outlay

i^* = the risk-adjusted discount rate

n = the project's expected life

VI. Methods for measuring a project's systematic risk

A. Theoretically, we know that systematic risk is the "priced" risk, and thus, the risk that affects the stock's market price and thus, the appropriate risk with which to be concerned. However, if there are bankruptcy costs (which are assumed away by the CAPM), if there are undiversified shareholders who are concerned with more than just systematic risk, if there are factors that affect a security's price beyond what the CAPM suggests, or if we are unable to confidently measure the project's systematic risk, then the project's individual risk carries relevance. Moreover, in general, a project's individual risk, is highly correlated with the project's systematic risk making it a reasonable proxy to use.

B. In spite of problems in confidently measuring an individual firm's level of systematic risk, if the project appears to be a typical one for the firm, then using the CAPM to determine the appropriate risk-return tradeoffs and then judging the project against them may be a warranted approach.

C.   If the project is not a typical project, we are without historical data and must either estimate the beta using accounting data or use the pure-play method for estimating beta.

   1.   Using historical accounting data to substitute for historical price data in estimating systematic risk: To estimate a project's beta using accounting data, we need run only a time series regression of the division's return on assets on the market index. The regression coefficient from this equation would be the project's accounting beta and serves as an approximation for the project's true beta.

   2.   The pure-play method for estimating a project's beta: The pure-play method attempts to find a publicly-traded firm in the same industry as the capital-budgeting project. Once the proxy or pure-play firm is identified, its systematic risk is determined and then used as a proxy for the project's systematic risk.

VII.   Examining a project's risk through simulation

A.   A simulation imitates the performance of the project being evaluated by randomly selecting observations from each of the distributions that affect the outcome of the project, combining those observations to determine the final output of the final project, and continuing with this process until a representative record of the project's probable outcome is assembled.

   1.   The firm's management then examines the resultant probability distribution, and, if management considers enough of the distribution lies above the normal cutoff criterion, it will accept the project.

   2.   The use of a simulation approach to analyze investment proposals offers two major advantages:

      a.   The financial managers are able to examine and base their decisions on the whole range of possible outcomes rather than just point estimates.

      b.   They can undertake subsequent sensitivity analysis of the project.

1. The R. T. Kleinman Corporation is considering selling one of its old assembly machines. The machine, purchased for $40,000 five years ago, had an expected life of 10 years and an expected salvage value of 0. Assume Kleinman uses simplified straight-line depreciation, creating depreciation of $4,000 per year, and could sell this old machine for $45,000. Also assume a 34% marginal tax rate.

   (a) What would be the taxes associated with this sale?

   (b) If the old machine were sold for $40,000, what would be the taxes associated with this sale?

   (c) If the old machine were sold for $20,000, what would be the taxes associated with this sale?

   (d) If the old machine were sold for $17,000, what would be the taxes associated with this sale?

SOLUTION

   (a) Tax payments associated with the sale for $45,000:

   Recapture of depreciation

   $$= (\$45,000 - \$20,000)\,(0.34) = \$8,500$$

   (b) Tax payments associated with sale for $40,000:

   Recapture of depreciation

   $$= (\$40,000 - \$20,000)\,(0.34) = \$6,800$$

   (c) No taxes, because the machine would have been sold for its book value.

   (d) Tax savings from sale below book value:

   Tax savings $= (\$20,000 - \$17,000)\,(0.34) = \$1,020$

2.   The G. Wolfe Corporation is introducing a new product and which is expected to result in change in EBIT of $900,000. The firm has a 34 percent marginal tax rate. This product will also produce $200,000 of depreciation per year. In addition, this product will cause the following changes:

	Without the product	With the product
Accounts receivable	$60,000	$70,000
Inventory	55,000	65,000
Accounts payable	45,000	50,000

What is the product's free cash flow?

SOLUTION

Initial Outlay

Change in net working capital equals the increase in accounts receivable and inventory less the increase in accounts receivable = $10,000 + $10,000 - $5,000 = $15,000.

The change in taxes will be EBIT X marginal tax rate = $900,000 X .34 = $306,000.

A project's free cash flows =

Change in earnings before interest and taxes
- change in taxes
+ change in depreciation
- change in net working capital
- change in capital spending

= $900,000
-   $306,000
+ $200,000
-   $15,000
-   $0
= $779,000

3.   A firm is considering introducing a new product that has an expected life of 5 years. Since this product is much riskier than a typical project for this firm, the management feels that the normal required rate of return of 12% is not sufficient; instead, the minimally acceptable rate of return on this project should be 20%. The initial outlay would be $100,000 and the expected cash flows from this project are as given below:

Year	Expected Cash Flow
1	$40,000
2	40,000
3	40,000
4	40,000
5	40,000

Should this project be accepted?

SOLUTION

Discounting this annuity back to present at 20% yields a present value of the future cash flows of $119,640. Since the initial outlay on this project is $100,000, the net present value becomes $19,640. The project should be accepted.

Self Tests

TRUE-FALSE

_____ 1. Cash flow, not income, is what is important in capital budgeting.

_____ 2. One way of evaluating risky projects is by discounting the expected cash flows at a risk-adjusted discount rate.

_____ 3. The interest payments should be subtracted from the cash flows in evaluating projects financed with debt.

_____ 4. While depreciation is not a cash flow item, it affects taxes which are a cash flow item.

_____ 5. Any changes in inventory or working capital need not be considered in capital budgeting because these cash flows never leave the firm.

_____ 6. Other things held constant, the use of accelerated depreciation causes profits to be less in the earlier years; therefore, taxes are lower in the earlier years, and, thus, cash flows are higher in the earlier years.

_____ 7. The use of risk-adjusted discount rates is based on the concept that investors require a higher rate of return for more risky projects.

_____ 8. As the salvage value of the equipment being replaced increases, all else held constant, the net present value of the project will increase.

MULTIPLE CHOICE

1. Which of the following is not a method for adjusting for or measuring risk in capital budgeting?

   a. Simulation
   b. Risk-adjusted discount rate
   c. Inverse profitability index

2. An investment project will be more desirable

   a. the smaller the standard deviation.
   b. the less positive its correlations with existing average cash flows.
   c. the larger the coefficient of variation of its cash flow.
   d. a and b.

3. Which of the following is important to capital budgeting decisions?

   a. Depreciation method
   b. Salvage value
   c. Timing of cash flows
   d. Taxes
   e. All of the above.

4. If the federal income tax rate were increased, the result would be to

   a. decrease the net present value.
   b. increase the net present value.
   c. increase the payback period.
   d. a and c.

CHAPTER 11

The Cost of Capital

Orientation: In Chapters 7 and 8, we considered the valuation of debt and equity securities. The concepts advanced there serve as a foundation for determining the required rate of return for the firm and for specific investment projects. The objective in this chapter is to determine the required rate of return to be used in evaluating investment projects which is an average of the required rates of return of the creditor who loan money to the firm and the stockholders who own the firm.

I.   The concept of the cost of capital

    A.   Defining the cost of capital:

        1.   The rate that must be earned in order to satisfy the required rate of return of the firm's investors.

        2.   The rate of return on investments at which the price of a firm's common stock will remain unchanged.

    B.   Type of investors and the cost of capital.

        1.   Each source of capital used by the firm (debt, preferred stock, and common stock) should be incorporated into the cost of capital, with the relative importance of a particular source being based on the percentage of the firm's total financing provided by each source.

        2.   Using the cost of a single source of capital as the hurdle rate for a new investment is often tempting to management where all the financing for the investment comes from that source (e.g., the retention of earnings or borrowing). This is a mistake and can lead to serious errors in the firm's investment decisions. For example, in periods when the firm is borrowing funds to finance

projects the cost of debt becomes the hurdle rate whereas in periods when the firm is issuing equity they use the much higher cost of equity. Consequently, the hurdle rate varies with the source of finance the firm uses and ignores the fact that the firm is actually balancing its debt and equity offerings to maintain a stable capital structure.

II. Factors determining the cost of capital

    A. <u>General economic conditions</u>. These include the demand for and supply of capital within the economy and the level of expected inflation. These are reflected in the riskless rate of return.

    B. <u>Market conditions</u>. Not all firms can sell their debt and/or equity securities when they might want to do it. The market for equity offerings, especially for firms that have never issued equity (i.e., IPOs) is only open to new firms under very optimistic market periods. Thus, general market conditions can have an important impact on a firm's ability to raise funds at various times.

    C. <u>A firm's operating and financing decisions</u>. A firm's choice of how to finance its assets and when to raise new capital is influenced by the underlying risk that investors see in the firm. In large part this risk results from the decisions made within the company and can be divided into two classes:

        1. <u>Business risk</u> is the variability in returns on assets and is affected by the company's investment decisions.

        2. <u>Financial risk</u> is the increased variability in firm earnings and correspondingly the returns to the common stockholders that results from the firm's use of debt and preferred stock financing as opposed to common equity.

III. Computing the weighted cost of capital. A firm's weighted cost of capital is a function of (1) the individual costs of capital and (2) the capital structure mix.

    A. Determining individual costs of capital.

        1. The <u>before-tax cost of debt</u> is found by solving for k_d in

$$NP_d = \sum_{t=1}^{n} \frac{\$I_t}{(1+k_d)^t} + \frac{\$M}{(1+k_d)^n}$$

167

where NP_d = the market price of the debt less flotation costs (i.e., the net proceeds from the issue)

I_t = the annual dollar interest paid to the investor each year,

M = the maturity value of the debt,

k_d = before-tax cost of the debt (before-tax required rate of return on debt)

n = the number of years to maturity.

The <u>after-tax cost of debt</u> equals:

$$k_d(1 - T)$$

2. Cost of preferred stock (required rate of return on preferred stock), k_{ps}, equals the dividend yield based upon the net price (market price less flotation costs) or

$$k_{ps} = \frac{\text{dividend}}{\text{net price}} = \frac{D}{NP_{ps}}$$

3. Cost of Common Stock. We use two measurement techniques to obtain estimates of the required rate of return on common stock.

a. dividend-growth model

b. capital asset pricing model

4. Dividend-growth model

a. Cost of internally generated common equity, k_{cs}

$$k_{cs} = \frac{\text{dividend in year 1}}{\text{market price}} + \left(\begin{array}{c}\text{annual growth} \\ \text{in dividends}\end{array}\right)$$

$$k_{cs} = \frac{D_1}{P_{cs}} + g$$

168

b.   Cost of new common stock, k_{ncs}

$$k_{ncs} = \frac{D_1}{P_{ncs}} + g$$

where NP_{cs} = the market price of the common stock less flotation costs incurred in issuing new shares.

5.   Capital asset pricing model

$$k_{cs} = k_{rf} + \beta(k_m - k_{rf})$$

where k_{cs} = the cost of common stock

k_{rf} = the risk-free rate

β = beta, measure of the stock's systematic risk

k_m = the expected rate of return on the market

6.   It is important to notice that the major difference between the equations presented here and the equations from Chapter 5 is that the <u>firm</u> incurs flotation costs when it issues any security. Thus, the cost of a particular source of capital to the firm will exceed the investor's required rate of return due to the costs of issuing the security that are paid to investment banks and other financial intermediaries that help the firm sell its securities.

B.   <u>Selection of weights</u>. The individual costs of capital will be different for each source of capital in the firm's capital structure. To use the cost of capital in investment analyses, we must compute a weighted or overall cost of capital.

1.   We have assumed that the company's current financial mix resulting from the financing of previous investments is relatively stable and that these weights will closely approximate future financing patterns.

2.   In computing weights, a question arises as to whether we should use current market values of the firm's securities or the book

values as shown in the balance sheet. Since we will be issuing new securities at their <u>current</u> market value, and not at book (historical) values, we should use the market value of the securities in calculating our weights.

IV. PepsiCo approach to weighted average cost of capital

    A. PepsiCo calculates the divisional cost of capital for its snack, beverage, and restaurant organizations by first finding peer-group firms for each division and using their average betas, after adjusting for differences in financial leverage, to compute the division's cost of equity. They also use accounting betas in estimating the cost of equity. They then compute the cost of debt for each division. Finally, they calculate a weighted cost of capital for each division.

    B. PepsiCo's WACC basic computation

$$k_{wacc} = k_{cs}\left(\frac{E}{D+E}\right) + k_d[1\text{-}T]\left(\frac{D}{D+E}\right)$$

where:

k_{wacc}	=	the weighted average cost of capital
k_{cs}	=	the cost of equity capital
k_d	=	the before-tax cost of debt capital
T_c	=	the firm's tax rate
E/(D+E)	=	percentage of financing from equity
D/(D+E)	=	percentage of financing from debt

    C. Calculating the Cost of Equity

Based on capital assets pricing model:

$$k_{cs} = k_{rf} + \beta\,(k_m - k_{rf})$$

where:

k_{cs}	=	the cost of common stock
k_{rf}	=	the risk-free rate
β	=	beta, measure of the stock's systematic risk
k_m	=	the expected rate of return on the market

Betas for each division are estimated by calculating an average unlevered beta from a group of divisional peers.

The average beta for each division's peer group is adjusted so that it reflects the division's target debt-to-equity ratio.

D. Calculating the Cost of Debt

The after-tax cost of debt is equal to:

$k_d (1 - T_c)$

where:

k_d	=	before-tax cost of debt
T_c	=	marginal tax rate

V. Market Value Added, Wealth Creation and Economic Profit

A. We can tell whether a firm has created value by comparing the market value of all its outstanding securities (the market value of the right hand side of its balance sheet) with the total amount of money that has been invested in the firm (approximately the book value of the firm's assets). This difference is commonly referred to as Market Value Added or MVA.

B. MVA is used to rank firms in order of their wealth creation and the 1,000 largest U.S. firms are published in the financial press each spring.

C. MVA is analogous to the net present value of the firm in that it compares the market value of the firm (i.e., the present value of the firm's anticipated future cash flows) to the total money invested in the firm (analogous to the initial outlay in a capital budgeting exercise). Technically, this is correct only when the book value of the firm's invested capital equals the cost of replacing those assets.

D. MVA, in turn, is related to the firm's annual economic profit. Economic profit (Stern-Stewart use the term Economic Value Added) for year t is defined as follows:

$$\text{Economic Profit}_t = \text{Net Operating Income}_t \left(1 - \text{Tax Rate}\right) - \left(\begin{array}{c}\text{Cost} \\ \text{of} \\ \text{Capital}\end{array}\right)\left(\text{Invested Capital}_{t-1}\right)$$

Note that economic profit is a flow measure like net income whereas MVA is a stock measure like retained earnings. The relationship between MVA measured today and Economic profit is the following:

$$MVA = \sum_{t=1}^{\infty} \frac{Economic\ Profit_t}{\left(1 + \frac{Cost\ of}{Capital}\right)^t}$$

That is, MVA is nothing more than the market's assessment of the value of the firm's future economic profits. Consequently, economic profit is often used to measure the contribution to shareholder wealth for the period.

VI.   Paying for Performance

A.   Economic profit or EVA® is used by a growing number of U.S. and foreign corporations as the basis for evaluating financial performance and consequently for determining incentive compensation.

B.   The following relationship offers a simple way to connect economic profit to incentive pay:

$$\frac{Incentive}{Compensation_t} = \frac{Base}{Pay_t} \times \frac{Percent}{\frac{Incentive}{Compensation}} \times \frac{Actual\ Economic\ Profit_t}{Target\ Economic\ Profit_t}$$

The idea here is that the fraction of a manager's pay that is tied to performance will vary with higher levels of management having a larger proportion of their pay tied to performance and the actual level of incentive pay corresponds to a comparison of actual and target performance.

1. A $1,000 par-value bond will sell in the market for $1,072 and carries a coupon interest rate of 9%. Issuance costs will be 7.5%. The number of years to maturity is .15, and the firm's tax rate is 46%. What is the after-tax cost for this security (K_d)?

    SOLUTION

    Use your financial calculator following the procedure on page 366 to calculate $K_d = 9.11\%$.

2. The current market price of ABC Company's common stock is $32.50. The firm expects to pay a dividend of $1.90, and the growth rate is projected to be 7% annually. The company is in a 40% tax bracket. Flotation costs would be 6% if new stock were issued. What is the cost of (a) internal and (b) external common equity?

    SOLUTION

    $$
    \begin{aligned}
    \text{Let } k_{cs} &= \text{cost of internal common} \\
    k_{ncs} &= \text{cost of external (new) common} \\
    D_1 &= \text{next dividend to be paid} \\
    P_{cs} &= \text{market price} \\
    g &= \text{growth rate} \\
    NP_o &= \text{market price less flotation costs}
    \end{aligned}
    $$

    (a) $\quad k_{cs} = \dfrac{D_1}{P_o} + g$

    $\quad\quad k_{cs} = \dfrac{\$1.90}{\$32.50} + 0.07 = 12.85\%$

    (b) $\quad k_{ns} = \dfrac{D_1}{NP_o} + g$

    $\quad\quad k_{ncs} = \dfrac{\$1.90}{\$32.50(1-0.06)} + 0.07 = 13.22\%$

3. Pharr, Inc.'s preferred stock pays a 16% dividend. The stock is selling for $62.75, and its par value is $40. Issuance costs are 5% and the firm's tax rate is 46%. What is the cost of this source of financing?

SOLUTION

$$k_{ps} = \frac{D}{NP_o}$$

$$k_{ps} = \frac{\$40(0.16)}{\$62.75(1-0.05)} = \frac{\$6.40}{\$59.61} = 10.74\%$$

4. The current capital structure of Smithhart, Inc. is as follows:

Bonds (7%, $1,000 par, 15 years)	$ 750,000
Preferred stock ($100 par, 7.25% dividend)	1,000,000

Common stock:

Par value ($2.50 par)	$500,000	
Retained earnings	350,000	850,000
Total		$2,600,000

The market price is $975 for the bonds, $60 for the preferred stock, and $21 for common stocks. Flotation costs are 9% for bonds and 5 percent for preferred stock. The firm's tax rate is 46%. Common stock will pay a $2.80 dividend which is not expected to grow. What is the weighted cost of capital using only internal common equity?

SOLUTION

Source of Financing	Market Value	Weight
Bonds	$731,250[1]	13.22%
Preferred stock	600,000[2]	10.85%
Common stock	4,200,000[3]	75.93%
	$5,531,250	100.00%

[1] 750 bonds at $975 value each
[2] 10,000 shares at $60 value each
[3] 200,000 shares at $21 value each

Cost of debt

$$\$975(1 - 0.09) \text{ or } \$887.25 = \sum_{t=1}^{15} \frac{\$70}{(1+k_d)}t + \frac{\$1,000}{(1+k_d)}15$$

Using a financial calculator, k_d equals 8.35%

k_d = 8.35% (1 - 0.46)

k_d = 4.51%

Cost of preferred stock

$$k_{ps} = \frac{\$7.25}{\$60(1-0.05)} = 12.72\%$$

Cost of internal common equity

$$k_{cs} = \frac{\$2.80}{\$21} + 0 = 13.33\%$$

Weighted Cost of Capital

Source of Financing	Cost	Weight	Weighted Costs
Bonds	4.51%	.1322	0.596%
Preferred stock	12.72	.1085	1.381
Common stock	13.33	.7593	10.124
			12.101%

Self Tests

TRUE-FALSE

_____ 1. The cost of capital is defined as the rate of return that the firm must earn on its investments if the investments are to leave the price of the firm's common stock unchanged.

_____ 2. Book values from the firm's balance sheet should be used when calculating a firm's weighted average cost of capital.

_____ 3. The firm's cost of capital is an appropriate investment hurdle only for investments whose risk is similar risk to that of the existing assets.

_____ 4. Financial risk is the risk that the price of a security may vary significantly.

_____ 5. Only those projects whose expected return equals or exceeds the cost of capital should be accepted.

_____ 6. The cost of preferred stock, like the cost of debt, must be adjusted for taxes.

_____ 7. In using a firm's weighted average cost of capital to evaluate new investments, we are assuming that the company's current capital structure will not change over the life of the investment.

_____ 8. As a general rule, new common stock is issued only if internal common equity (retained earnings) does not provide sufficient equity capital.

_____ 9. The capital asset pricing model (CAPM) is based on three variables: The risk-free rate, the firm's beta coefficient, and the market risk premium.

_____ 10. The beta for a firm's common stock measures the volatility of the project returns relative to that of a widely diversified portfolio of all other risky assets.

MULTIPLE CHOICE

1. What is/are the reason(s) for computing a firm's cost of capital?

    a. To determine the firm's future financing needs
    b. To assure the investors that their required rate of return is being met
    c. To use the cost of capital as an investment criterion
    d. b and c
    e. a and c
    f. a, b, and c

2. The cost of capital can be defined as

    a. the rate that must be earned in order to satisfy the required rate of return of the firm's investors.
    b. the rate of return on investments at which the price of the firm's common stock remains unchanged.
    c. the rate of return on investments which will increase the price of the firm's common stock.
    d. a and b.
    e. a and c.

3. All of the following variables are required to compute the cost of debt *except*

    a. the market price of debt.
    b. issuance or flotation costs.
    c. the tax rate for the firm.
    d. the growth rate in future dividends.
    e. the principal amount of the debt issue.

4. Adjustment for taxes is required for estimating which of the following?

    a. Cost of preferred stock
    b. Cost of debt
    c. Cost of common equity
    d. Cost of retained earnings.

5.   An investment with a beta of 0.80 means that the returns of the investment

    a.   are more volatile than market returns.
    b.   are less volatile than the market returns.
    c.   have no correlation with the market returns.
    d.   are perfectly correlated with the market returns.
    e.   None of the above.

6.   If a firm's Market Value Added (MVA) for the end of the most recent fiscal year were $140 million and the it had invested capital totaling $100 million, the market value of the firm's assets (debt plus equity) would be:

    a. $40 million.
    b. $180 million
    c. $240 million.
    d.   ($40 million)
    e.   None of the above

7.   The appropriate set of weights used in calculating a firm's weighted average cost of capital should reflect:

    a.   The firm's financial policies regarding the sources of financing it will use in the future.
    b.   The mix of financing sources used to fund the particular set of projects being analyzed.
    c.   The average mix of financing sources in the firm's current balance sheet.
    d.   All of the above
    e.   None of the above

8.   When firms operate in multiple industries for which the risk characteristics and financial structures vary significantly they should

    a.   Use a company wide weighted average cost of capital to evaluate all new investments so as to hold each operating division to the same standard.
    b.   Calculate divisional costs of capital for use in evaluating each division's investment opportunities.
    c.   Try to adjust the capital structures used in each of the divisions such that the weighted average cost of capital in each is the same.
    d.   All of the above
    e.   None of the above

9. The cost of common equity is more difficult to estimate than the cost of bonds or preferred stock because

    a. Common dividends are not contractually specified and must be estimated

    b. Common equity does not have a finite maturity like debt

    c. Common equity can be raised from two sources: the retention of earnings and the issuance of new common shares

    d. All of the above

    e. None of the above

10. The dividend growth model estimates the cost of common equity as

    a. the sum of the current dividend yield and the anticipated rate of growth in future dividends

    b. the sum of the risk free rate of interest and a market risk premium

    c. the reciprocal of the firm's price to earnings ratio

    d. all of the above

    e. none of the above

CHAPTER 12

Determining the Financing Mix

Orientation: This chapter focuses on useful aids to the financial manager in his or her determination of the firm's proper financial structure. It includes the definitions of the different kinds of risk, a review of break-even analysis, the concepts of operating leverage, financial leverage, the combination of both leverages, and their effect on EPS (earnings per share). Then the chapter concentrates on the way the firm arranges its sources of funds. The cost of capital-capital structure argument is highlighted in a straightforward manner without dwelling excessively on pure theory. A moderate view of the effect of financial leverage on the firm's overall cost of capital is highlighted and explained. Later, techniques useful to the financial officer faced with the determination of an appropriate financing mix are described. Agency theory and the concept of free cash flow as they relate to capital structure determination are also discussed. An overview of actual practice is also included.

I. Business risk and financial risk

   A. Risk has been defined as the likely variability associated with expected revenue streams.

      1. Focusing on the financial decision, the variations in the income stream can be attributed to:

         a. The firm's exposure to business risk.

         b. The firm's decision to incur financial risk.

   B. Business risk can be defined as the variability of the firm's expected earnings before interest and taxes (EBIT).

      1. Business risk is measured by the firm's corresponding expected coefficient of variation (i.e., the larger the ratio, the more risk a firm is exposed to).

2.   Dispersion in operating income does not cause business risk. It is the result of several influences, for example, the company's cost structure, product demand characteristics, and intra-industry competition. These influences are a direct result of the firm's investment decision.

C.   Financial risk is a direct result of the firm's financing decision. When the firm is selecting different financial alternatives, financial risk refers to the additional variability in earnings available to the firm's common shareholders and the additional chance of insolvency borne by the common shareholders caused by the use of financial leverage.

    1.   Financial leverage is the financing of a portion of the firm's assets with securities bearing a fixed (limited) rate of return in hopes of increasing the ultimate return to the common shareholders.

    2.   Financial risk, is to a large extent, passed on to the common shareholders who must bear almost all of the potential inconsistencies of returns to the firm after the deduction of fixed payments.

II.   Break-even analysis

A.   The objective of break-even analysis is to determine the break-even quantity of output by studying the relationships among the firm's cost structure, volume of output, and operating profit.

    1.   The break-even quantity of output is the quantity of output (in units) that results in an EBIT level equal to zero.

B.   Use of the model enables the financial officer to:

    1.   Determine the quantity of output that must be sold to cover all operating costs.

    2.   Calculate the EBIT that will be achieved at various output levels.

C. Some actual and potential applications of break-even analysis include:

1. Capital expenditure analysis as a complementary technique to discounted cash flow evaluation models.

2. Pricing policy.

3. Labor contract negotiations.

4. Evaluation of cost structure.

5. The making of financial decisions.

D. Essential elements of the break-even model are:

1. Fixed costs are costs that do not vary in total amount as the sales volume or the quantity of output changes over some relevant range of output. For example, administrative salaries are considered fixed because these salaries are generally the same month after month. Other examples are:
   a. Depreciation.
   b. Insurance premiums.
   c. Property taxes.
   d. Rent.

   The total fixed cost is unchanged regardless of the quantity of product output or sales, although, over some relevant range, these costs may be higher or lower (i.e., in the long run).

2. Variable costs are costs that tend to vary in total as output changes. Variable costs are fixed per unit of output. For example, direct materials are considered a variable cost because they vary with the amount of products produced. Other variable costs are:
   a. Direct labor.
   b. Energy cost associated with the production area.
   c. Packaging.
   d. Freight-out.
   e. Sales commissions.

3.	To implement the behavior of the break-even model, it is necessary for the financial manager to:

   a.	Identify the most relevant output range for his or her planning purposes.

   b.	Approximate all costs in the semifixed-semivariable range and allocate them to the fixed and variable cost categories.

4.	Total revenue and volume of output

   a.	Total revenue from sales is equal to the price per unit multiplied by the quantity sold.

   b.	The volume of output is the firm's level from operations and is expressed as sales dollars or a unit quantity.

E.	Finding the break-even point

   1.	The break-even model is just a simple adaptation of the firm's income statement expressed in the following format:

   sales - (total variable costs + total fixed costs) = profit

   a.	Trial and error

      (1)	Select an arbitrary output level.

      (2)	Calculate the corresponding EBIT amount.

      (3)	When EBIT equals zero, the break-even point has been found.

   b.	Contribution margin analysis

      (1)	The difference between the unit selling price and the unit variable cost equals the contribution margin.

      (2)	Then, the fixed cost divided by the contribution margin equals the break-even quantity in units.

c. Algebraic analysis

    (1) Q_B = the break-even level of units sold,

            P   = the unit sales price,

            F   = the total fixed cost for the period,

            V   = unit variable cost.

    (2)   Then,

$$Q_B = \frac{F}{P - V}$$

F. The break-even point in sales dollars:

1. Computing a break-even point in terms of sales dollars rather than units of output is convenient, especially if the firm deals with more than one product. Also, if the analyst cannot get unit cost data, he or she can compute a general break-even point in sales dollars by using the firm's annual report.

2. Since variable cost per unit and the selling price per unit are assumed constant, the ratio of total sales to total variable costs (VC/S) is a constant for any level of sales. So, if the break-even level of sales is denoted S*, the corresponding equation is:

$$S^* = \frac{F}{1 - \dfrac{VC}{S}}$$

G. Limitations of break-even analysis:

1. The cost-volume-profit relationship is assumed to be linear.

2. The total revenue curve is presumed to increase linearly with the volume of output.

3. A constant production and sales mix is assumed.

4. The break-even computation is a static form of analysis.

III. Operating Leverage

    A.   Operating leverage is the responsiveness of a firm's EBIT to fluctuations in sales. Operating leverage results when fixed operating costs are present in the firm's cost structure. It should be noted here that fixed operating costs do *not* include interest charges incurred from the firm's use of debt financing.

    B.   Implications of operating leverage:

        1.   At each point above the break-even level, the degree of operating leverage decreases (i.e., the greater the sales level, the lower the DOL_s).

        2.   At the break-even level of sales, the degree of operating leverage is undefined.

        3.   Operating leverage is present anytime the percentage change in EBIT divided by the percentage change in sales is greater than one.

        4.   The degree of operating leverage can be attributed to the business risk that a firm faces.

IV. Financial leverage

    A.   Financial leverage, as defined earlier, is the practice of financing a portion of the firm's assets with securities bearing a fixed rate of return in hopes of increasing the ultimate return to the common stockholders. To see if financial leverage has been used to benefit the common shareholders, the discussion here will focus on the responsiveness of the company's earnings per share (EPS) to changes in its EBIT. It should be noted here that not all analysts rely exclusively on this type of relationship. In fact, the weakness of such an approach will be examined in the following chapter.

    B.   The firm is using financial leverage and is exposing its owners to financial risk when:

$$\frac{\% \text{ change in EPS}}{\% \text{ change in EBIT}} \text{ is greater than } 1.00$$

V. Combining operating and financial leverage

    A. Since changes in sales revenues cause greater changes in EBIT, and if the firm chooses to use financial leverage, changes in EBIT turn into larger variations in both EPS and EAC (earnings available to common shareholders). Then, combining operating and financial leverage causes rather large variations in EPS.

    B. The combined effects of operating and financial leverage is reflected in the following ratio:

$$= \frac{\%\ \text{change in EPS}}{\%\ \text{change in sales}}$$

If the DCL is equal to 5.0 times, then it is important to understand that a 1% change in sales will result in a 5% change in EPS.

    C. Implications of combining operating and financial leverage

        1. The total risk exposure that the firm assumes can be managed by combining operating and financial leverage in different degrees.

        2. Knowledge of the various leverage measures that have been examined here aids the financial officer in his or her determination of the proper level of overall risk that should be accepted.

VI. Introduction to financing mix determination

    A. A distinction can be made between the terms financial structure and capital structure.

        1. Financial structure is the mix of all items that appear on the right-hand side of the firm's balance sheet.

        2. Capital structure is the mix of the long-term, sources of funds used by the firm.

        3. In this chapter, we do *not* dwell on the question of dealing with an appropriate maturity composition of the firm's sources of funds. Our main focus is on capital structure management, (i.e., determining the proper proportions relative to the total in which the permanent forms of financing should be used).

B. The *objective* of capital structure management is to mix the permanent sources of funds in a manner that will maximize the company's common stock price. This will minimize the firm's composite cost of capital. This proper mix of funds sources is referred to as the *optimal capital structure*.

VII. Capital structure theory

    A. The cost of capital-capital structure argument may be characterized by this question:

        1. Can the firm affect its overall cost of funds, either favorably or unfavorably, by varying the mixture of financing sources used?

    B. The argument deals with the postulated effect of the use of financial leverage on the overall cost of capital of the company.

    C. If the firm's cost of capital can be affected by the degree to which it uses financial leverage, then capital structure management is an important subset of business financial management.

VIII. Capital structure theory: A moderate position

    A. The moderate position on capital structure importance admits to the facts that (1) interest expense is tax-deductible in the world of corporate activity and (2) the probability of the firm's suffering bankruptcy costs is directly related to the company's use of financial leverage.

    B. When interest expense is tax-deductible, the *sum* of the cash flows that the firm could pay to *all* contributors of corporate capital (debt investors and equity investors) is affected by its financing mix. This is *not* the case when an environment of no corporate taxation is presumed.

        1. The amount of the *tax shield on interest* may be calculated as:

$$\text{Tax shield} = r_d(D)(T)$$

where r_d = the interest rate paid on outstanding debt,

D = the principal amount of the debt,

T = the firm's tax rate.

2.   The moderate position presents the view that the tax shield must have value in the marketplace. After all, the government's take is decreased, and the investor's take is increased because of the deductibility of interest expense.

3.   Therefore, according to this position, financial leverage affects firm value, and it must also affect the cost of corporate capital.

C.   To use too much financial leverage, however, would be imprudent. It seems reasonable to offer that the probability that the firm will be unable to meet the financial obligations contained in its debt contracts will increase the more the firm uses leverage-inducing instruments (debt) in its capital structure. The likelihood of firm failure, then, carries with it certain costs (bankruptcy costs) that rise as leverage use increases. There will be some point at which the expected cost of default will be large enough to outweigh the tax shield advantage of debt financing. At that point, the firm will turn to common equity financing.

D.   Figure 12.1 depicts the moderate view on capital structure importance. This view of the cost of capital-capital structure argument produces a saucer-shaped or U-shaped average cost of capital curve. In Figure 12.1, the firm's optimal range of financial leverage use lies between points A and B. It would be imprudent for the firm to use additional financial leverage beyond point B because (1) the average cost of capital would be higher than it has to be and (2) the firm's common stock price would be lower than it has to be. Therefore, we can say that point B represents the firm's *debt capacity*.

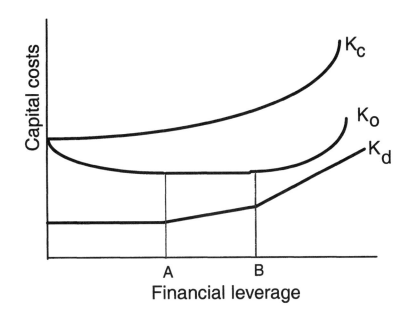

Figure 12.1
Capital Costs and Financial Leverage: The Moderate View Which Considers Taxes and Financial Distress

E. We conclude that the determination of the firm's financing mix *is* centrally important to both the financial manager and the firm's owners.

IX. Firm value and Agency Costs

A. Agency problem results in costs to the firm's owners to monitor management actions.

B. Capital structure management given risk to agency costs associated with conflict between firms stockholders and bondholders.

   1. Covenants in bond contracts may reduce potential conflicts.

   2. Costs associated with protective covenants are borne by shareholders.

   3. Monitoring costs rise as firm's use of financial leverage increases.

   4. With higher degrees of financial leverage, costs associate with financial distress increases.

C. Market value of levered firm is the sum of the market value of the unlevered firm plus the present value of tax shields less the present value of the financial distress costs and of agency costs.

D. Agency costs, free cash flow, and capital structure

1. Free cash flow's cash flow in excess of that required to fund all positive NPV projects.

2. Substantial free cash flow can lead to managerial misbehavior and poor discounts associated with expenditures of the cash.

X. Basic tools of capital structure management

A. Recall that the use of financial leverage has two effects on the earnings stream flowing to the firm's common stockholders: (1) the added variability in the earnings per share (EPS) stream that accompanies the use of fixed-charge securities, and (2) the level of EPS at a given earnings before interest and taxes level (EBIT) associated with a specific capital structure. The first effect is quantified by the degree of financial leverage measure. The second effect is analyzed by means of what is generally referred to as *EBIT-EPS* analysis.

B. The objective of EBIT-EPS analysis is to find the EBIT level that will equate EPS regardless of the financing plan chosen (from among two plans) by the financial manager.

1. A graphic analysis or an algebraic analysis can be used.

2. Study problems at the end of this chapter illustrate the nature of EBIT-EPS analysis.

3. EBIT-EPS analysis considers only the level of the earnings stream and ignores the variability (riskiness) in it. In other words, this tool of capital structure management disregards the implicit costs of debt financing. Therefore, it must be used with caution and in conjunction with other basic tools of capital structure management.

C. *Comparative leverage ratios* provide another tool of capital structure management. This involves the computation of various balance sheet leverage ratios and coverage ratios. Information for the latter comes essentially from the income statement. The ratios that would exist under alternative financing plans can then be computed and examined for their suitableness to management.

D. The use of *industry norms* in conjunction with comparative leverage ratios can aid the financial manager in arriving at an appropriate financing mix. Industry norms can be thought of as standards for comparison. We recognize that industry groupings contain firms whose basic business risk may differ widely. Nevertheless, corporate financial analysts, investment bankers, commercial loan officers, and bond rating agencies rely on industry classes in order to compute such "normal" ratios. Since so many observers are interested in industry standards, the financial officer must be too.

XI. A glance at actual capital structure management

A. The opinions and practices of financial executives reinforce the major topics covered in this chapter. Most senior financial officers, for example, *do* believe there is an optimum capital structure for the corporation.

B. *Target debt ratios* are widely used by financial officers. Surveys indicate that the firm's actual target debt ratio is affected by several factors including (1) the firm's ability to adequately meet its financing charges, (2) maintaining a desired bond rating, (3) providing an adequate borrowing reserve, and (4) exploiting the perceived advantages of financial leverage. In practice, the firm's *own management group and staff of analysts* seem to be the most important influence on actually setting the target debt ratio.

C. In this chapter, we defined *debt capacity* as the maximum proportion of debt that the firm can include in its capital structure and still maintain its lowest composite cost of capital. Executives operationalize this concept in different ways. The most popular approach is to define the firm's debt capacity as a target percent of total capitalization (i.e., total long-term debt divided by the sum of all long-term debt, preferred equity, and common equity).

D.   In the opinion of your authors, the single most important factor that should affect the firm's financing mix is the underlying nature of the business in which it operates. This also means the firm's *business risk* must be carefully assessed. This means the firm's capital structure cannot be properly designed without a thorough understanding of its commercial (business) strategy.

XII.   Multinational firm: Business Risk and Global Sales

A.   Business risk for multinational firm is directly affected by

1.   sensitively of firm's product demand to general economic conditions.

2.   degree of competition.

3.   product deversification.

4.   growth prospects.

5.   global sales volume and productive output.

B.   Multinational firm expansion into foreign markets increase the firm's business risk.

Study Problems

1.   Columbia Products will earn $231,000 next year after taxes. Sales for Columbia will be $4,400,000. The firm operates in modern facilities near Columbia, South Carolina. The firm specializes in the production of furniture for lawyers' offices, accountants' offices, and college dormitories. The average unit sells for $220 and has an associated variable cost per unit of $165. Columbia experiences a 30% tax rate.

(a)   What will fixed costs (in total) be next year for Columbia?

(b)   Calculate Columbia's break-even point both in units and dollars.

(c)   Generate the analytical income statement at the break-even level of sales dollars.

SOLUTION

(a) All that we have to do here is use our knowledge of the break-even model *and* the analytical income statement model (both are discussed in detail in Chapter 12 of your text). The calculations follow:

$$\{(P \cdot Q) - [V \cdot Q + (F)]\} \ (1\text{-}T) = \$231,000$$

$$\left\{4,400,000 - \left[\$1.65 \times \frac{\$4,400,000}{\$220} \right] + F \right\} (1 - T) = 231,000$$

$$[(\$4,400,000) - (\$3,300,000) - F] \ (\cdot 7) = \$231,000$$

$$(\$1,100,000 - F) \ (.7) = \$231,000$$

$$\$770,000 - \cdot 7F = \$231,000$$

$$.7F = \$539,000$$

$$F = \underline{\$770,000}$$

(b)
$$Q_B = \frac{F}{P - V} = \frac{\$770,000}{\$55} = 14,000 \text{ units}$$

$$S^* = \frac{F}{1 - \dfrac{VC}{S}} = \frac{\$770,000}{1 - .75} = \frac{\$770,000}{.25}$$

$$= \$3,080,000$$

We have shown that the firm will break even (i.e., EBIT= 0) when it sells 14,000 units. With a selling price of $220 per unit, the break-even sales level is $3,080,000.

(c) The analytical income statement at the break-even level of sales would appear as follows:

Sales	$3,080,000
Variable costs	2,310,000
Revenue before fixed costs	$ 770,000
Fixed costs	770,000
EBIT	$ 0

2. Woody's Carry-Out Pizza expects to earn $16,000 next year before interest and taxes. Sales will be $130,000. The store is the only pizza parlor near the fraternity-row district of Gardiner University. The owner, Eric Nemeth, makes only one variety and size of pizza (the House Special) and it sells for $10. The variable cost per pizza is $6. Woody's Carry-Out Pizza experiences a 48% tax rate.

   (a) What are the pizza parlor's fixed costs expected to be next year?

   (b) Calculate the parlor's break-even point in units and dollars.

SOLUTION

   (a) To compute fixed costs:

   $S - (VC + FC) = EBIT$

   $\$130,000/\$10 = 13,000$ units sold

   $\$130,000 - [(13,000)(\$6) + FC] = \$16,000$

   $\$130,000 - \$78,000 - FC = \$16,000$

   $FC = \$36,000$

   (b) First, the break-even point in units:

   $$Q_B = \frac{F}{P-V} = \frac{\$36,000}{\$10-\$6} = 9,000 \text{ units}$$

   Then, the break-even point in dollars:

   $$S^* = \frac{F}{1-VC/S} = \frac{\$36,000}{1-\dfrac{\$78,000}{\$130,000}} = \$90,000$$

3. The ESM Corporation projects that next year its fixed costs will total $120,000. Its only product sells for $17 per unit, of which $9 is a variable cost. The management of ESM is considering the purchase of a new machine that will lower the variable cost per unit to $7. The new machine, however, will add to fixed costs through an increase in depreciation expense.

   (a) How large can the addition to fixed costs be in order to keep the firm's break-even point in units produced and sold unchanged?

SOLUTION

 (a) Compute the present level of break-even output:

$$Q_B = \frac{F}{P - V}$$

$$= \frac{\$120,000}{8} = 15,000 \text{ units}$$

Compute the new level of fixed costs at the break-even output:

F + (7) (15,000)	=	(17) (15,000)
F + 105,000	=	255,000
F	=	$150,000

Compute the addition to fixed costs:

$150,000 - $120,000 = *$30,000 addition*

4. The Moose Hobby Company manufactures a full line of gold-plated model airplanes. The average selling price of a finished unit is $25. The associated variable cost is $15 per unit. Fixed costs for the company average $70,000 per year. What would be the company's profit or loss at the following units of production sold: 5,000? 7,000? 9,000 units?

SOLUTION

The company's profit or loss:

	@ 5,000 units	@ 7,000 units	@ 9,000 units
Sales (P X Q)	$125,000	$175,000	$225,000
− VC (VC/unit X Q)	75,000	105,000	135,000
− FC	70,000	70,000	70,000
Profit (loss)	($ 20,000)	-0-	$ 20,000

5.   An analytical income statement for the D. A. Bauer Corporation is shown below. It is based on an output level of 69,000 units.

Sales	$1,035,000
Variable costs	552,000
Revenue before fixed costs	$ 483,000
Fixed costs	183,000
EBIT	$ 300,000
Interest expense	80,000
Earnings before taxes	$ 220,000
Taxes	77,000
Net income	$ 143,000

(a)   Calculate net income for a 10% increase in sales where variable costs increase in proportion to sales.

(b)   What is the effect of the firm's operating leverage on the firm's EBIT?

(c)   What is the effect of the firm's financial leverage on net income?

(d)   What is the combined effect of operating and financial leverage on the firm?

SOLUTION

		+10%	% Change
Sales	$1,035,000	$1,138,500	10%
Variable costs	552,000	907,200	
Revenue before fixed costs	$ 483,000	$ 531,300	
Fixed costs	183,000	183,001	
EBIT	$ 300,000	348,299	16%
Interest expense	80,000	80,001	
Earnings before taxes	$ 220,000	$ 268,298	
Taxes	77,000	93,904	
Net income	$ 143,000	$ 174,394	22%

(a)   The 10% increase in sales increases firm net income from $143,000 to $174,394. Note that fixed costs and interest expense do not change and this fact is the source of operating and financial leverage.

(b)   The 10% increase in sales is magnified to a 16% increase in EBIT by the firm's use of operating leverage.

(c) The firm's use of financial leverage made the 16% increase in EBIT into a 22% increase in net income.

(d) Combined the effects of operating and financial leverage are to make the increase in net income 2.2 times larger than the percent change in sales.

6. E. Wrok and Associates, Inc., are planning to open a small manufacturing corporation. The company will manufacture a full line of solar-energized home products. The investors of the company have proposed two financing plans. Plan I is an all common equity alternative. Under this plan, 200,000 common shares will be sold to net the firm $20 per share. Financial leverage is stipulated in Plan II, and 100,000 shares will be sold. A debt issue with a 30-year maturity period will be privately placed. The interest rate on the debt issue will be 18% while the principal borrowed will amount to $2,000,000. The corporate tax rate is 50%.

(a) Find the EBIT indifference level associated with the two financing proposals.

(b) Prepare an income statement that shows that EPS will be the same regardless of the plan chosen at the EBIT level found in part a.

(c) If a detailed financial analysis projects that long-term EBIT will always be close to $1,000,000 annually, which plan would be chosen? Why?

SOLUTION

(a) In the following equation, E = EBIT.

$$\frac{(E-\$0)(1-0.5)-0}{200,000} = \frac{(E-\$360,000)(1-0.5)-0}{100,000}$$

$$\frac{0.5E}{200,000} = \frac{0.5E-\$180,000}{100,000}$$

$$\$50,000E = 100,000E - \$36,000,000,000$$

$$E = \underline{\$720,000}$$

(b)

$$\text{Income Statement}$$

	With C/S Financing	Financing With C/S and Debt
EBIT	$720,000	$720,000
Less: Interest Expense	0	360,000
Earnings before taxes	$720,000	$360,000
Less: Taxes @ 50%	360,000	180,000
Earnings available to common	$360,000	$180,000
C/S Outstanding	200,000	100,000
EPS	$1.80	$1.80

(c) Plan II, because at any level above the indifference point, the more heavily levered financing plan will generate a higher EPS.

7. Albina's Ice Cream Factory's capital structure for the past year of operations is shown below:

First Mortgage bonds at 15%	$ 4,000,000
Debentures at 17%	3,500,000
Common stock (1,500,000 shares)	10,500,000
Retained earnings	2,000,000
Total	$20,000,000

The federal income tax rate is 50%. Albina's Ice Cream Factory, home-based in San Antonio, wants to raise an additional $1,500,000 to open new facilities in Houston and Dallas. The firm can accomplish this via two alternatives. That is, it can sell a new issue of 20-year debentures with 18% interest; alternatively, 30,000 new shares of common stock can be sold to the public to net the ice cream factory $50 per share. A recent study performed by an outside consulting organization projected Albina's Ice Cream's long-term EBIT level at approximately $13,575,000.

(a) Find the indifference level of EBIT (with regard to earnings per share) between the suggested financing plans.

(b) Which alternative do you recommend that Albina's Ice Cream Factory pursue?

SOLUTION

(a) In the following equations, E = EBIT

$$\frac{(E - \$1,195,000)(0.5)}{1,530,000} = \frac{(E - \$1,465,000)(0.5)}{1,500,000}$$

$$\frac{0.5E - \$597,500}{153} = \frac{0.5E - \$732,500}{150}$$

75E - \$89,625,000 = 76.5E - \$112,072,500

E = \$14,965,000 indifference level of EBIT

(b) The consulting firm projected Albina's Ice Cream Factory's long-term EBIT at \$13,575,000. Since this projected level of EBIT is less than the indifference level of \$14,965,000, the earnings per share of the firm will be greater if the common stock is issued.

Self Test

TRUE-FALSE

_____ 1. Dispersion in operating income causes business risk.

_____ 2. Your firm adds to its facilities a completely automated product line. This will have no effect on the break-even point (in units of output).

_____ 3. Variable costs are fixed per unit of output but vary in total as output changes.

_____ 4. Your firm expects a 7% increase in sales for the next year. The degree of operating leverage will decrease for your firm.

_____ 5. When the firm uses more financial leverage, its stockholders expect a greater return.

_____ 6. The break-even model enables the financial officer to determine the quality of output that must be sold to cover all operating costs.

_____ 7. If EBIT were to remain constant while the firm incurred additional interest expense, the degree of financial leverage would increase.

_____ 8. The incurrence of fixed operating costs in the firm's income stream is referred to as financial leverage.

_____ 9. Break-even analysis is a long-run concept since all costs are variable in the long run.

_____ 10. Operating leverage is the responsiveness of the firm's EBIT to fluctuations in net income.

_____ 11. Earnings per share is the most appropriate criterion for all financing decisions.

_____ 12. The decision to use financial leverage by the firm magnifies its variation in earnings per share, compared to the use of no financial leverage.

_____ 13. Variable costs are fixed per unit of output.

_____ 14. Fixed costs per unit vary with units of output.

_____ 15. Combining operating and financial leverage magnifies variations in earnings per share in response to changes in sales.

_____ 16. A firm faces a greater chance of insolvency with an increase in the use of financial leverage (other factors held constant).

_____ 17. The decision to use debt or preferred stock in the financial structure of a corporation means that those who own the common shares are exposed to financial risk.

_____ 18. Semi-variable costs may be fixed over a range of output then rise sharply as a higher output level is reached and remain fixed over this higher range of output.

_____ 19. Break-even analysis _must_ include allowance for all non-cash expenses.

_____ 20. Financial risk is a direct result of the firm's investment decisions.

_____ 21. Financial leverage is a result of the financing of the firm's assets with securities bearing a fixed rate of return over a specific time period.

_____ 22. Firms can affect their total risk exposures by combining operating and financial leverage in different degrees.

_____ 23. The ratio of total variable costs to total sales is presumed constant in ordinary break-even analysis.

_____ 24. Capital structure is defined by the mix of all items that appear on the right-hand side of the firm's balance sheet.

_____ 25. The major influence on the maturity structure of the financing plan is the nature of the assets owned by the firm.

_____ 26. The optimal capital structure can be defined as the mix of permanent sources of funds that minimize the company's common stock price.

_____ 27. The EBIT-EPS analysis measures the variability (riskiness) of the earnings stream, thereby recognizing the implicit costs of debt financing.

_____ 28. The tax shield on interest represents additional cash flow to a firm's security holders resulting from tax savings on interest payments to the firm.

_____ 29. In computing the firm's tax bill, the interest expense is assumed not to be tax-deductible.

_____ 30. Inputs to the coverage ratios generally come from the firm's balance sheet.

_____ 31. According to the moderate position of capital structure theory, financial leverage affects firm value but not the cost of corporate capital.

_____ 32. Above a critical level of EBIT, the firm's earnings per share will be lower if greater degrees of financial leverage are employed.

_____ 33. Industry norms, used with other tools of capital structure management, can be helpful in determining an appropriate financing mix.

_____ 34. In practice, as more financial leverage is used, it will increase the firm's value indefinitely and lower its cost of capital continuously.

_____ 35. The EBIT-EPS analysis chart tells us that EPS will be greater than zero, if the EBIT level just covers the plan's financing cost.

_____ 36. At a point below the EBIT indifference level, the financing plan involving less leverage will generate a higher EPS.

_____ 37. Capital structure is equal to the financial structure less current liabilities.

_____ 38. Debt capacity is the maximum proportion of debt that a company can include in its capital structure without affecting the cost of common equity.

_____ 39. Agency costs refer to those expenses paid to lawyers, accountants, etc. during bankruptcy proceedings.

_____ 40. Financial managers must frequently use coverage ratios to operationalize debt capacity concepts.

_____ 41. External economic factors are an important influence on determining a firm's target debt ratio, but firm-specific factors have to be considered as well.

_____ 42. The purpose of EBIT-EPS analysis is to determine the level of operating income at which EBIT equals EPS for a single financing plan.

MULTIPLE CHOICE

1. Which of the following is *not* a limitation of break-even analysis?

    a. The price of the product is assumed to be constant.
    b. In multiple product firms, the product mix is assumed to be constant.
    c. It provides a method for analyzing operating leverage.
    d. Variable costs per unit are assumed to be constant.

2. Which of the following is not considered a fixed cost?

    a   Depreciation
    b. Rent
    c. Electricity
    d. Administrative salaries

3. At the break-even level of sales, the degree of operating leverage is

    a. zero.
    b. undefined.
    c. a positive number.
    d. Not enough information is given.

4. In the context of break-even point in sales dollars, if the variable cost per unit rises and if all other variables remain constant, the break-even level of sales will

    a.   fall.
    b.   rise.
    c.   stay the same.
    d.   either a or c.

5. The firm is exposing itself to financial risk when its percent change in EPS divided by percent change in EBIT is

    a.   less than 1.
    b.   greater than 1.
    c.   equal to 1.
    d.   between 0 and 1.

6. A firm that incurs a low level of fixed operating costs might prudently use
    a.   a low degree of financial leverage.
    b.   a high degree of financial leverage.
    c.   a low degree of combined leverage.
    d.   None of the above.

7. As the firm's sales revenue increases over time,

    a.   it can lessen its business risks.
    b.   it can lessen its operating leverage.
    c.   both a and b.
    d.   None of the above.

8. The practice of financing a portion of a firm's assets with securities bearing a fixed rate of return in hopes of increasing the ultimate return to shareholders refers to

    a.   operating leverage.
    b.   financial leverage.
    c.   break-even sales level.

9.   The selling price of a product is $25, and the unit variable cost is $17. If a firm's fixed costs are $20,000, what is the break-even level in units?

     a.   800 units
     b.   2,000 units
     c.   2,500 units
     d.   4,300 units

10. Business risk is the residual effect of
     a.   the company's cost structure.
     b.   product demand characteristics.
     c.   intra-industry competitive position.
     d.   All of the above.
     e.   None of the above.

11. The break-even model assumes that if sales increase by 10%, variable costs

     a.   remain unchanged.
     b.   rise by 10%.
     c.   rise by 20%.
     d.   The break-even model makes no assumptions about variable costs and sales.

12. The break-even level for the number of units sold is defined as

     a.   (unit sales price minus unit variable cost) divided by total fixed costs.
     b.   unit sales minus (unit variable costs divided by total fixed costs).
     c.   (total fixed costs divided by unit sales price) minus unit variable costs.
     d.   trial and error analysis.
     e.   All are acceptable techniques.

13. As the quantity of product increases, the fixed cost per unit of output

     a.   increases.
     b.   decreases.
     c.   remains constant.
     d.   increases to a certain level and then decreases.

14. Operating leverage can be attributed to _____ that a firm assumes.

   a. the financial risk
   b. the business risk
   c. both a and b
   d. none of the above

15. Break-even analysis and its assumptions can help the financial officer determine the

   a. level of output that must be sold to recover all operating costs.
   b. EBIT that will be achieved at various output levels.
   c. Both a & b.
   d. None of the above.

16. The firm's capital structure consists of

   a. long-term debt.
   b. common equity.
   c. preferred equity.
   d. Only b and c.
   e. All of the above.

17. A firm will turn to common equity financing when
   a. the stock market is looking favorable.
   b. the expected cost of default is greater than the tax advantage of debt financing.
   c. it reaches optimal capital structure.
   d. only a and b

18. The objective of capital structure management is to

   a. minimize the composite cost of capital.
   b. determine the optimal capital structure.
   c. maximize the common stock price.
   d. All of the above.

19. The cost of debt financing is _____ by the effects of income taxes

    a. increased
    b. decreased
    c. not affected
    d. either increased or decreased depending on the level of the tax rate

20. Which of the following assumptions does capital structure theory not include?

    a. Corporate income is not subject to any tax.
    b. Transaction costs of selling securities are prevalent.
    c. The expected values of all investors' forecasts of the future levels of EBIT for each firm are identical.
    d. The capital structures consist only of stocks and bonds.

21. Which of the following is not a limitation of EBIT-EPS analysis?
    a. It disregards the explicit cost of debt financing.
    b. It ignores the level of the firm's earnings stream.
    c. There are no limitations of the EBIT-EPS analysis.
    d. None of the above.

22. Which of the following is not true about capital structure theory (moderate position)?

    a. Firm's bankruptcy cost is related to its use of financial leverage.
    b. The sum of the cash flows that the firm could pay to all contributors of corporate capital is not affected by its financing mix.
    c. Financial leverage affects the firm's value.
    d. a and c

23. Which of the following is *not* a basic tool of capital structure management?

    a. EBIT-EPS analysis
    b. Comparative leverage ratios
    c. Use of industry norms
    d. None of the above.

23. Which of the following are ways of analyzing capital structure:

   a. EBIT-EPS analysis
   b. Comparative leverage ratios
   c. Analysis of cash flows
   d. a and b
   e. All of the above.

25. The optimal capital structure refers to a capital structure that
   a. is comprised of 99.9% debt capital.
   b. will minimize the composite cost of a firm's capital for raising a given amount of funds.
   c. will minimize the firm's common stock price.
   d. All of the above.

26. The target debt ratio is affected by the firm's ability to

   a. adequately meet its financing charges.
   b. maintain a desired bond rating.
   c. provide an adequate borrowing reserve.
   d. exploit the perceived advantages of financial leverage.
   e. All of the above.

CHAPTER 13

Dividend Policy and Internal Financing

Orientation: In determining the firm's dividend policy, two issues are important: the dividend payout ratio and the stability of the dividend payment over time. In this regard, the financial manager should consider the investment opportunities available to the firm and any preference that the company's investors have for dividend income or capital gains. Also, stock dividends, stock splits, or stock repurchases can be used to supplement or replace cash dividends.

I.   The tradeoffs in setting a firm's dividend policy

    A.   If a company pays a large dividend, it will

        1.   have a low retention of profits within the firm, and

        2.   need to rely heavily on a new common stock issue for equity financing.

    B.   If a company pays a small dividend, it will

        1.   have a high retention of profits within the firm, and

        2.   will not need to rely heavily on a new common stock issue for equity financing since the profits retained for reinvestment will provide the needed equity financing.

II.   The importance of a firm's dividend policy depends on the impact of the dividend decision on the firm's stock price. That is, given a firm's capital budgeting and borrowing decisions, what is the impact of the firm's dividend policies on the stock price?

III. Three views about the importance of a firm's dividend policy.

    A.   View 1:   Dividends do not matter

        1.   Assume that the dividend decision does not change the firm's capital budgeting and financing decisions.

        2.   Assume perfect markets, which means:

            a.   There are no brokerage commissions when investors buy and sell stocks.

            b.   New securities can be issued without incurring any flotation cost.

            c.   There is no income tax—personal or corporate.

            d.   Information is free and equally available to all investors.

            e.   There are no conflicts of interest between management and stockholders.

        3.   Under the foregoing assumptions, it may be shown that the market price of a corporation's common stock is unchanged under different dividend policies. If the firm increases the dividend to its stockholders, it has to offset this increase by issuing new common stock in order to finance the available investment opportunities. If, on the other hand, the firm reduces its dividend payment, it has more funds available internally to finance future investment projects. In either policy, the present value of the resulting cash flows to be accrued to the current investors is independent of the dividend policy. By varying the dividend policy, only the type of return is affected (capital gains versus dividend income), not the total return.

B.   View 2:   High dividends increase stock value

    1.   Dividends are more predictable than capital gains because management can control dividends, while they cannot dictate the price of the stock. Thus, investors are less certain of receiving income from capital gains than from dividend income. The incremental risk associated with capital gains relative to dividend income should, therefore, cause us to use a higher required rate in discounting a dollar of capital gains than the rate used for discounting a dollar of dividends. In so doing, we would give a higher value to the dividend income than we would the capital gains.

    2.   Criticisms of view 2

        a.   Since the dividend policy has no impact on the volatility of the company's overall cash flows, it has no impact on the riskiness of the firm.

        b.   Increasing a firm's dividend does not reduce the basic riskiness of the stock; rather, if dividend payment requires management to issue new stock, it only transfers risk *and* ownership from the current owners to new owners.

C.   View 3:   Low dividends increase value

Stocks that allow us to defer taxes (low dividends-high capital gains) will possibly sell at a premium relative to stocks that require us to pay taxes currently (high dividends-low capital gains). Only then will the two stocks provide comparable after tax returns, which suggests that a policy to pay low dividends will result in a higher stock price. That is, high dividends hurt investors, while low dividends-high retention help the firm's investors.

But wait, then came 2003 and Congress again felt the need to change the tax code as it pertained to both dividend income and capital gains income. On May 28 President Bush signed into law the "Jobs and Growth Tax Relief Reconciliation Act of 2003." Recall that part of the impetus for this Act was the recession that commenced in 2001 and the slow rate of payroll jobs creation that followed that recession.

In a nutshell this 2003 Act lowered the top tax rate on dividend income to 15 percent from a previous top rate of 38.6 percent, and also lowered the top rate paid on realized long-term capital gains to the same 15 percent from a previous 20 percent. Thus, you can see that the so-called investment playing field was (mostly) leveled for dividend income relative to qualifying capital gains. This rather dramatic change in the tax code will immediately remind you of **Principle 8: Taxes Bias Business Decisions.** In effect, A major portion of the previous bias against paying cash dividends to investors was mitigated. But, not all of it.

D. Additional thoughts about the importance of a firm's dividend policy

1. <u>Residual dividend theory</u>: Because of flotation costs incurred in issuing new stock, firms must issue a larger amount of securities in order to receive the amount of capital required for investments. As a result, new equity capital will be more expensive than capital raised through retained earnings. Therefore, financing investments internally (and decreasing dividends) instead of issuing new stock may be favored. This is embodied in the *residual dividend theory*, where a dividend would be paid only when any internally generated funds remain after financing the equity portion of the firm's investments.

2. <u>The clientele effect</u>: If investors do in fact have a preference between dividends and capital gains, we could expect them to seek out firms that have a dividend policy consistent with these preferences. They would in essence "sort themselves out" by buying stocks which satisfy their preferences for dividends and/or capital gains. In other words, there would be a "clientele effect," where firms draw a given clientele, given the stated dividend policy. However, unless there is a greater aggregate demand for a particular policy than is being satisfied in the market, dividend policy is still unimportant, in that one policy is as good as the other. The clientele effect tells us only to avoid making capricious changes in a company's dividend policy.

3. The information effect

    a.   We know from experience that a large, unexpected change in dividends can have significant impact on the stock price. Despite such "evidence," it is not unreasonable to hypothesize that dividend policy only appears to be important because we are not looking at the real cause and effect. It may be that investors use a change in dividend policy as a *signal* about the firm's "true" financial condition, especially its earning power.

    b.   Some would argue that management frequently has inside information about the firm that it cannot make available to the investors. This difference in accessibility to information between management and investors, called *information asymmetry,* may result in a lower stock price than would be true if we had conditions of certainty. Dividends become a means in a risky market place to minimize any "drag" on the stock price that might come from differences in the level of information available to managers and investors.

4. Agency costs: Conflicts between management and stock-holders may exist, and the stock price of a company owned by investors who are separate from management may be less than the stock value of a closely-held firm. The difference in price is the cost of the conflict to the owners, which has come to be called *agency costs.* A firm's dividend policy may be perceived by owners as a tool to minimize agency costs. Assuming the payment of a dividend requires management to issue stock to finance new investments, then new investors will be attracted to the company only if management provides convincing information that the capital will be used profitably. Thus, the payment of dividends indirectly results in a closer monitoring of management's investment activities. In this case, dividends may provide a meaningful contribution to the value of the firm.

5. Expectations theory: As the time approaches for management to announce the amount of the next dividend, investors form expectations as to how much the dividend will be. When the actual dividend decision is announced, the investor compares the actual decision with the expected decision. If the amount of the dividend is as expected, even if it represents an increase from prior years, the market price of the stock will remain unchanged. However, if the dividend is higher or lower than expected, the investors will reassess their perceptions about the firm and the value of the stock.

E. The empirical evidence about the importance of dividend policy

1. Statistical tests: To test the relationship between dividend payments and security prices, we could compare a firm's dividend yield (dividend/stock price) and the stock's total return; the question being, "Do stocks that pay high dividends provide higher or lower returns to the investors?" Such tests have been conducted using a variety of the most sophisticated statistical techniques available. Despite the use of these extremely powerful analytical tools involving intricate and complicated procedures, the results have been mixed.

   However, over long periods of time, the results have given a slight advantage to the low-dividend stocks; that is, stocks that pay lower dividends appear to have higher prices. The findings are far from conclusive, however, owing to the relatively large standard errors of the estimates.

2. Reasons for inconclusive results from the statistical tests

   a. To be accurate, we would need to know the amount of dividends investors *expect* to receive. Since these expectations cannot be observed, we can use only historical data, which may or may not relate to expectations.

   b. Most empirical studies have assumed a linear relationship between dividend payments and stock prices. The actual relationship may be nonlinear, possibly even with discontinuities in the relationship.

213

3. Since our statistical prowess does not provide us with any conclusive evidence, researchers have surveyed financial managers about their perceptions of the relevance of dividend policy. In such surveys, the evidence favors the relevance of dividend policy, but not overwhelmingly so. For the most part, managers are divided between believing that dividends are important and having no opinion in the matter.

F. Conclusions about the importance of dividend policy

1. As a firm's investment opportunities increase, the dividend payout ratio should decrease.

2. The firm's dividend policy appears to be important; however, appearances may be deceptive. The real issue may be the firm's *expected* earnings power and the riskiness of these earnings.

3. If dividends influence stock price, it probably comes from the investor's desire to minimize and/or defer taxes and from the role of dividends in minimizing agency costs.

4. If the expectations theory has merit, which we believe it does, it behooves management to avoid surprising the investors when it comes to the firm's dividend decision.

IV. Dividend policy decisions

A. Other practical considerations

1. Legal restrictions

a. A corporation may not pay a dividend

(1) If the firm's liabilities exceed its assets.

(2) If the amount of the dividend exceeds the accumulated profits (retained earnings).

(3) If the dividend is being paid from capital invested in the firm.

b. Debtholders and preferred stockholders may impose restrictive provisions on management, such as common dividends not being paid from earnings prior to the payment of interest or preferred dividends.

2. Liquidity position: The amount of a firm's retained earnings and its cash position are seldom the same. Thus, the company must have adequate *cash* available as well as retained earnings to pay dividends.

3. Absence or lack of other sources of financing: All firms do not have equal access to the capital markets. Consequently, companies with limited financial resources may rely more heavily on internally generated funds.

4. Earnings predictability: A firm that has a stable earnings trend will generally pay a larger portion of its earnings in dividends. If earnings fluctuate significantly, a larger amount of the profits may be retained to ensure that enough money is available for investment projects when needed.

5. Ownership control: For many small firms, and certain large ones, maintaining the controlling vote is very important. These owners would prefer the use of debt and retained profits to finance new investments rather than issue new stock.

6. Inflation: Because of inflation, the cost of replacing equipment has increased substantially. Depreciation funds tend to become insufficient. Hence, greater profit retention may be required.

B. Alternative dividend policies

1. Constant dividend payout ratio: The percentage of earnings paid out in dividends is held constant. Therefore, the dollar amount of the dividend fluctuates from year to year.

2. Stable dollar dividend per share: Relatively stable dollar dividend is maintained. The dividend per share is increased or decreased only after careful investigation by the management.

3. Small, regular dividend plus a year-end extra: Extra dividend is paid out in prosperous years. Management's objective is to avoid the connotation of a permanent dividend increase.

C. Bases for stable dividends

    1. Investors may use the dividend policy as a surrogate for information that is not easily accessible. The dividend policy may be useful in assessing the company's long-term earnings prospects.

    2. Many investors rely on dividends to satisfy personal income need. If dividends fluctuate from year to year, investors may have to sell or buy stock to satisfy their current needs, thereby incurring expensive transaction costs.

    3. Legal listings stipulate that certain types of financial institutions may invest only in companies that have a consistent dividend payment.

    4. Conclusion: An investor who prefers stable dividends will assign a lower required rate of return (a higher P/E ratio) for a stock paying a stable dividend. This results in a higher market price for the stock.

D. Dividend policy and corporate strategy: Things will change—even dividend policy

    1. The recessions of 1990 to 1991 and 2001 induced a large number of American corporations to revisit their broadest corporate strategies, including adjusted dividend policies.

    2. One firm that altered its dividend policy in response to new strategies was the W.R. Grace & Co., headquartered in Columbia, Maryland.

    3. Table 13-1 in the text reviews W.R. Grace's actual dividend policies over the 1992 to 1996 time frame. The firm's payout ratio and the absolute amount of the cash dividend paid per share declined in a significant fashion over this period.

V. Dividend payment procedures

A. Dividends are generally paid quarterly.

B. The *declaration date* is the date on which the firm's board of directors announces the forthcoming dividends.

C. The *date of record* designates when the stock transfer books are to be closed thus identifying who is entitled to the dividend.

D. Brokerage firms terminate the right of ownership to the dividend two working days prior to the date of record. This date is called the *ex-dividend date*.

E. Dividend checks are mailed on the *payment date*.

VI. Stock dividends and stock splits

A. Both a stock dividend and a stock split involve issuing new shares of stock to current stockholders.

B. The investor's percentage ownership in the firm remains unchanged. The investor is neither better nor worse off than before the stock split/dividend.

C. On an economic basis, there is no difference between a stock dividend and a stock split.

D. For accounting purposes, the stock split has been defined as a stock dividend exceeding 25%.

E. Accounting treatment

1. For a stock dividend, the dollar amount of the dividend is transferred from retained earnings to the capital accounts.

2. In the case of a split, the dollar amounts of the capital accounts do not change. Only the number of shares is increased, while the par value of each share is decreased proportionately.

F. Rationale for a stock dividend or split

1. The price of stock may not fall precisely in proportion to the share increase; thus, the stockholders' value is increased.

2. If a company is encountering cash problems, it can substitute a stock dividend for a cash dividend. Investors will probably look beyond the dividend to determine the underlying reasons for conserving cash.

VII.   Stock repurchases

A.   The following benefits justify stock repurchases instead of dividend payment:

1.   To provide an internal investment opportunity.

2.   To modify the firm's capital structure.

3.   To impact earnings per share, thus increasing stock price.

B.   Share repurchase as a dividend decision

1.   A firm may decide to repurchase its shares, increasing the earnings per share which should be reflected in a higher stock price.

2.   The investor's choice

a.   For tax purposes, the investor may prefer the firm to repurchase stock in lieu of a dividend. Dividends are taxed as ordinary income, whereas any price appreciation resulting from the stock repurchase would be taxed as a capital gain.

b.   The investor may still prefer dividend payment because

(1)   Dividends are viewed as more dependable than potential stock price appreciation resulting from stock repurchases.

(2)   The price the firm must pay for its stock may be too high.

(3)   Riskiness of the firm's capital structure may increase, lowering the P/E ratio and, thus, the stock price.

C.   Financing or investment decision

1.   A stock repurchase effectively increases the debt-equity ratio towards higher debt; thus, repurchase is viewed as a financing decision.

2. Buying its own stock at depressed prices, a firm may consider the repurchase as an investment decision. However, this action is not a true investment opportunity, as the extreme result would mean the company would consume itself.

D. The repurchase procedure

1. A public announcement should be made detailing the amount, purpose, and procedure for the stock repurchase.

2. Open market purchase—at the current market price.

3. Tender offer—more formal and at a specified price.

4. Negotiated basis—repurchasing from specific large shareholders.

VIII. Multinational firm: Dividend payments versus reinvesting in the firm

A. During economic expansion periods, firms tend to focus on growth strategies and invest more earnings into positive NPV projects rather than dividend payments.

B. Multinational firms look to international markets for high NPV projects to

1. spread country-related economic risks by geographically diversifying, and

2. achieve cost advantage over competitors.

C. The United States multinational firms tend to

1. invest in opportunities in the United Kingdom and Canada,

2. concentrate investments in manufacturing industries.

Study Problems

1. Philips Limited treats dividends as a residual variable in its financial decisions (see residual dividend theory). Net income has been forecasted for the upcoming year to be $600,000, which may be used for reinvesting in the firm or for paying dividends. The firm has only equity in its capital structure, and its cost of internally generated equity capital is 10%. If, however, new common stock were issued, flotation costs would raise this cost to 11%. If the firm considers the 10% cost of internal equity to be the opportunity cost of retained earnings,

    (a)   (1)   How much in dividends should be paid if the company has $500,000 in projects with expected returns exceeding 10%?

            (2)   How much should the dividend be if $600,000 in investments are available having expected returns greater than 10%?

    (b)   How much should be paid in dividends if the firm has $1 million in projects whose expected returns exceed 11%?

    (c)   How would your answer change in part b if the firm's optimal debt-equity mix is 40% debt and 60% common equity and the cost of capital remains the same?

SOLUTION

    (a)   (1)   According to the residual dividend theory, the firm should pay dividends only when it has exhausted its investments whose returns exceed the firm's cost of capital. Therefore, the firm should pay $100,000 in dividends ($600,000 income available for investing less $500,000 investments).

            (2)   The firm should use all of the $600,000 for investing in the projects and should not pay any dividends.

    (b)   If the firm has investment opportunities with returns exceeding the cost of capital, the firm should undertake these investments. In this example, the cost of capital increases (to 11%) when new equity is issued. Since the returns on the available investment projects (totaling $1 million) exceed the cost of equity capital, the firm should use up its internally generated funds ($600,000) and raise the remaining $400,000 by issuing new common stock. Therefore, no dividends would be paid.

(c) We would need $400,000 in new debt, (i.e., 40% of $1 million). The remaining $600,000 (which is 60% of the needed capital) will be supplied by internally generated funds. No dividend will be paid.

2. Beardsell Products and Voltas Products are identical firms in terms of (1) being in the same industry, (2) producing the same products, (3) being subject to the same risks, and (4) having equivalent earnings per share. Beardsell pays a constant cash dividend, whereas Voltas follows a constant percentage payout ratio of 50%. However, Voltas' common stock price has been lower than Beardsell's in spite of Voltas' dividend being substantially larger than Beardsell's in certain years. Given the data below:

| | Beardsell Products | | | Voltas Products | | |
| | | | Market | | | Market |
Year	EPS	Dividend	Price	EPS	Dividend	Price
1998	$2.50	$0.65	9	$2.50	$1.25	6 ¾
1999	-0.25	0.65	8 ¾	-0.25	0	6 ½
2000	3.00	0.65	9 ¼	3.00	1.50	9
2001	2.00	0.65	9	2.00	1.00	10

(a) What might account for the differences in the market prices of the two companies?

(b) What might both companies do in order to enhance the market prices of their respective shares?

SOLUTION

(a) The dissimilarity between market prices might be a function of the different dividend policies, with a lower capitalization rate, and, accordingly, a higher price being assigned to Beardsell as a result of the stable dividend stream.

(b) It appears that neither company would appear to be growth-oriented. If both firms are valued in terms of their dividend yield, which seems to be the case, higher dividend payouts might produce higher prices.

3. Rexall Corporation is considering 5 investment opportunities. The required investment outlays and expected rates of return for these investments are shown below. The cost of capital for the firm is 13%. Investments are to be financed with 30% debt and 70% equity. Internally generated funds available for reinvestment equal $1 million.

(a) Which investments should be accepted?

(b) According to the residual dividend theory, what amount should be paid out in dividends?

Investment	Cost	Internal Rate of Return
A	$200,000	20%
B	300,000	15
C	900,000	14
D	100,000	10
E	400,000	7

SOLUTION

(a) Investments A, B, and C should be accepted because their expected returns exceed the firm's cost of capital.

(b) Dividends to be paid:

Total cost of three projects:

$200,000 + $300,000 + $900,000	=	$1,400,000
Equity financing: $1,400,000 x 70%	=	980,000
Debt financing: $1,400,000 - $980,000	=	420,000

Internally generated funds available:	$1,000,000
Less equity necessary for projects:	980,000
Funds available for dividend payment:	$ 20,000

TRUE-FALSE

_____ 1. If dividend policy is treated as a passive residual, dividends are paid only if the firm has any remaining capital after financing attractive investments.

_____ 2. In practice, the firm should invest retained earnings as long as the required rate of return exceeds the expected rate of return from the investment.

_____ 3. The greater the ability of a firm to borrow, the less is its ability to pay a cash dividend.

_____ 4. If a firm has sporadic investment opportunities, it might be expected to pay out more dividends.

_____ 5. The introduction of flotation costs to the "dividend irrelevance" concept favors the retention of earnings in the firm.

_____ 6. Dividend income and capital gains from the sale of stock are taxed at the same personal income tax rate. Thus, there is no advantage to capital gains over dividend income for the investor.

_____ 7. An "expected" change in the dividend policy of a firm may not affect the price of the firm's stock when the change is actually announced.

_____ 8. A stock repurchase increases the debt-to-equity ratio.

_____ 9. Stock repurchases offer an attractive investment alternative for the firm any time its stock price is depressed.

_____ 10. The "bird-in-the-hand" theory assigns a higher value to capital gains than to dividend income.

_____ 11. A firm's dividend policy affects the variability of the firm's overall cash flows, even when we do not allow the dividend policy to impact investment decisions.

_____ 12. Stocks that allow us to defer taxes will not sell at a premium.

MULTIPLE CHOICE

1. Which of the following is not an assumption of the "dividend irrelevance" theory?

    a.   No taxes
    b.   Efficient capital markets
    c.   No flotation costs
    d.   Costless information

2. An argument for the relevance of dividends would be

    a.   informational content.
    b.   resolution of uncertainty
    c.   preference for current income.
    d.   All of the above.
    e.   None of the above.

3. An advantage of a stock dividend is that it

    a.   may help to conserve cash.
    b.   tends to increase the market price.
    c.   keeps the price of the stock within a desired trading range.
    d.   All of the above.

4. When the assumption of no taxes is removed from the "dividend irrelevance" theory

    a.   there is a preference for the retention of earnings.
    b.   there is a preference for paying out dividends.
    c.   the preference depends on the individual investor's tax status, but generally there is a preference for retention of earnings.

5. The following factors may influence the dividend policy that a firm undertakes:

    a.   The liquidity of the firm.
    b.   Capital structure.
    c.   Legal restrictions.
    d.   a and c
    e.   a and b

6. An advantage of a stock repurchase may be

   a. a means to modify capital structure.
   b. to impact earnings per share.
   c. the elimination of a particular minority group.
   d. All of the above.

7. A firm may not legally pay dividends if

   a. its liabilities exceed its assets.
   b. the dividend is being paid from capital invested in the firm.
   c. debtholders' contracts are not satisfied.
   d. All of the above.
   e. a and b

8. For tax purposes, a corporation may exclude _____ of the dividend income received from another corporation.

   a. 0%
   b. 10%
   c. 50%
   d. 70%
   e. none of the above

9. When real-world considerations are taken into account, the amount of a firm's dividend payment depends on the following factors:

   a. Profitability of investment opportunities.
   b. Investor's preference for capital gains or dividend income.
   c. Debt-to-equity ratio.
   d. Trading range of the firm's stock.
   e. a and b

10. Small-sized firms generally use retained earnings for investment purposes because

   a. they do not have easy access to the capital markets.
   b. ownership control is an important factor.
   c. their earnings fluctuate widely.
   d. inflation has greater impact on small companies.
   e. None of the above.
   f. a and b

11. Which one of the following dividend policies is the most popular?

    a.   Constant dividend payout ratio
    b.   Stable dividend (dollar) per share
    c.   Small, regular dividend plus a year-end extra

12. The ex-dividend date is

    a.   the same as the date of record.
    b.   two working days prior to date of record.
    c.   eight days prior to the payment date.
    d.   five days after the declaration date.
    e.   None of the above.

13. Properly viewed, a stock repurchase should be used as:

    a.   a dividend decision.
    b.   an investment decision.
    c.   a refinancing decision.
    d.   both a and c
    e.   All of the above.

CHAPTER 14
Short-Term Financial Planning

<u>Orientation</u>: In this chapter, we develop predictions of the firm's future financing needs based on a sales forecast. This entails construction of a pro forma income statement and balance sheet. The chapter also reviews the preparation and use of the cash budget as an essential tool of financial planning.

I.   Financial forecasting and planning

    A.   The need for forecasting in financial management arises whenever the future financing needs of the firm are being estimated. There are three basic steps involved in predicting financing requirements.

        1.   Project the firm's sales revenues and expenses over the planning period.

        2.   Estimate the levels of investment in current and fixed assets, which are necessary to support the projected sales level.

        3.   Determine the financing needs of the firm throughout the planning period.

    B.   The key ingredient in the firm's planning process is the sales forecast. This forecast should reflect (1) any past trend in sales that is expected to continue and (2) the effects of any events, which are expected to have a material effect on the firm's sales during the forecast period.

    C.   The traditional problem faced in financial forecasting begins with the sales forecast and involves making forecasts of the impact of predicted sales on the firm's various expenses, assets, and liabilities. The technique we use to make these forecasts is the <u>percent of sales</u> method. This involves projecting the financial variable as a percent of projected sales.

II. Profitability, Dividend Policy, and Discretionary Financing Needs (DFN)

    A. A firm's Discretionary Financing Needs (DFN) is the amount of financing the firm needs to obtain from discretionary (non-spontaneous) sources in order to finance its assets.

    B. Spontaneous sources of financing include accounts payable and other liabilities (e.g., wages payable) that arise "spontaneously" as the firm conducts its business plus the firm's net income less any dividends it pays. Consequently, the firm's dividend policy has a direct impact on its sources of spontaneous financing and consequently the firm's needs for discretionary financing, (i.e., discretionary financing needs or DFN).

III. Revenue Growth and DFN

    A. Revenue growth has two effects on DFN. First, as revenues grow this requires that the firm invest in additional working capital (current assets less current liabilities). Furthermore, with growing revenues the firm's profits generally increase with the effect of increasing the availability of funds to be retained and reinvested in the business.

VI. Financial planning and the cash budgeting

    A. The cash budget represents a detailed plan of future cash flows and can be broken down into four components: cash receipts, cash disbursements, net change in cash for the period, and new financing needed.

    B. Although no strict rules exist, as a general rule, the budget period shall be long enough to show the effect of management policies, yet short enough so that estimates can be made with reasonable accuracy. For instance, the capital expenditure budget may be properly developed for a 10-year period while a cash budget may cover only 12 months.

<u>Study Problems</u>

1. The most recent balance sheet for the Parino Manufacturing Co. is shown in the table below. The company is about to embark on an advertising campaign, which is expected to raise sales from the present level of $10 million to $12 million by the end of next year. The firm is presently operating at full capacity and will have to increase its investment in both current and fixed assets to support the projected level of new sales. In fact, the firm estimates that both categories of assets will rise in direct proportion to the projected increase in sales.

The firm's net profits were 4% of current year's sales but are expected to rise to 5% of next year's sales. To help support its anticipated growth in asset needs next year, the firm has suspended plans to pay cash dividends to its stockholders. In past years, a $1.50 per share dividend has been paid annually.

Parino Manufacturing Co., Inc. ($ millions)

	Present Level	Percent of Sales	Projected Level
Current assets	$2.0		
Net fixed assets	3.0		
Total	$5.0		
Accounts payable	$0.5		
Accrued expenses	0.5		
Notes payable	- -		
Current liabilities	$1.0		
Long-term debt	$2.0		
Common stock	0.5		
Retained earnings	1.5		
Common equity	$2.0		
Total	$5.0		

Parino's payables and accrued expenses are expected to vary directly with sales. In addition, notes payable will be used to supply the funds needed to finance next year's operations that are not forthcoming from other sources.

Fill in the table and project the firm's needs for discretionary financing. Use notes payable as the balancing entry for future discretionary financing needed.

SOLUTION ($ millions)

Current sales	$10		
Predicted sales	12		
Net profit margin	5%		

	Present Level	Percent of Sales	Projected Level
Current assets	$2.00	0.20	$2.40
Net fixed assets	3.00	0.30	3.60
Total	5.00	0.50	6.00
Accounts payable	0.50	0.05	0.60
Accrued expenses	0.50	0.05	0.60
Notes payable			
Current liabilities	1.00	0.10	1.20
Long-term debt	2.00	No Change	2.00
Common stock	0.50	No Change	0.50
Retained earnings	1.50	Ret. Earnings + NI	2.10
Common equity	2.00		2.60
Total	$5.00		
Total financing provided			$5.80
Discretionary financing needed			$ .20

2. The Horn Corporation's projected sales for the first 8 months of 2007 are as follows:

January	$300,000		May	$1,200,000
February	450,000		June	1,000,000
March	540,000		July	900,000
April	960,000		August	700,000

Twenty percent of Horn's sales are for cash, another 40% is collected in the month following sale, and 40% is collected in the second month following sale. November and December sales for 2000 were $800,000 and $650,000, respectively.

Horn purchases raw materials equal to 60% of sales, and it makes its purchases 2 months in advance of sales. The supplier is paid 1 month after the purchase. For example, purchases for April sales are made in February and are paid for in March.

Furthermore, Horn pays $42,000 per month for rent and $90,000 per month for other expenditures. Finally, tax deposits of $85,000 are made each quarter, beginning in March.

The company's cash balance at December 31, 2003, was $80,000, and a minimum balance of $50,000 must be maintained at all times. Assume that any short-term financing needed to maintain the minimum cash balance would be paid off in the month following the month of financing with interest paid at a 12% annual rate.

Prepare a cash budget for Horn covering the first 6 months of 2007.

SOLUTION

	January	February	March	April	May	June	July
Sales	$300,000	$450,000	$540,000	$960,000	$1,200,000	$1,000,000	$ 900,000
Cash sales	60,000	90,000	108,000	192,000	240,000	200,000	180,000
Collections 1 month later	260,000	120,000	180,000	216,000	384,000	480,000	400,000
2 months later	320,000	260,000	120,000	180,000	216,000	384,000	480,000
Total collections from sales	640,000	470,000	408,000	588,000	840,000	1,064,000	1,060,000
Purchases	324,000	576,000	720,000	600,000	540,000	420,000	
Payments on purchases	270,000	324,000	576,000	720,000	600,000	540,000	420,000
Cash receipts:							
Collections from sales	640,000	470,000	408,000	588,000	840,000	1,064,000	1,060,000
Cash disbursements:							
Payments on purchases	270,000	324,000	576,000	720,000	600,000	540,000	420,000
Other expenditures	90,000	90,000	90,000	90,000	90,000	90,000	90,000
Rent	42,000	42,000	42,000	42,000	42,000	42,000	42,000
Tax deposits			85,000			85,000	
Total disbursements	402,000	456,000	793,000	852,000	732,000	757,000	552,000
Net change for the month	238,000	14,000	(385,000)	(264,000)	108,000	307,000	
Beginning cash balance	80,000	318,000	332,000	50,000	50,000	50,000	
Plus: net change	238,000	14,000	(385,000)	(264,000)	108,000	307,000	
Borrowing (repayment)	-----	-----	103,000	265,000	(104,320)	(263,710)	
Interest for prior month's borrowing	-----	-----	-----	1,030*	3,680	2,637	
Ending cash balance	$318,000	$332,000	$ 50,000	$ 50,000	$ 50,000	$ 90,653	
Cumulative borrowing	-----	-----	-----	$368,030	$263,710	$ 90,653	

*0.12 x 103,000 x 1/12 = $1,030

232

TRUE-FALSE

_____ 1. Budgets perform the basic functions of (1) providing the basis for taking corrective action and (2) providing the basis for performance evaluation.

_____ 2. DFN is the acronym for Discretionary Financing Needs.

_____ 3. Depreciation expense is an essential element in the cash budget.

_____ 4. Performance evaluation is an important function that can be performed through the use of budgets.

_____ 5. Research and development expenditures do not impact a firm's cash budget.

_____ 6. Discretionary financing needs are defined by the rate at which a firm's sales and the availability of non-discretionary sources of financing.

_____ 7. The budget planning period should never exceed six-months so that estimates can be made with reasonable accuracy.

_____ 8. The plowback or retention ratio reflects the proportion of a firm's earnings that are paid in dividends.

_____ 9. The cash budget is only as useful as the accuracy of the forecasts that are used in its preparation.

_____ 10. Depreciation expense reduces a firm's cash flow for the year in which the expense is recognized and incorporated in the firm's income statement.

MULTIPLE CHOICE

1. The most important element in determining the accuracy of most cash budgets is the

    a. forecast of cash disbursements.
    b. forecast of the firm's collection schedule for accounts receivable.
    c. forecast of sales.
    d. Cannot be determined.
    e. None of the above.

2. The cash budget embodies

    a. forecasts of prospective future cash balances of the firm.
    b. forecasts of actual cash expenditures and receipts.
    c. forecasts of the firm's personnel requirements.
    d. all of the above.
    e. a and b only.

3. Which of the following items would be included in the cash budget?

    a. Depreciation charges
    b. Goodwill
    c. Patent amortization
    d. All of the above
    e. None of the above

4. The cash budget provides the following information:

    a. The exact amount of borrowing needed for the budget interval.
    b. The type of loan which should be obtained to meet the cash needs for the time interval.
    c. A point estimate of the borrowing needs for the budget interval.
    d. An estimate of the cash needed for depreciation expense.
    e. None of the above.

5. Spontaneous sources of financing include the following:

    a. Wages payable.
    b. Taxes payable.
    c. Short-term bank loans.
    d. Commercial paper.
    e. a and b only..

CHAPTER 15

Introduction to Working-Capital Management

Orientation: In this chapter, we introduce working-capital management in terms of managing the firm's liquidity. Specifically, net working capital is defined as the difference in current assets and current liabilities. The hedging principle is offered as one approach to addressing the firm's liquidity problems. In this chapter, we also discuss sources of short-term financing that must be repaid within one year.

I.   Managing current assets

    A.   The firm's investment in current assets (such as fixed assets) is determined by the marginal benefits derived from investing in them compared with their acquisition cost.

    B.   However, the current fixed-asset mix of the firm's investment in assets is an important determinant of the firm's liquidity. That is, the greater the firm's investment in current assets, other things remaining the same, the greater the firm's liquidity. This is generally true since current assets are usually more easily converted into cash.

    C.   The firm can invest in marketable securities to increase its liquidity. However, such a policy involves committing the firm's funds to a relatively low-yielding (in comparison to fixed assets) investment.

II. Managing the firm's use of current liabilities

    A.   The greater the firm's use of current liabilities, other things being the same, the less will be the firm's liquidity.

B. There are a number of <u>advantages</u> associated with the use of current liabilities for financing the firm's asset investments.

    1. <u>Flexibility</u>. Current liabilities can be used to match the timing of a firm's short-term financing needs exactly.

    2. <u>Interest cost</u>. Historically, the interest cost on short-term debt has been lower than that on long-term debt.

C. Following are the <u>disadvantages</u> commonly associated with the use of short-term debt:

    1. Short-term debt exposes the firm to an increased <u>risk of illiquidity</u> because short-term debt matures sooner and in greater frequency, by definition, than does long-term debt.

    2. Since short-term debt agreements must be renegotiated from year to year, the <u>interest cost</u> of each year's financing <u>is uncertain</u>.

III. Determining the appropriate level of working capital

A. Pragmatically, it is impossible to derive the "optimal" level of working capital for the firm. Such a derivation would require estimation of the potential costs of illiquidity which, to date, have eluded precise measurement.

B. However, the "hedging principle" provides the basis for the firm's working-capital decisions.

    1. The <u>hedging principle</u> or <u>rule of self-liquidating debt</u> involves the following: Those asset needs of the firm not financed by spontaneous sources (i.e., payables and accruals) should be financed in accordance with the following rule: Permanent asset investments are financed with permanent sources and temporary investments are financed with temporary sources, of financing.

    2. A <u>permanent investment in an asset</u> is one which the firm expects to hold for a period longer than one year. Such an investment may involve current or fixed assets.

    3. <u>Temporary asset investments</u> comprise the firm's investment in current assets that will be liquidated and <u>not</u> replaced during the year.

4. Spontaneous sources of financing include all those sources that are available upon demand (e.g., trade credit—accounts Payable) or that arise naturally as a part of doing business (e.g., wages payable, interest payable, taxes payable, etc.).

5. Temporary sources of financing include all forms of current or short-term financing not categorized as spontaneous. Examples include bank loans, commercial paper, and finance company loans.

6. Permanent sources of financing include all long-term sources such as debt having a maturity longer than one year, preferred stock, and common stock.

C. Although the hedging principle provides a useful guide to the firm's working-capital decisions, no firm will follow its tenets strictly. At times, a firm may rely too much on temporary financing for its cash needs, or it may have excess cash as a result of excessive use of permanent financing.

IV. Determining the appropriate level of short-term financing

A. The hedging concept was presented as one basis for determining the firm's use of short-term debt.

B. Hedging involves attempting to match temporary needs for funds with short-term sources of financing and permanent needs with long-term sources.

V. Selecting a source of short-term financing

A. In general, there are three basic factors that should be considered in selecting a source of short-term financing:

1. The effective cost of the credit source

2. The availability of credit

3. The effect of the use of a particular source of credit on the cost and availability of other sources

B. The basic procedure used in estimating the cost of short-term credit utilizes the basic interest equation, (i.e., interest = principal x rate x time).

C. The problem faced in assessing the cost of a source of short-term financing involves estimating the annual percentage rate (APR) where the interest amount, the principal sum, and the time for which financing will be needed is known. Thus, the basic interest equation is "rearranged" as follows:

$$APR = \frac{interest}{principal} \times \frac{1}{time}$$

D. Compound interest was not considered in the simple APR calculation. To consider compounding, the following relation is used:

$$APY = \left(1 + \frac{i}{M}\right)^M - 1$$

where APY is the <u>annual percentage yield</u>, i is the nominal rate of interest per year, and M is the number of compounding periods within one year. The effect of compounding is thus to raise the effective cost of short-term credit.

VI. Sources of short-term credit

A. The two basic sources of short-term credit are unsecured and secured credit.

   1. Unsecured credit consists of all those sources that have as their security only the lender's faith in the ability of the borrower to repay the funds when due.

   2. Secured funds include additional security in the form of assets that are pledged as collateral in the event the borrower defaults in payment of principal or interest.

B. There are three major sources of unsecured short-term credit: trade credit, unsecured bank loans, and commercial paper.

   1. Trade credit provides one of the most flexible sources of financing available to the firm. To arrange for credit, the firm need only place an order with one of its suppliers. The supplier then checks the firm's credit and if the credit is good, the supplier sends the merchandise.

2. Commercial banks provide unsecured short-term credit in two basic forms: lines of credit and transaction loans (notes payable). Maturities of both types of loans are usually one year or less with rates of interest depending on the credit-worthiness of the borrower and the level of interest rates in the economy as a whole.

3. A line of credit is generally an informal agreement or understanding between the borrower and the bank as to the maximum amount of credit that the bank will provide the borrower at any one time. There is no "legal" commitment on the part of the bank to provide the stated credit. There is another variant of this form of financing referred to as a revolving credit agreement whereby such a legal obligation is involved. The line of credit generally covers a period of one year corresponding to the borrower's "fiscal" year.

4. Transaction loans are another form of unsecured short-term bank credit. The transaction loan, in contrast to a line of credit, is made for a specific purpose.

5. Only the largest and most creditworthy companies are able to use commercial paper, which consists of unsecured promissory notes in the money market.

    a. The maturities of commercial paper are generally six months or less with the interest rate slightly lower than the prime rate on commercial bank loans. The new issues of commercial paper are either directly placed or dealer placed.

    b. There are a number of advantages that accrue to the user of commercial paper: interest rates are generally lower than rates on bank loans and comparable sources of short-term financing; no minimum balance requirements are associated with commercial paper; and, commercial paper offers the firm with very large credit needs a single source for all its short-term financing needs. Since it is widely recognized that only the most creditworthy borrowers have access to the commercial paper market, its use signifies a firm's credit status.

c. However, a very important "risk" is involved in using this source of short-term financing; the commercial paper market is highly impersonal and denies even the most creditworthy borrower any flexibility in terms of repayment.

C. Secured sources of short-term credit have certain assets of the firm, such as accounts receivable or inventories, pledged as collateral to secure a loan. Upon default of the loan agreement, the lender has first claim to the pledged assets.

    1. Generally, a firm's receivables are among its most liquid assets. Two secured loan arrangements are generally made with accounts receivable as collateral:

        a. Under the arrangement of <u>pledged accounts receivable</u>, the amount of the loan is stated as a percentage of the face value of the receivables pledged.

        b. <u>Factoring accounts receivable</u> involves the outright sale of a firm's accounts receivables to a factor.

    2. Four secured loan arrangements are generally made with inventory as collateral:

        a. Under the <u>floating lien agreement</u>, the borrower gives the lender a lien against all his or her inventories.

        b. The <u>chattel mortgage agreement</u> involves having specific items of inventory identified in the security agreement.

        c. The <u>field warehouse financing agreement</u> means that the inventories used as collateral are physically separated from the firm's other inventories and are placed under the control of a third-party field warehousing firm.

        d. <u>Terminal warehouse agreements</u> involve transporting the inventories pledged as collateral to a public warehouse that is physically removed from the borrower's premises.

Study Problems

1. In order to meet a temporary need for working capital during an upcoming seasonal peak in sales, Gregory Sales Co. needs $500,000. Gregory's bank has agreed to lend the funds for the necessary 3-month interval at a rate of 12% with a 20% compensating balance. Gregory Sales Co. normally maintains a demand deposit amount of $20,000. Estimate the annual (effective) cost of the loan to Gregory.

SOLUTION

To obtain the needed $500,000 and meet the compensating balance requirement, Gregory must borrow X dollars, where X is found as follows:

$$X - [0.20X - 20{,}000] = 500{,}000$$

$$0.80X = 480{,}000$$

$$X = \$600{,}000$$

Thus, Gregory borrows $600,000 for which it must maintain a compensating balance of 0.20 x 600,000 = $120,000, of which $20,000 will come from its normal demand deposit and $100,000 must be borrowed. This will leave the firm with the use of $500,000. The interest cost of the loan is computed as follows:

$$\text{Interest} = 0.12 \ \text{x} \ 600{,}000 \div 4 = \$18{,}000$$

We divide by 4 since the loan is for only 3 months or one-fourth of a year. The _effective_ annual cost of the loan is:

$$\text{Rate} = \frac{\$ \, \text{loan cost}}{\$ \, \text{funds available}} \times \frac{\text{loan maturity as a}}{\text{fraction of 1 year}}$$

$$= \frac{18{,}000}{500{,}000} \times \frac{1}{90/360} = \underline{0.144 \text{ or } 14.44\%}$$

2.   A factor has agreed to buy Thomas Brothers' receivables ($250,000 per month) which have an average collection period of 90 days. The factor will advance up to 80% of the face value of the receivables for an annual charge of 10% of the funds advanced. The factor also charges a handling fee of 5% of the face value of all accounts purchased. What is the effective annual cost of the factoring arrangement to Thomas Brothers if the maximum advance is taken every month?

SOLUTION

With an average collection period of 90 days and monthly credit sales, Thomas Brothers could build up a loan advance over 3 months of 0.80 x 750,000 = $600,000. This loan would be constantly rolling over as accounts were being collected and as new credit sales were being made. The 90-day interest cost of the loan would be computed:

$$\text{Interest} = \$600,000 \times \frac{0.10}{4} = \$15,000$$

The factor's fee is calculated as follows:

$$\text{Fee} = 0.05 \times \$750,000 = \$37,500$$

Thus, the effective annual cost of the 90-day loan would be:

$$\text{Rate} = \frac{\$15,000 + \$37,500}{\$600,000} \div \frac{3}{12}$$

$$= \underline{0.35 \text{ or } 35\%}$$

3. For the past 7 years Warden Company has been factoring its accounts receivables. The factor's fee is 3%, and the factor will lend up to 90% of the volume of receivables purchased for an additional 1% per month. The firm typically has sales of $200,000 per month; 75% are on credit. Warden Company will save credit department costs of $3,500, since it will no longer need to operate a credit department. In addition, there will no longer be bad-debt losses which previously were 1.25% per month.

The firm's bank has recently offered to lend the firm up to 90% of the face value of the receivables shown on the schedule of accounts. The bank would charge 9% per annum interest plus a 2% processing charge per dollar of receivables pledged. The firm extends terms of net 30, and all customers who plan to pay will do so by the thirtieth of the month. Should the firm discontinue its factoring arrangement in favor of the bank's offer if the firm borrows, on the average, $100,000 per month on its receivables?

SOLUTION

Factoring
The cost of factoring is:

Fee (0.03 x $200,000 x .75)	$4,500
Interest cost (0.01 x $100,000)	1,000
	$5,500 per month

Bank loan
The cost of the bank loan is:

Fee (0.02 x $100,000/.90)	$2,222
Interest (0.09 x $200,000 x 1/12)	750
	$2,972

Plus:

Credit department cost per month	$2,500
Bad-debt losses ($200,000 x .75 x 0.0125)	1,875
Total cost	$7,375 per month

No, in this case, factoring is much cheaper. Note that we assure that the factor will absorb all credit risks and perform all credit functions saving the firm $2,500 + 1,875 = $4,375 per month.

4. Calculate the effective cost of the following trade credit terms where payment is made on the net due date.

   (a) 2/10, net 30

   (b) 3/15, net 30

   (c) 3/15, net 45

   (d) 2/15, net 60

SOLUTION

(a) $\dfrac{0.02}{0.98} \times \dfrac{1}{20/360} = 0.36734$ or 36.73%

(b) $\dfrac{0.03}{0.97} \times \dfrac{1}{15/360} = 0.74226$ or 74.23%

(c) $\dfrac{0.03}{0.97} \times \dfrac{1}{30/360} = 0.37113$ or 37.11%

(d) $\dfrac{0.02}{0.98} \times \dfrac{1}{45/360} = 0.16327$ or 16.33%

5. Luft, Inc., recently acquired production rights to an innovative sailboard design but needs funds to pay for the first production run, which is expected to sell briskly. The firm plans to issue $450,000 in 180-day maturity notes. The paper will carry an 11% rate with discounted interest and will cost Luft $13,000 (paid in advance) to issue.

   (a) What is the effective cost of credit to Luft?

   (b) What other factors should the company consider in analyzing whether to issue the commercial paper?

SOLUTION

(a) $\text{RATE} = \dfrac{\text{interest}}{\text{principal}} \times \dfrac{1}{\text{time}}$

$\text{RATE} = \dfrac{\$24,750^{*}+13,000}{\$450,000-13,000-24,750} \times \dfrac{1}{180/360}$

$\quad = .1831$ or 18.31%

*Interest $= .11 \times \$450,000 \times \frac{1}{2}$

(b) The risk involved with the issue of commercial paper should be considered. This risk relates to the fact that the commercial paper market is highly impersonal and denies even the most creditworthy borrower any flexibility in terms of when repayment is made.

In addition, commercial paper is a viable source of credit to only the most creditworthy borrowers. Thus, it may simply not be available to the firm.

6.   DST, Inc., a producer of inflatable river rafts, needs $400,000 for the three-month summer season, ending September 30, 2001. The firm has explored two possible sources of credit.

(a) DST has arranged with its bank for a $400,000 loan secured by accounts receivable. The bank has agreed to advance DST 80% of the value of its pledged receivables at a rate of 11% plus a 1% fee based on all receivables pledged. DST's receivables average a total of $1 million year-round.

(b) An insurance company has agreed to lend the $400,000 at a rate of 9% per annum, using a loan secured by DST's inventory. A field warehouse agreement would be used, which would cost DST $2,000 a month.

Which source of credit should DST select? Explain.

SOLUTION

Pledged Receivables (A/R):

0.80 A/R   = $400,000 loan

A/R   = $400,000/.80 = $500,000

Fee   = (0.01) ($500,000) = $5,000

Interest cost = (0.11) ($400,000) x ¼ = $11,000

$$\text{Effective rate} = \left(\frac{\$11,000 + 5,000}{\$400,000} \right) \left(\frac{1}{90/360} \right) = .16 \text{ or } 16\%$$

Inventory loan:

Warehousing cost   = $2,000 x 3 months = $6,000

Interest cost = 0.09 x $400,000 x ¼ = $9,000

$$\text{Effective rate} = \left(\frac{\$6,000 + 9,000}{\$400,000} \right) \left(\frac{1}{90/360} \right) = .15 \text{ or } 15\%$$

The inventory loan would be preferred since its cost is lowest under the conditions presented.

TRUE-FALSE

_____ 1. Working capital has traditionally been defined as the sum of the firm's investment in assets (both current assets and long-term assets).

_____ 2. Generally, interest rates on short-term debt are higher than they are on long-term debt for any given borrower.

_____ 3. The guiding principle for the firm's working capital policies is referred to as the "principle of self-liquidating debt" or the "hedging principle."

_____ 4. The use of short-term sources of financing generally enhances the firm's liquidity and reduces the firm's rate of return on assets.

_____ 5. There are two basic problems encountered in attempting to manage the firm's use of short-term financing: determining how much short-term debt to use and determining what sources to select.

_____ 6. Investment decisions are undertaken in the expectation of receiving future benefits.

_____ 7. In order to reduce its risk of illiquidity, a firm should decrease its investment in cash and marketable securities.

_____ 8. Current liabilities generally provide a more flexible source of financing than long-term debt.

_____ 9. The "hedging principle" is well grounded in valuation theory.

_____ 10. Spontaneous financing consists of trade credit and other accounts payable which arise "automatically" in the firm's day-to-day operations.

_____ 11. The amount of trade credit available to the firm varies inversely with the size of the cash discount.

_____ 12. Compensating balances are never required when a firm has a line of credit with its bank.

_____ 13. A transaction loan is made for a specific purpose in mind for the funds involved.

_____ 14. An advantage of commercial paper to a creditworthy borrower is that repayment can be postponed if the firm finds itself in a liquidity squeeze.

_____ 15. Pledging involves selling accounts receivable to a financial intermediary known as a "factor".

_____ 16. The primary sources of collateral for secured short-term credit are accounts receivable and inventories.

_____ 17. Field warehouse financing agreements involve physically moving the pledged inventories to a public warehouse.

_____ 18. Commercial paper and trade credit are both forms of secured credit.

_____ 19. An advantage of trade credit is that the amount of credit extended expands and contracts with the needs of the firm.

MULTIPLE CHOICE

1. Which of the following is an advantage associated with the use of current versus long-term liabilities?

    a. The use of current liabilities subjects the firm to greater risk of illiquidity.
    b. The firm's interest costs can vary from year to year.
    c. The interest cost of current liabilities is generally higher than long-term debt.
    d. All of the above.
    e. None of the above.

2. Spontaneous financing consists of

    a. accounts payable.
    b. trade credit.
    c. short-term notes payable.
    d. All of the above.
    e. a and b only

3. Which of the following accounts would *not* be a prime consideration in working-capital management?

    a. Cash
    b. Accounts payable
    c. Bonds payable
    d. Marketable securities
    e. Accounts receivable

4. The greatest increase in margin of safety (liquidity) for a firm would be provided by

    a. more current assets and less current liabilities.
    b. more current assets and more current liabilities.
    c. less current assets and more current liabilities.
    d. less current assets and less current liabilities.
    e. none of the above

5. Which asset-liability combination would result in the firm having the greatest risk of not being able to pay its bills on time?

    a. More current assets and less current liabilities
    b. More current assets and more current liabilities
    c. Less current assets and more current liabilities
    d. Less current assets and less current liabilities
    e. None of the above.

6. Which of the following illustrates the use of the hedging approach?

    a. Temporary assets financed with long-term liabilities
    b. Permanent assets financed with long-term liabilities
    c. Temporary assets financed with short-term liabilities
    d. All of the above
    e. b and c

7. Which of the following is not a form of secured short-term credit?

    a. General lien
    b. Chattel mortgages
    c. Commercial paper
    d. Terminal warehouse receipt
    e. Factoring

8. Under which of the following agreements does the borrower retain physical possession of the inventory used as collateral for a loan?

   a. Field warehouse financing
   b. Chattel mortgage
   c. Terminal warehouse
   d. All of the above.
   e. None of the above.

9. An informal agreement between a bank and its customer with respect to the maximum amount of unsecured credit the bank will permit the firm to owe at any one time is a

   a. line of credit agreement.
   b. revolving credit agreement.
   c. transaction loan.
   d. None of the above.
   e. All of the above.

10. When a firm needs short-term funds for only one purpose it usually obtains

   a. a line of credit.
   b. a revolving credit agreement.
   c. a transaction loan.
   d. a compensating balance.
   e. None of the above.

CHAPTER 16

Current Asset Management

<u>Orientation</u>: This chapter initiates our study of liquidity management. Here, we focus on the cash flow process and the reasons why a firm holds cash balances. The objectives of a sound cash management system are identified. The concept of float is defined. Several techniques that firms can use to favorably affect their cash receipts and disbursement patterns are examined. Finally, the composition of the firm's marketable securities portfolio is discussed.

Additionally, the risk-return tradeoff associated with the firm's investment in accounts receivable is discussed. For accounts receivable this tradeoff occurs as less creditworthy customers with a higher probability of bad debts are taken on to increase sales. The analysis is similar for sound inventory management. Here, a larger investment in inventory leads to more efficient production and speedier delivery; this should result in increased sales. However, additional financing costs to support the increase in inventory and increased handling and carrying costs is required.

I.   Why a company holds cash

    A.   The firm's cash balance is constantly affected by a variety of influences. Sound cash management techniques are based on a thorough understanding of the cash flow process.

        1.   On an irregular basis, cash holdings are increased from several external sources, such as from the sale of securities.

        2.   In a similar fashion, irregular cash outflows reduce the firm's cash balance. Typical examples include cash dividend payments and the interest requirements on debt agreements.

        3.   Other major sources of cash arising from internal operations occur on a rather regular basis. Accounts receivable collections are an example.

B. Three motives for holding cash balances have been identified by Keynes.[1]

1. The <u>transactions motive</u> is the need for cash to meet payments that arise in the ordinary course of doing business. Holding cash to meet a payroll or to acquire raw materials characterizes this motive.

2. The <u>precautionary motive</u> describes the investment in liquid assets that are used to satisfy possible but as yet indefinite needs for cash. Precautionary balances are a buffer against all kinds of things that might happen to drain the firm's cash resources.

3. The <u>speculative motive</u> describes holding cash to take advantage of hoped-for, profit-making situations.

II. Variations in liquid asset holdings

A. Considerable variation is present in the liquid asset holdings of major industry groups and individual firms.

1. This is because (1) not all of the factors noted above affect every firm and (2) the executives in different firms who are ultimately responsible for cash management tasks have different risk-bearing preferences.

2. Some industries invest very heavily in liquid assets. For example, the total-liquid-assets-to-total-assets ratio of the contract construction industry greatly exceeds that of the utility industry.

B. Because assets are acquired, used, and sold every day, the management of liquid assets must be viewed as a dynamic process. The cash flow process is complex. In order to cut through this complexity, it is necessary that the firm's cash management system operate within clearly defined objectives.

---

[1]John Maynard Keynes, <u>The General Theory of Employment Interest and Money</u> (New York: Harcourt Brace Jovanovich, Inc., 1936).

III. Cash management objectives and decisions

    A.   A properly designed cash management program forces the financial manager to come to grips with a risk-return tradeoff.

        1.   He or she must strike an acceptable balance between holding too much cash and holding too little cash.

        2.   A large cash investment minimizes the chances of insolvency, but it penalizes company profitability.

        3.   A small cash investment frees excess (cash) balances for investment in longer-lived and more profitable assets, which increases the firm's profitability.

    B.   The firm's cash management system should strive to achieve two prime objectives:

        1.   Enough cash must be on hand to dispense effectively with the disbursal needs that arise in the course of doing business.

        2.   The firm's investment in idle cash balances must be reduced to a minimum.

    C.   In the attempt to meet the two objectives noted above, certain decisions dominate the cash management process. These decision areas can be reduced to the following questions:

        1.   What can be done to speed up cash collections and slow down or better control cash outflows?

        2.   What should be the composition of the marketable securities portfolio?

IV. Collection and disbursement procedures

    A.   Cash acceleration and deceleration techniques revolve around the concept of <u>float</u>. Float can be broken down into four elements:

        1.   <u>Mail float</u> refers to funds that are tied up as a result of the time that elapses from the moment a customer mails his or her remittance check until the firm begins to process the check.

2. Processing float refers to funds that are tied up as a result of the firm's recording and processing remittance checks prior to their deposit in the bank.

3. Transit float refers to funds that are tied up as a result of the time needed for a deposited check to clear through the commercial banking system and become "usable" funds to the firm.

4. Disbursing float refers to funds that are technically usable to the firm until its payment check has cleared through the banking system and has been charged against its deposit account.

B. Float reduction can result in considerable benefits in terms of (l) usable funds that are released for company use and (2) in the returns produced on these freed-up balances. A study problem at the end of this chapter illustrates the calculation of such savings.

In October of 2003, President Bush signed into law the Check Clearing for the 21st Century Act. The law took effect on October 28, 2004. This new law is now commonly referred to as "Check 21." Prior to this new regulation ordinary paper checks were physically transported by land carrier or air carrier from the depositing location to the financial institution that would eventually pay the check drawn against the firm's or individual's bank account.

Check 21 allow financial institutions the option of clearing a check image instead of the original check. Such digital substitutes can then be quickly processed within the banking clearing system in the same way that you use the internet on your personal computer. These digital substitutes are being referred to as substitute checks or image replacement documents.

The impetus for this new law was threefold: (1) bank regulators, like those at the Federal Reserve System, feel that Check 21 will accelerate check collection at the ultimate or payee bank, (2) it is forecast that out-of-pocket transportation costs to the banking system will be reduced, this increasing individual bank profitability, and (3) the high degree of physical risk exposure associated with airline service can be minimalized.

From the viewpoint of the firm's cash management system, "managing the float" will eventually be directly impacted. What is called "disbursing float" above could be dramatically reduced towards a few hours instead of a day or two. But, Check 21 did not require banks to alter their "hold" time on specific checks or substitute checks posted to the firm's account within the bank (these are ultimately cash inflows that become "good" funds).

So while the check may have cleared within the bank clearing mechanism, (i.e., from bank to bank), the firm may not have use of "good" funds until banks are forced by a yet-to-be-defined regulatory change to reduce their "hold" time on checks that have actually cleared. Thus, the effects of Check 21 on "transit float" (the third type of float mentioned above) will occur gradually as pressure is put on individual financial institutions to reduce hold times and make the funds available for disbursement by the receiving firm.

The upshot for the firm, and its cash management system, is that the greatest profitability opportunities are still associated with reducing mail float and processing float.

C. Several techniques are available to improve the management of the firm's cash inflows. These techniques may also provide for a reduction in float.

   1. The lock-box arrangement is a widely used commercial banking service for expediting cash gathering.

       a. The objective is to reduce <u>both</u> mail and processing float.

       b. The procedure behind a lock-box system is very simple. The firm rents a local post office box and authorizes a local bank in which a deposit account is maintained to pick up remittances from the box.

           (1) Customers are instructed to mail their payments to the numbered post office box.

           (2) A deposit form is prepared by the <u>bank</u> for each batch of processed checks.

           (3) The bank may notify the firm daily as to the amount of funds deposited on the firm's behalf.

           (4) The firm that receives checks from all over the country establishes several lock boxes.

c.   A lock-box arrangement provides for (1) increased working cash, (2) elimination of clerical functions, and (3) early knowledge of dishonored checks.

d.   The firm must carefully evaluate whether this or any cash management service is worth the added costs. Usually, the bank levies a charge for each check processed through the system. The marginal income generated from released funds must exceed the added costs of the system to make it economically beneficial. A study problem at the end of this chapter illustrates this kind of calculation.

D.   Techniques used by firms that hope to improve the management of their cash outflows include: (1) zero balance accounts, (2) payable-through drafts, and (3) remote disbursing.

1.   Zero balance accounts (ZBAs) permit centralized control (i.e., at the head office) over cash disbursements, but, at the same time, they allow the firm to maintain disbursing authority at the local or divisional level.

a.   The major objective of a ZBA system is to achieve better control over cash payments. A secondary benefit of this technique might be an increase in disbursement float.

b.   For the firm that has several operating units, the benefits from using a ZBA system include:

(1)   Centralized control over disbursements.

(2)   Reduction of time spent on superficial cash management activities.

(3)   Reduction of excess cash balances held in outlying accounts.

(4)   An increase in disbursement float.

2. <u>Payable-through drafts</u> (PTDs) have the physical appearance of ordinary checks but they are drawn on and paid by the issuing firm instead of the bank. The bank serves as a collection point for the documents and passes the documents on to the firm for inspection and authorization for payment.

    a. The objective of a payable-through draft system is to provide for effective control of field authorized payments. An example would be a claim settlement authorized by an insurance agent.

    b. Stop payment orders can be initiated by the firm's headquarters on any drafts considered inappropriate.

3. <u>Remote disbursing</u>, rather obviously, is intended to increase disbursing float.

    a. To implement such a procedure, the firm needs only to open and use a deposit account located in a city distant from its customers' banks.

    b. Since checks written on that account take longer to clear, the firm has use of its funds for a longer period of time.

    c. The major constraint on this procedure is the possible alienation of important customers who must wait longer for their remittance checks to become usable funds.

V. Evaluating the costs of cash management services

    A. Whether a particular cash management system will provide an economic benefit to the firm can be evaluated by use of this relationship:

added costs = added benefits

    B. Clearly, if the benefits exceed the costs of using the system, then the system is economically feasible.

C. On a per unit-basis, this relationship can be expressed as follows:

P = (D) (S) (i)

where P = increase in per-check processing cost, if the new system is adopted,

D = days saved in the collection process, (i.e., float reduction),

S = average check size in dollars,

i = the daily, before-tax opportunity cost (rate of return) of carrying cash.

D. The product of (D) (S) (i) must exceed P for the system to be beneficial to the firm. A study problem at the end of this chapter provides an example of this logic.

VI. Composition of the marketable securities portfolio

A. When selecting a proper marketable securities mix, five factors should be considered.

1. Financial risk is the uncertainty of expected returns from a security due to unforeseeable changes in the financial capacity of the security issuer to make future payments to the security owner.

2. Interest rate risk is the uncertainty in expected returns caused by possible changes in interest rates. This is particularly important for securities that have long, as opposed to short, terms of maturity. (See study problem 5 for an illustration of this point.)

3. Liquidity is the ability to transform a security into cash. Consideration should be given to (1) the time needed to sell the security and (2) the likelihood that the security can be sold at or near its prevailing market price.

4. The taxability of interest income and capital gains are seriously considered by some corporate treasurers.

a. The interest income from municipal obligations is tax-exempt.

257

b. The following equation may be used to determine an equivalent before-tax yield on a taxable security.

(1) Notation:

r = equivalent before-tax yield.

r* = after-tax yield on tax-exempt security.

T = firm's marginal income tax rate.

(2) Computation

$$r = \frac{r*}{(1-T)}$$

(3) Example: Suppose a firm has a choice between investing in a 1-year tax-free debt issue yielding 6% on a $1,000 outlay or a 1-year taxable issue that yields 7% on a $1,000 outlay. The firm pays federal taxes at the rate of 34%. Which security is more beneficial to the firm?

$$r = \frac{0.06}{(1-0.34)} = 9.09\%$$

(4) Clearly, this firm should choose the tax-exempt security.

5. The <u>yield</u> criterion involves a weighing of the risks and benefits inherent in the four previously mentioned factors. The higher the risks associated with a particular security, the higher the expected yield (risk-return tradeoff).

B. Marketable security alternatives

1. A <u>Treasury bill</u> is a direct obligation of the U.S. government sold on a regular basis by the U.S. Treasury.

a. These bills may now be purchased in denominations as small as $1,000.

b.   Since Treasury bills are backed by the U.S. government, they are considered risk-free and consequently sell at lower yields than those obtainable on other marketable securities.

c.   The income from Treasury bills is subject only to federal income taxes and is always taxed as an ordinary gain.

2.   <u>Federal agency securities</u> represent debt obligations of federal government agencies and were created to carry out lending programs of the U.S. government.

a.   The Federal National Mortgage Association (FNMA) renders supplementary assistance to the secondary market for mortgages.

b.   The Federal Home Loan Banks (FHLB) function as a credit reserve system for member banks.

c.   The Federal Land Banks grant loans to members of Federal Land Bank Associations who are engaged in agriculture, provide agricultural services, or own rural homes.

d.   The Federal Intermediate Credit Banks grant loans to and purchase notes originating from loans made to farmers by other financial institutions.

e.   The Banks for Cooperatives make loans to cooperative associations, which are owned and controlled by individuals involved in general farm business.

f.   Securities of these "big five" federally sponsored agencies are <u>not</u> directly backed by the U.S. government.

3.   <u>Bankers' acceptances</u> are largely concentrated in the financing of foreign transactions; this acceptance is a draft (order to pay) drawn on a specific bank by an exporter in order to obtain payment for goods shipped to a customer who maintains an account with that bank.

4. A <u>negotiable certificate of deposit</u> (CD), is a marketable receipt for funds that have been deposited in a bank for a fixed time period at a fixed interest rate.

5. <u>Commercial paper</u> refers to short-term, unsecured promissory notes sold by large businesses in order to raise cash.

6. <u>Repurchase agreements</u> are legal contracts that involve the actual sale of securities by a borrower to the lender, with a commitment on the part of the borrower to repurchase the securities at the contract price plus a stated interest charge.

7. <u>Money market mutual funds</u> usually invest in a diversified portfolio of short-term, high-grade debt instruments like those described in this section.

   a. These funds sell their shares to a large number of small investors in order to raise cash.

   b. The funds offer the investing firm a high degree of liquidity and investment expertise.

VII. Accounts receivable

A. Typically, accounts receivable represent just over 25% of a firm's assets.

B. The size of the investment in accounts receivable varies from industry to industry and is affected by several factors including the percentage of credit sales to total sales, the level of sales, and the credit and collection policies—more specifically the terms of sale, the quality of customer, and collection efforts.

C. Although all these factors affect the size of the investment, only the credit and collection policies are decision variables under the control of the financial manager.

D. The terms of sale are generally stated in the form **a/b** net **c**, indicating that the customer can deduct **a** percentage if the account is paid within **b** days; otherwise, the account must be paid within **c** days.

E. If the customer decides to forgo the discount and not pay until the final payment date, the annualized opportunity cost of passing up this **a%** discount and withholding payment until the **c**[th] day is determined as follows:

annualized opportunity

$$\text{cost of forgoing the discount} = \frac{a}{1-a} \times \frac{360}{c-b}$$

Example: Given the trade credit terms of 3/20 net 60, what is the annualized opportunity cost of passing up the 3% discount and withholding payment until the 60th day?

Solution: Substituting in the values from the example, we get

$$27.8\% = \frac{0.03}{1-0.03} \times \frac{360}{60-20}$$

F. A second decision variable in determining the size of the investment in accounts receivable in addition to the trade credit terms is the type of customer.

    1. The costs associated with extending credit to lower-quality customers include:

        a. Increased costs of credit investigation

        b. Increased probability of customer default

        c. Increased collection costs

G. Analyzing the credit application is a major part of accounts receivable management.

    1. Several avenues are open to the firm in considering the credit rating of an applicant. Among these are financial statements, independent credit ratings and reports, bank checking, information from other companies, and past experiences.

2. One commonly used method for credit evaluation is called credit scoring and involves the numerical evaluation of each applicant in which an applicant receives a score based upon the answers to a simple set of questions. The score is then evaluated relative to a predetermined standard, its level relative to that standard determining whether or not credit scoring should be extended to the applicant. The major advantage of credit scoring is that it is inexpensive and easy to perform.

3. Once the decision to extend credit has been made and if the decision is yes, a maximum credit line is established as a ceiling on the amount of credit to be extended.

H. The third and final decision variable in determining the size of the investment in accounts receivable is the firm's collection policies.

1. Collection policy is a combination of letter sending, telephone calls, personal visits, and legal actions.

2. The greater the amount spent on collecting, the lower the volume of bad debts.

a. The relationship is not linear, however, and beyond a point is not helpful.

b. If sales are independent of collection efforts, then methods of collection should be evaluated with respect to the reduction in bad debts against the cost of lowering those bad debts.

I. Credit should be extended to the point that marginal profitability on additional sales equals the required rate of return on the additional investment in receivables necessary to generate those sales.

J. Credit policy changes involve direct tradeoffs between costs and benefits. Determining whether the increased sales contribute more toward profits than the increased costs take away from them is the job of marginal or incremental analysis. Marginal analysis is performed as follows:

1. Estimate the change in profits from the new policy. This is equal to the increased sales times the profit contribution less any additional bad debts incurred.

2. Estimate the cost of the additional investment in accounts receivable and inventory.

3. Estimate the change in the cost of the cash discount (if a change in the cash discount is enacted).

4. Compare the incremental revenues with the incremental costs.

VIII. Inventory

A. Typically, inventory accounts for about 4.88% of a firm's assets.

B. The purpose of carrying inventories is to uncouple the operations of the firm, that is, to make each function of the business independent of each other function.

C. As such, the decision with respect to the size of the investment in inventory involves a basic tradeoff between risk and return.

D. The risk comes from the possibility of running out of inventory if too little inventory is held, while the return aspect of this tradeoff results because increased inventory investment costs money.

E. There are several general types of inventory.

1. Raw materials inventory consists of the basic materials that have been purchased from other firms to be used in the firm's productions operations. This type of inventory uncouples the production function from the purchasing function.

2. Work in process inventory consists of partially finished goods that require additional work before they become finished goods. This type of inventory uncouples the various production operations.

3. Finished goods inventory consists of goods on which the production has been completed but the goods are not yet sold. This type of inventory uncouples the production and sales function.

4. Stock of cash inventory serves to make the payment of bills independent of the collection of accounts due.

F.   In order to effectively manage the investment in inventory, two problems must be dealt with: the order quantity problem and the order point problem.

G.   The order quantity problem involves the determination of the optimal order size for an inventory item given its expected usage, carrying, and ordering costs.

H.   The economic order quantity (EOQ) model attempts to determine the order size that will minimize total inventory costs. The EOQ is given as:

$$Q^* = \sqrt{\frac{2SO}{C}}$$

where   C   =   carrying costs per unit

   O   =   ordering costs per order

   S   =   total demand in units over the planning period

   Q^* =   the optimal order quantity in units

I.   The order point problem attempts to answer the following question: How low should inventory be depleted before it is reordered?

J.   In answering this question, two factors become important:

   1.   What is the usual procurement or delivery time, and how much stock is needed to accommodate this time period?

   2.   How much safety stock does the management desire?

K.   Modification for safety stocks is necessary, since the usage rate of inventory is seldom stable over a given timetable.

L.   This safety stock is used to safeguard the firm against changes in order time and receipt of shipped goods.

M.   The greater the uncertainty associated with forecasted demand or order time, the larger the safety stock.

   1.   The costs associated with running out of inventory will also determine the safety stock levels.

2.   A point is reached where it is too costly to carry a larger safety stock given the associated risk.

N.   Inflation can also have an impact on the level of inventory carried.

1.   Goods may be purchased in large quantities in anticipation of price rises.

2.   The cost of carrying goods may increase, causing a decline in Q^*, the optional order quantity.

O.   The just-in-time inventory control system is more than just an inventory control system; it is a production and management system.

1.   Under this system, inventory is cut down to a minimum, and the time and physical distance between the various production operations are also minimized.

2.   Actually, the just-in-time inventory control system is just a new approach to the EOQ model which tries to produce the lowest average level of inventory possible.

3.   Average inventory is reduced by locating inventory supplies in convenient locations and setting up restocking strategies that cut time and thereby reduce the needed level of safety stock.

Study Problems

1.   Buckeye Equipment has $3,000,000 in excess cash that it might invest in marketable securities. In order to buy and sell the securities, though, the company must pay a transactions fee of $67,500.

(a)   Would you recommend purchasing the securities if they yield 13% annually and are held for:

1.   1 month?
2.   2 months?
3.   3 months?
4.   6 months?
5.   1 year?

(b)   What minimum required yield would the securities have to return for the firm to hold them for 3 months?

SOLUTION

(a)   It is necessary to calculate the dollar value of the estimated return for each holding period and compare it with the transactions fee. This will allow you to determine if a gain can be made by investing in the securities. The calculations and recommendations are shown below:

			Recommendation
1. $3,000,000(.13)(1/12)	=	$32,500 < $67,500	No
2. $3,000,000(.13)(2/12)	=	$65,000 < $67,500	No
3. $3,000,000(.13)(3/12)	=	$97,500 > $67,500	Yes
4. $3,000,000(.13)(6/12)	=	$195,000 > $67,500	Yes
5. $3,000,000(.13)(12/12)	=	$390,000 > $67,500	Yes

(b)   Now we find the break-even yield for a 3-month holding period. Let (%) be the required yield. With $3,000,000 to invest for three months, we have:

$3,000,000 (%) (3/12) = $ 67,500
$3,000,000 (%) = $270,000
(%) = $270,000/$3,000,000 = 9%

2.   Portland Energy Products is evaluating whether or not to use an additional lock box. If the lock box is used, check processing costs will rise by $.20 a check. The average check size that will be mailed to the lock-box location is $1,000. Funds that are freed by using the lock box will be invested in marketable securities to yield an *annual* before-tax return of 7%. The firm uses a 365-day year in its analysis procedures. What reduction in check-collection time is required to justify use of the lock box?

SOLUTION

Solve the following relationship for D:

$$P = (D)(S)(i)$$

$$\$.20 = (D)(\$1,000)\left(\frac{0.07}{365}\right)$$

$$\$.20 = (D)(\$.192)$$

$$\frac{\$.20}{\$.192} = D = \underline{1.0417 \text{ days}}$$

Thus, the lock box is justified if it can speed up collections by *more* than 1.0417 days.

3.   Annual sales for Austin Drilling Supply will total $250,000,000 next year. What would be the annual value of one day's float reduction to this firm if it could invest the freed-up balances at 8% per year?

SOLUTION

Compute Austin's sales per day:

$$\frac{\text{annual revenues}}{\text{days in years}} = \frac{250,000,000}{365} = \$684,932$$

Compute the annual value of the 1-day float reduction:

($684,932) (0.08) = $54,795

4.   The corporate treasurer of Buckeye Bottling is considering purchasing a municipal obligation with a 7% coupon and a $1,000 par value. Mr. Inside Info has telephoned the treasurer about another $1,000 par value offering which provides a 12% yield. This latter offering is, however, fully taxable. Buckeye is taxed at a 48% rate.

(a)   Should the treasurer take Mr. Info's advice and purchase the 12% security?

(b)   What is the equivalent before-tax yield on the municipal, assuming Buckeye is in a 48% tax bracket?

SOLUTION

(a)   The after-tax yield to Buckeye on the 12% offering is (0.12) (1-0.48) = 6.24%. Since the yield on the municipal is already stated on an after-tax basis, the treasurer should ignore Mr. Info's advice and purchase the municipal offering.

(b)   The equivalent before-tax yield is:

$$r = \frac{0.07}{(1-0.48)} = 13.46\%$$

Thus, the taxable issue would have to yield in excess of 13.46% to be more attractive than the municipal to Buckeye.

5. Tech Electronics, manufacturers of fine calculators, has recently purchased 10-year bonds at their par value of $1,000 per security. Texas Parts, a close competitor, has just purchased 5-year bonds at their $1,000 par value. Both securities have a coupon rate set at 8%, are compounded annually, and have a maturity value of $1,000. Suppose the prevailing interest rate 1 year from now rises to 10%. What would the decline in market price be for each bond in 1 year?

SOLUTION

One year from now, the 5-year issue has 4 years remaining to maturity. The market price in 1 year can be found by computing P according to the following:

$$P = \sum_{t=1}^{4} \frac{\$80}{(1 + 0.10)^t} + \frac{\$1,000}{(1+0.10)^4} = \$936.60$$

where $80 = (0.08) ($1,000). Similarly, for the 10-year issue, which now has 9 years to maturity,

$$P = \sum_{t=1}^{9} \frac{\$80}{(1 + 0.10)^t} + \frac{\$1,000}{(1+0.10)^9} = \$884.82$$

Thus the 10-year security declines in price $115.18 ($1,000 - $884.82), while the 5-year security declines in price by only $63.40 ($1,000-$936.60). This illustrates the concept of *interest rate risk*, discussed in the text in Chapter 15.

6. Gavin International expects to generate sales of $74,000,000 in the coming year. All sales are done on a credit basis, net 30 days. Gavin has estimated that it takes an average of 4 days for payments to reach their central office and an additional day to process the payments. What is the opportunity cost of the funds tied up in the mail and processing? Gavin uses a 360-day year in all calculations and can invest free funds at 7%.

SOLUTION

Daily collections = 74,000,000/360 = $ 205,555.56

Opportunity Cost = (205,555.56) (5) (.07) = $71,944

7. The corporate treasurer of Chester Motors is considering the purchase of either an offering carrying a 7.6% coupon or a municipal obligation with a 5% coupon. Both bonds have a $1,000 par value. The company is currently in the 34% marginal tax bracket. Which security should the treasurer recommend?

SOLUTION

The after-tax yield to Chester Motors on the 7.6% offering is (1-.34) (.076) = 5%. The municipal's after-tax rate is the stated 5%. There is no difference in yield. If the risk is considered equal for each security, then the treasurer would be indifferent between the two.

8. The Swank Furniture Company is trying to determine the optimal order quantity for sofas. Annual sales for sofas are 800, and the retail price is $300 per sofa. The cost of carrying sofas is $50 per sofa per year. It costs $35 to prepare and receive an order. The inventory planning period is one year.

(a) Determine the EOQ (assuming a one-year planning period).

(b) If the annual sales are 1200, what is the EOQ? If the annual sales are 300, what is the EOQ?

SOLUTION

(a) $\text{EOQ} = \sqrt{\dfrac{2(800)(35)}{50}} = \sqrt{1120} = 33.47 = 33 \text{ sofas}$

(b) $\text{EOQ} = \sqrt{\dfrac{2(1200)(35)}{50}} = \sqrt{1680} = 40.99 = 41 \text{ sofas}$

$\sqrt{\dfrac{2(300)(35)}{50}} = \sqrt{420} = 20.49 = 20 \text{ sofas}$

9. What is the effective annualized cost of forgoing a trade discount with terms 4/40, net 60?

SOLUTION

The annualized opportunity cost of foregoing the trade discount $= \dfrac{a}{1-a} \times \dfrac{360}{c-b}$

where the terms of sale are stated in the form **a/b** net **c**, indicating that they can deduct **a**% if the account is paid within **b** days; otherwise, the account must be paid within **c** days.

Thus,

annualized opportunity cost of foregoing the trade discount $= \dfrac{a}{1-a} \times \dfrac{360}{c-b}$

$= \dfrac{.04}{1-.04} \times \dfrac{360}{60-40}$

$= 0.75$

$= 75\%$

TRUE-FALSE

_____ 1. Accounts receivable are included on the balance sheet as current liabilities.

_____ 2. Holding cash to pay for next week's labor bill (payroll) is an example of the precautionary motive for holding cash.

_____ 3. Ready borrowing power enables the firm to reduce the cash balances actually held for precautionary purposes.

_____ 4. A firm is insolvent when it is able to meet its short-term obligations on time.

_____ 5. Cash flow forecasting is the initial step in any effective cash management program.

_____ 6. The major objective of using payable-through drafts is to extend disbursing float.

_____ 7. The major reason for using lock boxes is to enjoy a reduction in transit float.

_____ 8. Zero balance accounts are used to accelerate cash receipts.

_____ 9. Although they have a lower yield, agency securities are more readily marketable by the purchasing corporation than are Treasury bills.

_____ 10. Bankers' acceptances generally mature from 9 to 12 months after "sight."

_____ 11. Commercial paper is backed by specific assets of the firm.

_____ 12. The most common denomination for the negotiable CD is $10,000.

_____ 13. The longer the term of maturity, the less sensitive the price of a security to changes in interest rates.

_____ 14. Long-term bonds may serve as a useful (comfortable) hedge against interest rate risk.

_____ 15. Because of their higher financial risk, agency securities always yield more than Treasury securities of a comparable maturity.

_____ 16. The higher the marginal tax bracket, the lower the after-tax rate of return on a taxable security.

_____ 17. Bankers' acceptances provide for a steady flow of interest payments to the investor in the form of coupon payments.

_____ 18. With respect to interest risk, Treasury securities are risk-free.

_____ 19. The lock-box system is the most widely used commercial banking service for expediting cash gathering.

_____ 20. A concentration bank is one where the firm generally maintains several minor disbursing accounts.

_____ 21. There is an inverse relationship between a financial instrument's chance of default and financial risk.

_____ 22. The contract price of the securities that make up the repurchase agreement is fixed for the duration of the transaction.

_____ 23. According to Keynes, the demand for cash can be divided into three categories: transactions, precautionary, and speculative.

_____ 24. To calculate the annual savings due to float reduction, you would multiply the sales per day by the days of float reduction.

_____ 25. Payable-through drafts provide control over field payments.

_____ 268. Increases in cash holdings from external sources of funds tend to be more regular than internal generation of cash.

_____ 27. The motives for holding cash apply equally to all firms. Variations in cash holdings from firm to firm result from differing management risk preferences.

_____ 28. The prime objectives of cash management are to reduce idle cash balances and to have sufficient cash on hand to meet disbursal needs.

_____ 29. Under the lock-box arrangement, a deposit form is prepared by the _depositor_ for each batch of processed checks.

_____ 30. The use of payable-through drafts will usually increase disbursing float to the issuing firm.

_____ 31. The expression "5/10, net 30" means that the customers receive a 10% discount if they pay within 5 days; otherwise, they must pay within 30 days.

_____ 32. There is no one level of inventory that is efficient for all firms.

_____ 33. In determining the level of safety stock, it is important to evaluate the tradeoff between the cost of carrying the additional inventory with the risk of running out of inventory.

_____ 34. The EOQ provides for an optimal safety stock determination.

MULTIPLE CHOICE

1. Indicate the item that is not an advantage of the lock-box system.

    a. The cost is minimal.
    b. Speeds up the flow of cash to the firm.
    c. Remittances are collected sooner.
    d. All of the above are advantages.

2. Zero balance accounts

    a. permit centralized control over disbursements.
    b. provide for effective control over field payments.
    c. are an integral part of the lock-box system.
    d. are the same thing as pre-authorized checks.

3. Generally, the least important component of a firm's preference for liquidity is

    a. the transaction motive.
    b. the precautionary motive.
    c. the speculative motive.
    d. all motives are of equal importance.

4. Which of the following is *not* an objective of the lockbox system?

    a. Reduce mail float.
    b. Reduce processing float.
    c. Reduce transit float.
    d. Reduce disbursing float.

5. The uncertainty of expected returns from a security attributable to possible changes in the financial capacity of the security issuer to make future payments to the security owner refers to

    a. interest rate risk.
    b. liquidity.
    c. financial risk.
    d. taxability.
    e. yield.

6. The fact that funds are available in the company's bank account until its payment check has cleared through the banking system refers to

    a. mail float.
    b. processing float.
    c. transit float.
    d. disbursing float.

7. Which is *not* an objective of zero balance accounts?

    a. Achieve better control over cash payments.
    b. Reduce excess cash balances held in regional banks for disbursing purposes.
    c. Decrease disbursing float.

8. Interest rate risk is of concern to a firm's financial officer, because

    a. it is more difficult to issue securities when interest rates are low.
    b. changes in interest rates affect the expected return of financial instruments.
    c. federal government taxation increases as interest rates rise, reducing the cash available to the firm.
    d. inflationary periods may reduce the real earnings of the firm.

9.   Which of the following does *not* describe U.S. Treasury bills?

  a.   Maturities include 3-month, 6-month, and 1-year securities.
  b.   Discount instrument
  c.   Issued only in bearer form
  d.   Income subject to federal, state and local income tax
  e.   All of the above describe U.S. Treasury bills.

10.   Which security (assuming identical maturities) would be expected to have the highest yield based on recent experience?

  a.   Banker's acceptances
  b.   Agencies
  c.   CDs
  d.   Commercial paper
  e.   Treasury bills

11.   Which of the following is *not* a motive for holding cash balances?

  a.   Transactions motive
  b.   Speculative motive
  c.   Convenience motive
  d.   Precautionary motive

12.   A concentration bank is

  a.   a bank that has the most deposit accounts.
  b.   a bank that concentrates its service in one geographic area.
  c.   a bank that concentrates on one type of service.
  d.   a bank in which the firm maintains a major disbursing account.

13.   Which of the following is not part of the firm's credit and collection policy decisions?

  a.   The credit period
  b.   The cash discount given
  c.   The dividend decision
  d.   The level of collection expenditures
  e.   The quality of account accepted

14. All of the following are relationships that exist for safety stock, except

  a. The greater the risk of running out of stock, the larger the safety stock.
  b. The larger the opportunity cost of the funds invested in inventory, the smaller the safety stock.
  c. The greater the uncertainty associated with future forecasts of use, the larger the safety stock.
  d. The higher the profit margin per unit, the lower the safety stock necessary.

15. In the basic model, the optimal inventory level is the point at which

  a. total depreciation is minimized.
  b. total cost is minimized.
  c. total revenue is maximized.
  d. carrying costs are minimized.
  e. ordinary costs are minimized.

163. Determine the effective annualized cost of forgoing the trade discount on terms 2/10, net 45 (round to nearest .01%).

  a. 21.0%
  b. 16.3%
  c. 16.0%
  d. 20.6%

17. The Janjigian Company uses approximately 4,000 oxygen tanks in its manufacturing process each year. The carrying cost of the oxygen tanks inventory is $.60 per tank, and the ordering cost per order is $20. What is Janjigian's economic ordering quantity of tanks (round to the nearest unit)?

  a. 15
  b. 365
  c. 417
  d. 516

CHAPTER 17

International Business Finance

Orientation: This chapter introduces some of the financial techniques and strategies necessary to the efficient operation of an international business. Problems inherent to these firms include multiple currencies, differing legal and political environments, differing economic and capital markets, and internal control problems. The difficulties arising from multiple currencies are stressed here, including the dimensions of foreign exchange risk and strategies for reducing this risk. We also cover working-capital management and direct foreign investment for international firms.

I.   The globalization of product and financial markets

    A.   World trade has grown faster over the last few decades than has aggregate world GNP.

    B.   In less-developed countries, long-run overseas investments of the United States' companies have yielded high returns.

    C.   Many American *multinational corporations* (MNC) have significant assets, sales, and profits attributable to foreign investments.

    D.   Many foreign MNCs have significant operations in the United States.

    E.   Many firms, investment companies, and individuals invest in the capital markets of foreign companies in the hopes of realizing

        1.   higher returns than those available in domestic capital markets, and

        2.   reduced portfolio risk through international diversification.

    F.   Companies are increasingly turning to the Eurodollar market to raise funds.

II.   Exchange rates

    A.   Recent history of exchange rates

        1.   Exchange rates between the major currencies were fixed from 1949 and 1970.

        2.   Countries were required to set a *parity rate* with the U.S. dollar, around which the daily exchange rate could narrowly fluctuate.

        3.   In order to effect a major adjustment, a currency had to undergo either a *devaluation* (reducing the cost relative to the dollar) or an *up-valuation/revaluation* (increasing the cost relative to the U.S. dollar).

        4.   Since 1973, a *floating rate* international currency system has operated, wherein the currencies are allowed to fluctuate freely.

        5.   Two major types of transactions now occur in the foreign exchange markets: *spot* and *forward transactions*.

    B.   Spot exchange rates

        1.   The rate at which one currency can be immediately exchanged for another currency

        2.   *Direct quote* expresses the exchange rate in the units of home currency required to buy one unit of foreign currency. For example, 1.4845 U.S. dollars per pound.

        3.   *Indirect quotes* indicate the number of foreign currency units needed to purchase one unit of home currency. For example, .6691 pounds per U.S. dollar.

        EXAMPLE

        Using the rates listed above, how many dollars would a U.S. manufacturer pay for a part costing 250 pounds?

        250 (pounds) x 1.4845 ($/pound) = $371.13

4. The direct and indirect quotes should have a reciprocal relationship. In formula

$$\text{Direct Quote} = \frac{1}{\text{Indirect Quote}}$$

or

$$\text{Indirect Quote} = \frac{1}{\text{Direct Quote}}$$

5. When these quotes are not equal, *arbitrage* will occur, where a trader (or arbitrageur) makes a riskless profit, by exchanging currency in two markets.

6. The *asked rate* is the rate which the bank or foreign exchange trader "asks" the buyer to pay for the foreign currency.

7. The *bid rate* is the rate at which the bank or foreign exchange trader buys the foreign currency from the customer.

8. The *spread* is the difference in the bid and the asked rates.

9. The narrower the spread, the greater the efficiency in the spot exchange market.

10. A *cross rate* is the result of an indirect computation of one currency's exchange rate from the exchange rate of two other currencies. For example, the calculation of marks per pound from U.S. dollars per pound and marks per U.S. dollars.

11. Triangular arbitrage will occur when the cross rates are not equal to the exchange rates offered.

C. Forward exchange rates

1. A *forward exchange rate* specifies *today* the rate at which currencies will be exchanged in the future, usually 30, 90, or 180 days from today.

2. Rates are quoted in both the direct and indirect form.

3. Forward rates are often quoted at a *premium* or a *discount* to the existing spot rate. This is also referred to as the forward-spot differential.

4. These differentials may be stated either in absolute terms or as an annualized percent premium or discount.

5. The use of forward contracts allows for risk reduction, in that future cash outlays are known with certainty.

III. Interest rate parity

A. Theorem states that the forward premium or discount should be equal and opposite in sign to the difference in the national interest rates for securities of the same maturity (except for the effects of small transaction costs). Notationally, this is expressed as

$$P \text{ (or D)} \quad = \quad -\left(\frac{I^f - I^d}{1 + I^f}\right) = \left(\frac{I^d - I^f}{1 + I^f}\right)$$

where

$P \text{ (or D)}$ = the percent-per-annum premium or discount on the forward rate

I^f = the annual interest rate on a foreign instrument having the same maturity as the forward contract

I^d = the annualized interest rate on a domestic instrument having the same maturity as the forward contract

EXAMPLE

The premium (P) on 30-day forward mark contracts is 4.368%. If the 30-day T-bill is yielding 10%, what must the 30-day German instrument yield?

$$P \quad = \quad \left(\frac{I^f - I^d}{1 + I^f}\right)$$

$$0.04368 \quad = \quad \frac{I^f - .10}{1 + I^f}$$

$$I^f \quad = \quad .1502 \text{ or } 15.02\%$$

B.   If the forward differentials are not those predicted by the interest parity theorem, then *covered interest arbitrage* can occur and be profitable at no risk.

IV.   Purchasing power parity

A.   According to purchasing power parity, exchange rates will adjust over time so that the currencies of different countries will have the same purchasing power. The exchange rates will adjust to cover the inflation rate differential between the two countries.

B.   Purchasing power parity can be demonstrated by the equation

$$S_{t+1} \;=\; S_t(1 + P_d) \,/\, (1 + P_f)^n$$

$$\;=\; S_t(1 + P_d - P_f)^n$$

where

S_t	=	units of domestic currency per unit of the foreign currency at time t,
P_f	=	the foreign inflation rate,
P_d	=	the domestic inflation rate, and
n	=	the number of time periods.

EXAMPLE

The inflation rate in Great Britain is 6%, and, in the United States, it is 10%. The current spot rate of the pound is \$2.00. According to purchasing power parity, what will be the expected value of the pound at the end of the year?

$$S \;=\; \$2.00\,(1 + .10 - .06)^1$$

$$\;=\; \$2.00\,(1.04)^1$$

$$\;=\; \$2.08$$

C.   The law of one price

The law of one price underlies purchasing power parity. This law suggests that where there are no transportation costs or barriers to trade, the same good sold in different countries should sell for the same price if all the different prices are expressed in terms of the same currency.

D. International Fisher effect

1. According to the Fisher effect, interest rates reflect not only the real rate of return but also the expected inflation rate.

2. The Fisher effect can be expressed as

$$= P + I_r + (P)(I_r)$$

$$r_{nom} = r_{inf} + r_{real} + (r_{inf})(r_{real})$$

where

r_{nom} = the nominal interest rate

r_{real} = the real rate of return

r_{inf} = the expected inflation rate

3. The international Fisher effect suggests that the exchange rate adjusts to cover the interest rate differential between two countries.

4. This theory suggests that in efficient markets, with rational expectations, the forward rate is an unbiased forecast of the future spot rate.

V. Exchange rate risk

A. Risk arises from not knowing today the value of the future spot rate.

B. Types of exchange risk

1. Risk in international trade contracts: when an agreement exists to purchase some good at a future date in foreign currency, uncertainty exists as to the future cash outlay.

2. Risk in foreign portfolios: because of exchange rate fluctuations in foreign securities, the returns are more variable and, thus, more risky than investment in domestic securities.

3. Risk in direct foreign investment (DFI): the balance sheet and income statement are dominated in foreign currency. Thus, for the parent company, risk arises from the fluctuations in both the asset's value and the profit streams.

C. Exposure to exchange rate risk

1. Transaction exposure refers to the net total foreign currency transactions whose monetary value was fixed at a time different from when the transactions are actually completed. Examples of transactions exposed to this kind of risk are receivables, payables, and fixed price sales or purchase contracts. Fluctuations in exchange rates can affect the value of these assets and liabilities.

2. Translation exposure is actually a paper gain or loss. Translation exposure refers to gains or losses caused by the translation of foreign currency assets and liabilities into the currency of the parent company for accounting purposes.

3. Economic exposure refers to the extent to which the economic value of a company can decline due to exchange rate changes. It is the overall impact of exchange rate changes on the value of the firm. A decline in value can be attributed to an exchange-rate-induced decline in the level of expected cash flows and/or by an increase in the riskiness of these cash flows.

D. Hedging strategies

1. The standard procedure to hedge is to match the amount and the duration of the asset (liability) position.

2. The *money market hedge* offsets the exposed position in a foreign currency by borrowing or lending in the foreign and domestic money markets. This may be costly for small or infrequent users.

3. The *forward market hedge* matches the asset (liability) position with an offsetting forward contract of equal value and maturity. Generally, this is less costly than the money market hedge.

4. Foreign currency futures contracts and foreign currency options are two relatively new instruments used for hedging. Futures contracts are similar to forward contracts in that they provide a fixed price for the required delivery. Options, on the other hand, *permit* a fixed price anytime before their expiration date. Options and futures both differ from forward contracts in that they are traded in standardized amounts with standardized maturity dates

and are traded through organized exchanges and individual dealers. The difference between the futures contract and the currency option is that the option requires delivery only if it is exercised. The option can be exercised anytime before its maturity date; this can provide additional flexibility for a company.

VI. Multinational working-capital management

    A. The MNC must be careful to make decisions concerning working-capital management that are optimal for the corporation as a whole and not just the best for the individual entities.

    B. *Leading* and *lagging* are important risk reduction techniques for a MNC's working-capital management.

        1. When holding an *asset* in a:

            a. strong (appreciating) currency, we should lag (delay) conversion to the domestic currency.

            b. weak (depreciating) currency, we should lead (expedite) conversion to the domestic currency.

        2. When holding a *liability* in a:

            a. strong currency, we should lead (expedite) payment of the liability.

            b. weak currency, we should lag (delay) payment of the liability.

    C. Cash management

        1. An MNC may wish to position funds in a specific subsidiary in another country such that the foreign exchange exposure and the tax liability of the MNC are minimized as a whole. This strategy may not, however, be the optimal strategy for the subsidiary.

        2. The transfer of funds is effected by royalties, fees, and transfer-pricing. The *transfer price* is the price charged for goods or services transferred from a subsidiary or parent company to another subsidiary.

VII. International financing decisions

    A. A multinational corporation (MNC) may have a lower cost of capital than a domestic firm due to its ability to tap a larger number of financial markets.

        1. A multinational company has access to financing sources in the countries in which it operates.

        2. Host countries often provide access to low-cost subsidized financing to attract foreign investment.

        3. An MNC may enjoy preferential credit treatment due to its size and investor preference for its home currency.

        4. An MNC may be able to access third country capital markets.

        5. An MNC has access to external currency markets variously known as Eurodollar, Eurocurrency, or Asiandollar markets. These markets are unregulated and, because of their lower spread, can offer attractive rates for financing and investment.

    B. To increase their visibility in foreign capital markets, MNCs are increasingly listing their stocks in the foreign capital markets.

    C. An MNC's capital structure should reflect its wider access to financial markets, the ability to diversify economic and political risks, and several of its other advantages over domestic firms.

VIII. Direct foreign investment

    A. Risk in international capital budgeting

        1. Political risk arises from operating a business in a different and possibly less stable business climate than the United States.

        2. Exchange risk incorporates changes in the future earnings stream because of currency fluctuations, possibly in both foreign and domestic currencies.

        3. Business risk is affected by the response of business and the MNC to economic conditions within the foreign country.

4. Financial risk arises from the financial structure of the firm and its effect on the profit stream.

B. Cash flows must be estimated considering the potential effects of exchange rate changes, governmental policy, and other items that determine product demand and sales.

C. A foreign investment can be evaluated from either a parent or a local firm perspective. If a firm uses a local perspective, the initial investment and all of its cash flows should be discounted at a rate that reflects the local inflation rate and the riskiness of the project. When using the parent company perspective, the discount rate should reflect the expected inflation rate in the parent currency, and foreign currency cash flows should be converted to the parent currency cash flows using projected exchange rates.

D. The net present value (NPV) must be calculated using the preceding factors.

1. If NPV is greater than zero, accept direct foreign investments.

2. If NPV is less than zero, the MNC may decide to

a. Reject direct foreign investment.

b. Establish a sales office in the foreign country.

c. License a local company to manufacture the product, where the MNC receives royalty payments.

Study Problems

1. An American manufacturer owes 5,000 marks to a German supplier. How much does he owe in U.S. dollars, if the exchange rate is 0.661 U.S. dollars per mark?

SOLUTION

Exchange rate = 0.6601 U.S. dollar per mark

5,000 (marks) x 0.6601 (U.S. dollar/mark) = $3,300.50 U.S. dollars

2. A fashion designer in France owes $65,000, due in 30 days, to a counterpart in the United States. How much is the foreign liability today if the exchange rates for 30-day forward contracts is 5.2070 francs per U.S. dollar?

SOLUTION

> 30-day forward exchange rate - 5.2070 francs per U.S. dollar
>
> 65,000 ($) x 5.2070 (francs per U.S. dollar) = 338,455 francs

3. You own $20,000. The dollar rate in London is 0.5201. The pound rate is given in the textbook. Are arbitrage profits possible? Set up an arbitrage scheme with your capital. What is the gain (loss) in dollars?

SOLUTION

The London rate is 0.5201 pounds/U.S. dollar. The indirect New York rate is 0.5349 pounds/U.S. dollar.

Assuming no transaction costs, the rates between London and New York are out of line. Arbitrage profits are possible.

Pounds are cheaper in New York. Buy pounds in New York with the $20,000.

> 20,000 ($) x .5349 (pounds/dollars) = 10,698 pounds.

Sell pounds in London.

> 10,698 (pounds) ÷ .5201 (pounds/U.S. dollars) = $20,569.12.

Your net gain is $20,569.12 - $20,000 = $569.12

4. Interest rates on the 30-day instruments in the United States and Germany are 12 and 10% (annualized), respectively. What is the correct price of the 30-day forward mark? Use spot rates from textbook.

SOLUTION

The spot rate is .6601 U.S. dollar per mark. The annual premium via equation discussed on page 276 is

$$= \frac{.12 - .10}{1 + .10} = \frac{.02}{1.10} = .0182$$

$$P = 1.82\%$$

Using this premium in equation (16-2), compute the "correct" forward price.

$$\frac{F - .6601}{.6601} \times \frac{12}{1} = .0182 \quad \underline{F = .6611}$$

TRUE-FALSE

_____ 1. One of the most difficult aspects of operating a business in a foreign country is the problem of multiple currencies.

_____ 2. International business affairs affect very few firms and, therefore, are of little concern to most businesses.

_____ 3. Exchange rates are fixed according to the U.S. dollar and must be maintained within the narrow margins unless a major adjustment is enacted.

_____ 4. The forward contract states the exchange rate to be used in the spot market on a specific date in the near future.

_____ 5. A narrow spread between the bid and asked rates indicates an efficient spot market.

_____ 6. The interest parity theorem states that (except for effect of transaction costs) the forward premium or discount should be equal and opposite in sign to the difference in the respective country's interest rates for securities of the same maturities.

_____ 7. Extensive profit opportunities exist for arbitrageurs in the foreign exchange markets.

_____ 8. Exchange rate risk constitutes only a small portion of the risk associated with international business.

_____ 9. An investor with foreign currency liabilities may want to hedge against exchange rate changes in the money markets.

_____ 10. Leading and lagging are strategies for optimal working capital management.

_____ 11. Covered interest arbitrage can be taken advantage of when the premiums in the forward rate are not equal to the interest rate differentials.

_____ 12. Purchasing power parity suggests that exchange rates in countries with high inflation rates tend to decline.

_____ 13. Translation exposure results in exchange-rate-related losses or gains that have little or no impact on taxable income.

_____ 14. Futures contracts are customized with regard to the amount and maturity date of the contract.

_____ 15. Receivables and payables are subject to transaction exposure.

_____ 16. The objective of a hedging strategy is to have a positive net asset position in the foreign currency.

MULTIPLE CHOICE

1. A direct 30-day forward quote of 1.4957 U.S. dollars per pound is equivalent to what 30-day indirect quote?

   a. .6686 U.S. dollars per pound
   b. .6671 pounds per U.S. dollar
   c. 1.4957 U.S. dollars per pound
   d. .6686 pounds per U.S. dollar
   e. .6671 pounds per U.S. dollar

2. An example of a cross rate, when the exchange rates are given in U.S. dollars, would be

   a. marks per U.S. dollar.
   b. pounds per yen.
   c. yen per mark.
   d. U.S. dollars per yen.
   e. both b and c

3. Forward rate contracts are used in international transactions to

   a. reduce the risk for the buyer.
   b. reduce the risk for the seller.
   c. both a and b
   d. neither a nor b

4. If an investor noticed a discrepancy in the exchange rates of two countries and acted upon it, he would be engaging in

    a. money market hedging.
    b. forward hedging.
    c. arbitrage.
    d. sabotage.
    e. leading strategies.

5. If your firm held liabilities in a strong currency, it would be wise to

    a. lead.
    b. lag.
    c. engage in money market hedging.
    d. engage in forward hedging.
    e. All of the above.

6. Direct foreign investment involves

    a. political risk.
    b. business risk.
    c. financial risk.
    d. exchange rate risk.
    e. All of the above.

7. If the net present value of a direct foreign investment project for an MNC is less than zero, they should

    a. reject it.
    b. open a sales office.
    c. license a foreign company.
    d. accept it.
    e. a, b, and c are all possibilities

8. If the U.S. experiences a 7% inflation rate while France is experiencing a 4% inflation rate, then according to purchasing power parity

    a. the value of the U.S. dollar should increase by approximately 3% against the French franc.
    b. the U.S. dollar should decline against the French franc by 3%.
    c. the French franc would decline by 3% against the U.S. dollar.
    d. there would be no change in either currency.

9. A paper loss/gain best describes which type of risk:

    a. economic.
    b. transaction.
    c. interest rate.
    d. translation.

10. Which of the following do not provide a hedge against some risk?

    a. Forward contract
    b. Money market hedge
    c. Currency options
    d. Futures contracts
    e. All are forms of hedging

ANSWERS TO SELF TESTS

Chapter 1

True-False

1.	F	2.	T	3.	F	4.	T	5.	T
6.	F	7.	F	8.	F	9.	T	10.	F
11.	T								

Multiple Choice

1.	d	2.	e	3.	e	4.	e	5.	d
6.	d	7.	c	8.	d				

Chapter 2

True-False

1.	F	2.	T	3.	F	4.	F	5.	F
6.	F	7.	T	8.	T	9.	F	10.	T
11.	T	12.	F	13.	T	14.	F	15.	F
16.	T	17.	T	18.	F	19.	F	20.	T
21.	F	22.	T	23.	F	24.	F	25.	T
26.	F	27.	T	28.	T	29.	F		

Multiple Choice

1.	c	2.	d	3.	e	4.	b	5.	b
6.	a	7.	c	8.	d	9.	c	10.	c
11.	d	12.	b	13.	b	14.	c	15.	c
16.	d	17.	d	18.	b	19.	d	20.	c
21.	c	22.	c	23.	c	24.	b	25.	c

Chapter 3

True-False

1.	F	2.	T	3.	F	4.	T	5.	T
6.	F	7.	F	8.	F	9.	F	10.	T
11.	T	12.	T	13.	T	14.	F	15.	T

Multiple Choice

1.	d	2.	a	3.	b	4.	d	5.	d
6.	d	7.	b	8.	a	9.	c	10.	c

Chapter 4

True-False

1.	T	2.	F	3.	F	4.	T	5.	F
6.	T	7.	T	8.	F	9.	T	10.	T
11.	F	12.	F	13.	F	14.	F		

Multiple Choice

1.	b	2.	e	3.	c	4.	a	5.	e
6.	b	7.	b	8.	c	9.	b	10.	a

Chapter 5

True-False

1.	T	2.	T	3.	F	4.	T	5.	T
6.	T	7.	T	8.	F	9.	T	10.	F

Multiple Choice

1.	a	2.	c	3.	d	4.	c	5.	a

Chapter 6

True-False

1.	T	2.	T	3.	T	4.	F	5.	F
6.	F	7.	T	8.	T	9.	F	10.	F
11.	F	12.	F						

Multiple Choice

1.	b	2.	d	3.	c	4.	d	5.	b
6.	d	7.	b	8.	b	9.	a		

Chapter 7

True-False

1.	T	2.	F	3.	T	4.	T	5.	F
6.	T	7.	F	8.	T	9.	T	10.	F
11.	F	12.	F	13.	F	14.	F	15.	F
16.	T	17.	F						

Multiple Choice

1.	a	2.	e	3.	a	4.	b	5.	b
6.	c	7.	c	8.	a	9.	b	10.	d
11.	b	12.	a	13.	b	14.	b	15.	d
16.	c	17.	e						

Chapter 8

True-False

1.	T	2.	T	3.	F	4.	F	5.	F
6.	F	7.	F	8.	F	9.	F	10.	F
11.	T	12.	F	13.	F	14.	F	15.	T

Multiple Choice

1.	a	2.	b	3.	d	4.	c	5.	a
6.	c	7.	a	8.	b	9.	c	10.	d
11.	d	12.	b						

Chapter 9

True-False

1.	T	2.	T	3.	T	4.	T	5.	F
6.	T	7.	T	8.	F	9.	T	10.	T

Multiple Choice

1.	c	2.	a	3.	c	4.	b

Chapter 10

True-False

1.	T	2.	F	3.	F	4.	T	5.	F
6.	T	7.	T	8.	T				

Multiple Choice

1.	c	2.	d	3.	e	4.	d

Chapter 11

True-False

1.	F	2.	F	3.	T	4.	F	5.	T
6.	F	7.	T	8.	T	9.	T	10.	T

Multiple Choice

1.	d	2.	d	3.	d	4.	b	5.	b

Chapter 12

True-False

1.	F	2.	F	3.	T	4.	T	5.	T
6.	F	7.	T	8.	F	9.	F	10.	F
11.	F	12.	T	13.	T	14.	T	15.	T
16.	T	17.	T	18.	T	19.	F	20.	F
21.	T	22.	T	23.	T	24.	F	25.	T
26.	F	27.	F	28.	T	29.	F	30.	F
31.	F	32.	F	33.	T	34.	F	35.	F
36.	T	37.	T	38.	F	39.	F	40.	F
41.	T	42.	F						

Multiple Choice

1.	c	2.	c	3.	b	4.	b	5.	b
6.	b	7.	c	8.	b	9.	c	10.	d
11.	b	12.	d	13.	b	14.	b	15.	c
16.	e	17.	b	18.	d	19.	b	20.	b
21.	d	22.	b	23.	d	24.	e	25.	b
26.	e								

Chapter 13

True-False

1.	T	2.	F	3.	F	4.	F	5.	T
6.	F	7.	T	8.	T	9.	F	10.	F
11.	F	12.	F						

Multiple Choice

1.	b	2.	d	3.	d	4.	c	5.	d
6.	d	7.	d	8.	d	9.	e	10.	f
11.	b	12.	b	13.	d						

Chapter 14

True-False

1.	T	2.	T	3.	F	4.	T	5.	F
6.	T	7.	F	8.	F	9.	T	10.	F

Multiple Choice

1.	c	2.	e	3.	e	4.	c	5.	e

Chapter 15

True-False

1.	F	2.	F	3.	T	4.	F	5.	T
6.	T	7.	F	8.	T	9.	F	10.	T
11.	F	12.	F	13.	T	14.	F	15.	F
16.	T	17.	F	18.	F	19.	T		

Multiple Choice

1.	d	2.	e	3.	c	4.	a	5.	c
6.	e	7.	c	8.	b	9.	a	10.	c

Chapter 16

True-False

1.	F	2.	F	3.	T	4.	T	5.	T
6.	F	7.	F	8.	F	9.	F	10.	F
11.	F	12.	F	13.	F	14.	F	15.	T
16.	T	17.	F	18.	F	19.	T	20.	F
21.	F	22.	T	23.	T	24.	F	25.	T
26.	F	27.	F	28.	T	29.	F	30.	F
31.	F	32.	T	33.	T	34.	F		

Multiple Choice

1.	a	2.	c	3.	a	4.	c	5.	d
6.	c	7.	d	8.	e	9.	d	10.	c
11.	b	12.	b	13.	d	14.	c	15.	c
16.	d	17.	c	18.	c	19.	e	20.	d
21.	d	22.	b	23.	a	24.	d		

Chapter 17

True-False

1.	T	2.	F	3.	F	4.	F	5.	T
6.	T	7.	F	8.	F	9.	T	10.	T
11.	T	12.	T	13.	T	14.	F	15.	T
16.	F								

Multiple Choice

1.	d	2.	e	3.	c	4.	c	5.	a
6.	e	7.	e	8.	b	9.	d	10.	e

APPENDIX A
USING THE CALCULATOR TO COMPUTE TABLE VALUES

Note: See that the memory is cleared; you are in the correct mode for financial calculations; and have adequate decimal places.

Appendix B (Compound sum of $1): $FVIF_{i,n} = \$1(1 + i)^n$

Hewlett-Packard HP-12C

1 [CHS] [PV] → No. of periods (Days, mths., or yrs.) [N] → (Interest rate per period) [I] → 0 [PMT] → [FV] → ANSWER

Hewlett-Packard HP-17B II, HP-19B II

1 [+/-] [PV] → No. of periods (Days, mths., or yrs.) [N] → (Interest rate per period) [I%YR] → 0 [PMT] → [FV] → ANSWER

Texas Instruments BA-35

1 [+/-] [PV] → No. of periods (Days, mths., or yrs.) [N] → (Interest rate per period) [%I] → 0 [PMT] → [CPT] [FV] → ANSWER

Texas Instruments BAII

1 [+/-] [PV] → No. of periods (Days, mths., or yrs.) [N] → (Interest rate per period) [%I] → 0 [PMT] → [2nd] [FV] → ANSWER

Texas Instruments BAII Plus

1 [+/-] [PV] → No. of periods (Days, mths., or yrs.) [N] → (Interest rate per period) [I/Y] → 0 [PMT] → [CPT] [FV] → ANSWER

Appendix C (Present value of $1): $PVIF_{i,n} = \dfrac{\$1}{(1 + i)^n}$

Hewlett-Packard HP-12C

1 [CHS] [FV] → No. of periods (Days, mths., or yrs.) [N] → (Interest rate per period) [I] → 0 [PMT] → [PV] → ANSWER

Hewlett-Packard HP-17B II, HP-19B II

1 [+/-] [FV] → No. of periods (Days, mths., or yrs.) [N] → (Interest rate per period) [I%YR] → 0 [PMT] → [PV] → ANSWER

Texas Instruments BA-35

1 [+/-] [FV] → No. of periods (Days, mths., or yrs.) [N] → (Interest rate per period) [%I] → 0 [PMT] → [CPT] [PV] → ANSWER

Texas Instruments BAII

1 [+/-] [FV] → No. of periods (Days, mths., or yrs.) [N] → (Interest rate per period) [%I] → 0 [PMT] → [2nd] [PV] → ANSWER

Texas Instruments BAII Plus

1 [+/-] [FV] → No. of periods (Days, mths., or yrs.) [N] → (Interest rate per period) [I/Y] → 0 [PMT] → [CPT] [PV] → ANSWER

Appendix D (Sum of an annuity of $1): $FVIFA_{i,n} = \$1 \sum_{t=0}^{n-1}(1+i)^t$

Hewlett-Packard HP-12C

| 1 | CHS | PMT | N (No. of periods — Days, mths., or yrs.) | I (Interest rate per period) | 0 | PV | | FV | → | ANSWER |

Hewlett-Packard HP-17B II, HP-19B II

| 1 | +/- | PMT | N (No. of periods — Days, mths., or yrs.) | I%YR (Interest rate per period) | 0 | PV | | FV | → | ANSWER |

Texas Instruments BA-35

| 1 | +/- | PMT | N (No. of periods — Days, mths., or yrs.) | %I (Interest rate per period) | 0 | PV | CPT | FV | → | ANSWER |

Texas Instruments BAII

| 1 | +/- | PMT | N (No. of periods — Days, mths., or yrs.) | %I (Interest rate per period) | 0 | PV | 2nd | FV | → | ANSWER |

Texas Instruments BAII Plus

| 1 | +/- | PMT | N (No. of periods — Days, mths., or yrs.) | I/Y (Interest rate per period) | 0 | PV | CPT | FV | → | ANSWER |

Appendix E (Present value of an annuity of $1): $PVIFA_{i,n} = \left(\sum_{t=1}^{n}\frac{\$1}{(1+i)^t}\right)$

Hewlett-Packard HP-12C

| 1 | CHS | PMT | N (No. of periods — Days, mths., or yrs.) | I (Interest rate per period) | 0 | FV | | PV | → | ANSWER |

Hewlett-Packard HP-17B II, HP-19B II

| 1 | +/- | PMT | N (No. of periods — Days, mths., or yrs.) | I%YR (Interest rate per period) | 0 | FV | | PV | → | ANSWER |

Texas Instruments BA-35

| 1 | +/- | PMT | N (No. of periods — Days, mths., or yrs.) | %I (Interest rate per period) | 0 | FV | CPT | PV | → | ANSWER |

Texas Instruments BAII

| 1 | +/- | PMT | N (No. of periods — Days, mths., or yrs.) | %I (Interest rate per period) | 0 | FV | 2nd | PV | → | ANSWER |

Texas Instruments BAII Plus

| 1 | +/- | PMT | N (No. of periods — Days, mths., or yrs.) | I/Y (Interest rate per period) | 0 | FV | CPT | PV | → | ANSWER |

APPENDIX B: COMPOUND SUM OF $1

n	1%	2%	3%	4%	5%	6%	7%	8%	9%	10%
1	1.010	1.020	1.030	1.040	1.050	1.060	1.070	1.080	1.090	1.100
2	1.020	1.040	1.061	1.082	1.103	1.124	1.145	1.166	1.188	1.210
3	1.030	1.061	1.093	1.125	1.158	1.191	1.225	1.260	1.295	1.331
4	1.041	1.082	1.126	1.170	1.216	1.262	1.311	1.360	1.412	1.464
5	1.051	1.104	1.159	1.217	1.276	1.338	1.403	1.469	1.539	1.611
6	1.062	1.126	1.194	1.265	1.340	1.419	1.501	1.587	1.677	1.772
7	1.072	1.149	1.230	1.316	1.407	1.504	1.606	1.714	1.828	1.949
8	1.083	1.172	1.267	1.369	1.477	1.594	1.718	1.851	1.993	2.144
9	1.094	1.195	1.305	1.423	1.551	1.689	1.838	1.999	2.172	2.358
10	1.105	1.219	1.344	1.480	1.629	1.791	1.967	2.159	2.367	2.594
11	1.116	1.243	1.384	1.539	1.710	1.898	2.105	2.332	2.580	2.853
12	1.127	1.268	1.426	1.601	1.796	2.012	2.252	2.518	2.813	3.138
13	1.138	1.294	1.469	1.665	1.886	2.133	2.410	2.720	3.066	3.452
14	1.149	1.319	1.513	1.732	1.980	2.261	2.579	2.937	3.342	3.797
15	1.161	1.346	1.558	1.801	2.079	2.397	2.759	3.172	3.642	4.177
16	1.173	1.373	1.605	1.873	2.183	2.540	2.952	3.426	3.970	4.595
17	1.184	1.400	1.653	1.948	2.292	2.693	3.159	3.700	4.328	5.054
18	1.196	1.428	1.702	2.026	2.407	2.854	3.380	3.996	4.717	5.560
19	1.208	1.457	1.754	2.107	2.527	3.026	3.617	4.316	5.142	6.116
20	1.220	1.486	1.806	2.191	2.653	3.207	3.870	4.661	5.604	6.727
21	1.232	1.516	1.860	2.279	2.786	3.400	4.141	5.034	6.109	7.400
22	1.245	1.546	1.916	2.370	2.925	3.604	4.430	5.437	6.659	8.140
23	1.257	1.577	1.974	2.465	3.072	3.820	4.741	5.871	7.258	8.954
24	1.270	1.608	2.033	2.563	3.225	4.049	5.072	6.341	7.911	9.850
25	1.282	1.641	2.094	2.666	3.386	4.292	5.427	6.848	8.623	10.835
30	1.348	1.811	2.427	3.243	4.322	5.743	7.612	10.063	13.268	17.449
40	1.489	2.208	3.262	4.801	7.040	10.286	14.974	21.725	31.409	45.259
50	1.645	2.692	4.384	7.107	11.467	18.420	29.457	46.902	74.358	117.391

APPENDIX B: COMPOUND SUM OF $1 (Continued)

n	11%	12%	13%	14%	15%	16%	17%	18%	19%	20%
1	1.110	1.120	1.130	1.140	1.150	1.160	1.170	1.180	1.190	1.200
2	1.232	1.254	1.277	1.300	1.323	1.346	1.369	1.392	1.416	1.440
3	1.368	1.405	1.443	1.482	1.521	1.561	1.602	1.643	1.685	1.728
4	1.518	1.574	1.630	1.689	1.749	1.811	1.874	1.939	2.005	2.074
5	1.685	1.762	1.842	1.925	2.011	2.100	2.192	2.288	2.386	2.488
6	1.870	1.974	2.082	2.195	2.313	2.436	2.565	2.700	2.840	2.986
7	2.076	2.211	2.353	2.502	2.660	2.826	3.001	3.185	3.379	3.583
8	2.305	2.476	2.658	2.853	3.059	3.278	3.511	3.759	4.021	4.300
9	2.558	2.773	3.004	3.252	3.518	3.803	4.108	4.435	4.785	5.160
10	2.839	3.106	3.395	3.707	4.046	4.411	4.807	5.234	5.695	6.192
11	3.152	3.479	3.836	4.226	4.652	5.117	5.624	6.176	6.777	7.430
12	3.498	3.896	4.335	4.818	5.350	5.936	6.580	7.288	8.064	8.916
13	3.883	4.363	4.898	5.492	6.153	6.886	7.699	8.599	9.596	10.699
14	4.310	4.887	5.535	6.261	7.076	7.988	9.007	10.147	11.420	12.839
15	4.785	5.474	6.254	7.138	8.137	9.266	10.539	11.974	13.590	15.407
16	5.311	6.130	7.067	8.137	9.358	10.748	12.330	14.129	16.172	18.488
17	5.895	6.866	7.986	9.276	10.761	12.468	14.426	16.672	19.244	22.186
18	6.544	7.690	9.024	10.575	12.375	14.463	16.879	19.673	22.901	26.623
19	7.263	8.613	10.197	12.056	14.232	16.777	19.748	23.214	27.252	31.948
20	8.062	9.646	11.523	13.743	16.367	19.461	23.106	27.393	32.429	38.338
21	8.949	10.804	13.021	15.668	18.822	22.574	27.034	32.324	38.591	46.005
22	9.934	12.100	14.714	17.861	21.645	26.186	31.629	38.142	45.923	55.206
23	11.026	13.552	16.627	20.362	24.891	30.376	37.006	45.008	54.649	66.247
24	12.239	15.179	18.788	23.212	28.625	35.236	43.297	53.109	65.032	79.497
25	13.585	17.000	21.231	26.462	32.919	40.874	50.658	62.669	77.388	95.396
30	22.892	29.960	39.116	50.950	66.212	85.850	111.065	143.371	184.675	237.376
40	65.001	93.051	132.782	188.884	267.864	378.721	533.869	750.378	1051.668	1469.772
50	184.565	289.002	450.736	700.233	1083.657	1670.704	2566.215	3927.357	5988.914	9100.438

APPENDIX B: COMPOUND SUM OF $1 (Continued)

n	21%	22%	23%	24%	25%	26%	27%	28%	29%	30%
1	1.210	1.220	1.230	1.240	1.250	1.260	1.270	1.280	1.290	1.300
2	1.464	1.488	1.513	1.538	1.563	1.588	1.613	1.638	1.664	1.690
3	1.772	1.816	1.861	1.907	1.953	2.000	2.048	2.097	2.147	2.197
4	2.144	2.215	2.289	2.364	2.441	2.520	2.601	2.684	2.769	2.856
5	2.594	2.703	2.815	2.932	3.052	3.176	3.304	3.436	3.572	3.713
6	3.138	3.297	3.463	3.635	3.815	4.002	4.196	4.398	4.608	4.827
7	3.797	4.023	4.259	4.508	4.768	5.042	5.329	5.629	5.945	6.275
8	4.595	4.908	5.239	5.590	5.960	6.353	6.768	7.206	7.669	8.157
9	5.560	5.987	6.444	6.931	7.451	8.005	8.595	9.223	9.893	10.604
10	6.727	7.305	7.926	8.594	9.313	10.086	10.915	11.806	12.761	13.786
11	8.140	8.912	9.749	10.657	11.642	12.708	13.862	15.112	16.462	17.922
12	9.850	10.872	11.991	13.215	14.552	16.012	17.605	19.343	21.236	23.298
13	11.918	13.264	14.749	16.386	18.190	20.175	22.359	24.759	27.395	30.288
14	14.421	16.182	18.141	20.319	22.737	25.421	28.396	31.691	35.339	39.374
15	17.449	19.742	22.314	25.196	28.422	32.030	36.062	40.565	45.587	51.186
16	21.114	24.086	27.446	31.243	35.527	40.358	45.799	51.923	58.808	66.542
17	25.548	29.384	33.759	38.741	44.409	50.851	58.165	66.461	75.862	86.504
18	30.913	35.849	41.523	48.039	55.511	64.072	73.870	85.071	97.862	112.455
19	37.404	43.736	51.074	59.568	69.389	80.731	93.815	108.890	126.242	146.192
20	45.259	53.358	62.821	73.864	86.736	101.721	119.145	139.380	162.852	190.050
21	54.764	65.096	77.269	91.592	108.420	128.169	151.314	178.406	210.080	247.065
22	66.264	79.418	95.041	113.574	135.525	161.492	192.168	228.360	271.003	321.184
23	80.180	96.889	116.901	140.831	169.407	203.480	244.054	292.300	349.593	417.539
24	97.017	118.205	143.788	174.631	211.758	256.385	309.948	374.144	450.976	542.801
25	117.391	144.210	176.859	216.542	264.698	323.045	393.634	478.905	581.759	705.641
30	304.482	389.758	497.913	634.820	807.794	1025.927	1300.504	1645.505	2078.219	2619.996
40	2048.400	2847.038	3946.430	5455.913	7523.164	10347.175	14195.439	19426.689	26520.909	36118.865
50	13780.612	20796.561	31279.195	46890.435	70064.923	104358.362	154948.026	229349.862	338442.984	497929.223

APPENDIX B: COMPOUND SUM OF $1 (Continued)

n	31%	32%	33%	34%	35%	36%	37%	38%	39%	40%
1	1.310	1.320	1.330	1.340	1.350	1.360	1.370	1.380	1.390	1.400
2	1.716	1.742	1.769	1.796	1.823	1.850	1.877	1.904	1.932	1.960
3	2.248	2.300	2.353	2.406	2.460	2.515	2.571	2.628	2.686	2.744
4	2.945	3.036	3.129	3.224	3.322	3.421	3.523	3.627	3.733	3.842
5	3.858	4.007	4.162	4.320	4.484	4.653	4.826	5.005	5.189	5.378
6	5.054	5.290	5.535	5.789	6.053	6.328	6.612	6.907	7.213	7.530
7	6.621	6.983	7.361	7.758	8.172	8.605	9.058	9.531	10.025	10.541
8	8.673	9.217	9.791	10.395	11.032	11.703	12.410	13.153	13.935	14.758
9	11.362	12.166	13.022	13.930	14.894	15.917	17.001	18.151	19.370	20.661
10	14.884	16.060	17.319	18.666	20.107	21.647	23.292	25.049	26.925	28.925
11	19.498	21.199	23.034	25.012	27.144	29.439	31.910	34.568	37.425	40.496
12	25.542	27.983	30.635	33.516	36.644	40.037	43.717	47.703	52.021	56.694
13	33.460	36.937	40.745	44.912	49.470	54.451	59.892	65.831	72.309	79.371
14	43.833	48.757	54.190	60.182	66.784	74.053	82.052	90.846	100.510	111.120
15	57.421	64.359	72.073	80.644	90.158	100.713	112.411	125.368	139.708	155.568
16	75.221	84.954	95.858	108.063	121.714	136.969	154.003	173.008	194.194	217.795
17	98.540	112.139	127.491	144.804	164.314	186.278	210.984	238.751	269.930	304.913
18	129.087	148.024	169.562	194.038	221.824	253.338	289.048	329.476	375.203	426.879
19	169.104	195.391	225.518	260.011	299.462	344.540	395.996	454.677	521.532	597.630
20	221.527	257.916	299.939	348.414	404.274	468.574	542.514	627.454	724.930	836.683
21	290.200	340.449	398.919	466.875	545.769	637.261	743.245	865.886	1007.653	1171.356
22	380.162	449.393	530.562	625.613	736.789	866.674	1018.245	1194.923	1400.637	1639.898
23	498.012	593.199	705.647	838.321	994.665	1178.677	1394.996	1648.994	1946.885	2295.857
24	652.396	783.023	938.511	1123.350	1342.797	1603.001	1911.145	2275.611	2706.171	3214.200
25	854.638	1033.590	1248.220	1505.289	1812.776	2180.081	2618.268	3140.344	3761.577	4499.880
30	3297.151	4142.075	5194.566	6503.452	8128.550	10143.019	12636.215	15717.106	19518.391	24201.432
40	49074.042	66520.767	89963.354	121392.522	163437.135	219561.574	294321.973	393698.224	525523.341	700037.697
50	730406.758	1068308.196	1558052.359	2265895.716	3286157.879	4752754.903	6855329.878	9861757.523	14149464.787	20248916.240

APPENDIX C: PRESENT VALUE OF $1

n	1%	2%	3%	4%	5%	6%	7%	8%	9%	10%
1	0.990	0.980	0.971	0.962	0.952	0.943	0.935	0.926	0.917	0.909
2	0.980	0.961	0.943	0.925	0.907	0.890	0.873	0.857	0.842	0.826
3	0.971	0.942	0.915	0.889	0.864	0.840	0.816	0.794	0.772	0.751
4	0.961	0.924	0.888	0.855	0.823	0.792	0.763	0.735	0.708	0.683
5	0.951	0.906	0.863	0.822	0.784	0.747	0.713	0.681	0.650	0.621
6	0.942	0.888	0.837	0.790	0.746	0.705	0.666	0.630	0.596	0.564
7	0.933	0.871	0.813	0.760	0.711	0.665	0.623	0.583	0.547	0.513
8	0.923	0.853	0.789	0.731	0.677	0.627	0.582	0.540	0.502	0.467
9	0.914	0.837	0.766	0.703	0.645	0.592	0.544	0.500	0.460	0.424
10	0.905	0.820	0.744	0.676	0.614	0.558	0.508	0.463	0.422	0.386
11	0.896	0.804	0.722	0.650	0.585	0.527	0.475	0.429	0.388	0.350
12	0.887	0.788	0.701	0.625	0.557	0.497	0.444	0.397	0.356	0.319
13	0.879	0.773	0.681	0.601	0.530	0.469	0.415	0.368	0.326	0.290
14	0.870	0.758	0.661	0.577	0.505	0.442	0.388	0.340	0.299	0.263
15	0.861	0.743	0.642	0.555	0.481	0.417	0.362	0.315	0.275	0.239
16	0.853	0.728	0.623	0.534	0.458	0.394	0.339	0.292	0.252	0.218
17	0.844	0.714	0.605	0.513	0.436	0.371	0.317	0.270	0.231	0.198
18	0.836	0.700	0.587	0.494	0.416	0.350	0.296	0.250	0.212	0.180
19	0.828	0.686	0.570	0.475	0.396	0.331	0.277	0.232	0.194	0.164
20	0.820	0.673	0.554	0.456	0.377	0.312	0.258	0.215	0.178	0.149
21	0.811	0.660	0.538	0.439	0.359	0.294	0.242	0.199	0.164	0.135
22	0.803	0.647	0.522	0.422	0.342	0.278	0.226	0.184	0.150	0.123
23	0.795	0.634	0.507	0.406	0.326	0.262	0.211	0.170	0.138	0.112
24	0.788	0.622	0.492	0.390	0.310	0.247	0.197	0.158	0.126	0.102
25	0.780	0.610	0.478	0.375	0.295	0.233	0.184	0.146	0.116	0.092
30	0.742	0.552	0.412	0.308	0.231	0.174	0.131	0.099	0.075	0.057
40	0.672	0.453	0.307	0.208	0.142	0.097	0.067	0.046	0.032	0.022
50	0.608	0.372	0.228	0.141	0.087	0.054	0.034	0.021	0.013	0.009

APPENDIX C: PRESENT VALUE OF $1 (Continued)

n	11%	12%	13%	14%	15%	16%	17%	18%	19%	20%
1	0.901	0.893	0.885	0.877	0.870	0.862	0.855	0.847	0.840	0.833
2	0.812	0.797	0.783	0.769	0.756	0.743	0.731	0.718	0.706	0.694
3	0.731	0.712	0.693	0.675	0.658	0.641	0.624	0.609	0.593	0.579
4	0.659	0.636	0.613	0.592	0.572	0.552	0.534	0.516	0.499	0.482
5	0.593	0.567	0.543	0.519	0.497	0.476	0.456	0.437	0.419	0.402
6	0.535	0.507	0.480	0.456	0.432	0.410	0.390	0.370	0.352	0.335
7	0.482	0.452	0.425	0.400	0.376	0.354	0.333	0.314	0.296	0.279
8	0.434	0.404	0.376	0.351	0.327	0.305	0.285	0.266	0.249	0.233
9	0.391	0.361	0.333	0.308	0.284	0.263	0.243	0.225	0.209	0.194
10	0.352	0.322	0.295	0.270	0.247	0.227	0.208	0.191	0.176	0.162
11	0.317	0.287	0.261	0.237	0.215	0.195	0.178	0.162	0.148	0.135
12	0.286	0.257	0.231	0.208	0.187	0.168	0.152	0.137	0.124	0.112
13	0.258	0.229	0.204	0.182	0.163	0.145	0.130	0.116	0.104	0.093
14	0.232	0.205	0.181	0.160	0.141	0.125	0.111	0.099	0.088	0.078
15	0.209	0.183	0.160	0.140	0.123	0.108	0.095	0.084	0.074	0.065
16	0.188	0.163	0.141	0.123	0.107	0.093	0.081	0.071	0.062	0.054
17	0.170	0.146	0.125	0.108	0.093	0.080	0.069	0.060	0.052	0.045
18	0.153	0.130	0.111	0.095	0.081	0.069	0.059	0.051	0.044	0.038
19	0.138	0.116	0.098	0.083	0.070	0.060	0.051	0.043	0.037	0.031
20	0.124	0.104	0.087	0.073	0.061	0.051	0.043	0.037	0.031	0.026
21	0.112	0.093	0.077	0.064	0.053	0.044	0.037	0.031	0.026	0.022
22	0.101	0.083	0.068	0.056	0.046	0.038	0.032	0.026	0.022	0.018
23	0.091	0.074	0.060	0.049	0.040	0.033	0.027	0.022	0.018	0.015
24	0.082	0.066	0.053	0.043	0.035	0.028	0.023	0.019	0.015	0.013
25	0.074	0.059	0.047	0.038	0.030	0.024	0.020	0.016	0.013	0.010
30	0.044	0.033	0.026	0.020	0.015	0.012	0.009	0.007	0.005	0.004
40	0.015	0.011	0.008	0.005	0.004	0.003	0.002	0.001	0.001	0.001
50	0.005	0.003	0.002	0.001	0.001	0.001	0.000	0.000	0.000	0.000

APPENDIX C: PRESENT VALUE OF $1 (Continued)

n	21%	22%	23%	24%	25%	26%	27%	28%	29%	30%
1	0.826	0.820	0.813	0.806	0.800	0.794	0.787	0.781	0.775	0.769
2	0.683	0.672	0.661	0.650	0.640	0.630	0.620	0.610	0.601	0.592
3	0.564	0.551	0.537	0.524	0.512	0.500	0.488	0.477	0.466	0.455
4	0.467	0.451	0.437	0.423	0.410	0.397	0.384	0.373	0.361	0.350
5	0.386	0.370	0.355	0.341	0.328	0.315	0.303	0.291	0.280	0.269
6	0.319	0.303	0.289	0.275	0.262	0.250	0.238	0.227	0.217	0.207
7	0.263	0.249	0.235	0.222	0.210	0.198	0.188	0.178	0.168	0.159
8	0.218	0.204	0.191	0.179	0.168	0.157	0.148	0.139	0.130	0.123
9	0.180	0.167	0.155	0.144	0.134	0.125	0.116	0.108	0.101	0.094
10	0.149	0.137	0.126	0.116	0.107	0.099	0.092	0.085	0.078	0.073
11	0.123	0.112	0.103	0.094	0.086	0.079	0.072	0.066	0.061	0.056
12	0.102	0.092	0.083	0.076	0.069	0.062	0.057	0.052	0.047	0.043
13	0.084	0.075	0.068	0.061	0.055	0.050	0.045	0.040	0.037	0.033
14	0.069	0.062	0.055	0.049	0.044	0.039	0.035	0.032	0.028	0.025
15	0.057	0.051	0.045	0.040	0.035	0.031	0.028	0.025	0.022	0.020
16	0.047	0.042	0.036	0.032	0.028	0.025	0.022	0.019	0.017	0.015
17	0.039	0.034	0.030	0.026	0.023	0.020	0.017	0.015	0.013	0.012
18	0.032	0.028	0.024	0.021	0.018	0.016	0.014	0.012	0.010	0.009
19	0.027	0.023	0.020	0.017	0.014	0.012	0.011	0.009	0.008	0.007
20	0.022	0.019	0.016	0.014	0.012	0.010	0.008	0.007	0.006	0.005
21	0.018	0.015	0.013	0.011	0.009	0.008	0.007	0.006	0.005	0.004
22	0.015	0.013	0.011	0.009	0.007	0.006	0.005	0.004	0.004	0.003
23	0.012	0.010	0.009	0.007	0.006	0.005	0.004	0.003	0.003	0.002
24	0.010	0.008	0.007	0.006	0.005	0.004	0.003	0.003	0.002	0.002
25	0.009	0.007	0.006	0.005	0.004	0.003	0.003	0.002	0.002	0.001
30	0.003	0.003	0.002	0.002	0.001	0.001	0.001	0.001	0.000	0.000
40	0.000	0.000	0.000	0.000	0.000	0.000	0.000	0.000	0.000	0.000
50	0.000	0.000	0.000	0.000	0.000	0.000	0.000	0.000	0.000	0.000

APPENDIX C: PRESENT VALUE OF $1 (Continued)

n	31%	32%	33%	34%	35%	36%	37%	38%	39%	40%
1	0.763	0.758	0.752	0.746	0.741	0.735	0.730	0.725	0.719	0.714
2	0.583	0.574	0.565	0.557	0.549	0.541	0.533	0.525	0.518	0.510
3	0.445	0.435	0.425	0.416	0.406	0.398	0.389	0.381	0.372	0.364
4	0.340	0.329	0.320	0.310	0.301	0.292	0.284	0.276	0.268	0.260
5	0.259	0.250	0.240	0.231	0.223	0.215	0.207	0.200	0.193	0.186
6	0.198	0.189	0.181	0.173	0.165	0.158	0.151	0.145	0.139	0.133
7	0.151	0.143	0.136	0.129	0.122	0.116	0.110	0.105	0.100	0.095
8	0.115	0.108	0.102	0.096	0.091	0.085	0.081	0.076	0.072	0.068
9	0.088	0.082	0.077	0.072	0.067	0.063	0.059	0.055	0.052	0.048
10	0.067	0.062	0.058	0.054	0.050	0.046	0.043	0.040	0.037	0.035
11	0.051	0.047	0.043	0.040	0.037	0.034	0.031	0.029	0.027	0.025
12	0.039	0.036	0.033	0.030	0.027	0.025	0.023	0.021	0.019	0.018
13	0.030	0.027	0.025	0.022	0.020	0.018	0.017	0.015	0.014	0.013
14	0.023	0.021	0.018	0.017	0.015	0.014	0.012	0.011	0.010	0.009
15	0.017	0.016	0.014	0.012	0.011	0.010	0.009	0.008	0.007	0.006
16	0.013	0.012	0.010	0.009	0.008	0.007	0.006	0.006	0.005	0.005
17	0.010	0.009	0.008	0.007	0.006	0.005	0.005	0.004	0.004	0.003
18	0.008	0.007	0.006	0.005	0.005	0.004	0.003	0.003	0.003	0.002
19	0.006	0.005	0.004	0.004	0.003	0.003	0.003	0.002	0.002	0.002
20	0.005	0.004	0.003	0.003	0.002	0.002	0.002	0.002	0.001	0.001
21	0.003	0.003	0.003	0.002	0.002	0.002	0.001	0.001	0.001	0.001
22	0.003	0.002	0.002	0.002	0.001	0.001	0.001	0.001	0.001	0.001
23	0.002	0.002	0.001	0.001	0.001	0.001	0.001	0.001	0.001	0.000
24	0.002	0.001	0.001	0.001	0.001	0.001	0.001	0.000	0.000	0.000
25	0.001	0.001	0.001	0.001	0.001	0.000	0.000	0.000	0.000	0.000
30	0.000	0.000	0.000	0.000	0.000	0.000	0.000	0.000	0.000	0.000
40	0.000	0.000	0.000	0.000	0.000	0.000	0.000	0.000	0.000	0.000
50	0.000	0.000	0.000	0.000	0.000	0.000	0.000	0.000	0.000	0.000

APPENDIX D: SUM OF AN ANNUITY OF $1 FOR N PERIODS

n	1%	2%	3%	4%	5%	6%	7%	8%	9%	10%
1	1.000	1.000	1.000	1.000	1.000	1.000	1.000	1.000	1.000	1.000
2	2.010	2.020	2.030	2.040	2.050	2.060	2.070	2.080	2.090	2.100
3	3.030	3.060	3.091	3.122	3.153	3.184	3.215	3.246	3.278	3.310
4	4.060	4.122	4.184	4.246	4.310	4.375	4.440	4.506	4.573	4.641
5	5.101	5.204	5.309	5.416	5.526	5.637	5.751	5.867	5.985	6.105
6	6.152	6.308	6.468	6.633	6.802	6.975	7.153	7.336	7.523	7.716
7	7.214	7.434	7.662	7.898	8.142	8.394	8.654	8.923	9.200	9.487
8	8.286	8.583	8.892	9.214	9.549	9.897	10.260	10.637	11.028	11.436
9	9.369	9.755	10.159	10.583	11.027	11.491	11.978	12.488	13.021	13.579
10	10.462	10.950	11.464	12.006	12.578	13.181	13.816	14.487	15.193	15.937
11	11.567	12.169	12.808	13.486	14.207	14.972	15.784	16.645	17.560	18.531
12	12.683	13.412	14.192	15.026	15.917	16.870	17.888	18.977	20.141	21.384
13	13.809	14.680	15.618	16.627	17.713	18.882	20.141	21.495	22.953	24.523
14	14.947	15.974	17.086	18.292	19.599	21.015	22.550	24.215	26.019	27.975
15	16.097	17.293	18.599	20.024	21.579	23.276	25.129	27.152	29.361	31.772
16	17.258	18.639	20.157	21.825	23.657	25.673	27.888	30.324	33.003	35.950
17	18.430	20.012	21.762	23.698	25.840	28.213	30.840	33.750	36.974	40.545
18	19.615	21.412	23.414	25.645	28.132	30.906	33.999	37.450	41.301	45.599
19	20.811	22.841	25.117	27.671	30.539	33.760	37.379	41.446	46.018	51.159
20	22.019	24.297	26.870	29.778	33.066	36.786	40.995	45.762	51.160	57.275
21	23.239	25.783	28.676	31.969	35.719	39.993	44.865	50.423	56.765	64.002
22	24.472	27.299	30.537	34.248	38.505	43.392	49.006	55.457	62.873	71.403
23	25.716	28.845	32.453	36.618	41.430	46.996	53.436	60.893	69.532	79.543
24	26.973	30.422	34.426	39.083	44.502	50.816	58.177	66.765	76.790	88.497
25	28.243	32.030	36.459	41.646	47.727	54.865	63.249	73.106	84.701	98.347
30	34.785	40.568	47.575	56.085	66.439	79.058	94.461	113.283	136.308	164.494
40	48.886	60.402	75.401	95.026	120.800	154.762	199.635	259.057	337.882	442.593
50	64.463	84.579	112.797	152.667	209.348	290.336	406.529	573.770	815.084	1163.909

APPENDIX D: SUM OF AN ANNUITY OF $1 FOR N PERIODS (Continued)

n	11%	12%	13%	14%	15%	16%	17%	18%	19%	20%
1	1.000	1.000	1.000	1.000	1.000	1.000	1.000	1.000	1.000	1.000
2	2.110	2.120	2.130	2.140	2.150	2.160	2.170	2.180	2.190	2.200
3	3.342	3.374	3.407	3.440	3.473	3.506	3.539	3.572	3.606	3.640
4	4.710	4.779	4.850	4.921	4.993	5.066	5.141	5.215	5.291	5.368
5	6.228	6.353	6.480	6.610	6.742	6.877	7.014	7.154	7.297	7.442
6	7.913	8.115	8.323	8.536	8.754	8.977	9.207	9.442	9.683	9.930
7	9.783	10.089	10.405	10.730	11.067	11.414	11.772	12.142	12.523	12.916
8	11.859	12.300	12.757	13.233	13.727	14.240	14.773	15.327	15.902	16.499
9	14.164	14.776	15.416	16.085	16.786	17.519	18.285	19.086	19.923	20.799
10	16.722	17.549	18.420	19.337	20.304	21.321	22.393	23.521	24.709	25.959
11	19.561	20.655	21.814	23.045	24.349	25.733	27.200	28.755	30.404	32.150
12	22.713	24.133	25.650	27.271	29.002	30.850	32.824	34.931	37.180	39.581
13	26.212	28.029	29.985	32.089	34.352	36.786	39.404	42.219	45.244	48.497
14	30.095	32.393	34.883	37.581	40.505	43.672	47.103	50.818	54.841	59.196
15	34.405	37.280	40.417	43.842	47.580	51.660	56.110	60.965	66.261	72.035
16	39.190	42.753	46.672	50.980	55.717	60.925	66.649	72.939	79.850	87.442
17	44.501	48.884	53.739	59.118	65.075	71.673	78.979	87.068	96.022	105.931
18	50.396	55.750	61.725	68.394	75.836	84.141	93.406	103.740	115.266	128.117
19	56.939	63.440	70.749	78.969	88.212	98.603	110.285	123.414	138.166	154.740
20	64.203	72.052	80.947	91.025	102.444	115.380	130.033	146.628	165.418	186.688
21	72.265	81.699	92.470	104.768	118.810	134.841	153.139	174.021	197.847	225.026
22	81.214	92.503	105.491	120.436	137.632	157.415	180.172	206.345	236.438	271.031
23	91.148	104.603	120.205	138.297	159.276	183.601	211.801	244.487	282.362	326.237
24	102.174	118.155	136.831	158.659	184.168	213.978	248.808	289.494	337.010	392.484
25	114.413	133.334	155.620	181.871	212.793	249.214	292.105	342.603	402.042	471.981
30	199.021	241.333	293.199	356.787	434.745	530.312	647.439	790.948	966.712	1181.882
40	581.826	767.091	1013.704	1342.025	1779.090	2360.757	3134.522	4163.213	5529.829	7343.858
50	1668.771	2400.018	3459.507	4994.521	7217.716	10435.649	15089.502	21813.094	31515.336	45497.191

APPENDIX D: SUM OF AN ANNUITY OF $1 FOR N PERIODS (Continued)

n	21%	22%	23%	24%	25%	26%	27%	28%	29%	30%
1	1.000	1.000	1.000	1.000	1.000	1.000	1.000	1.000	1.000	1.000
2	2.210	2.220	2.230	2.240	2.250	2.260	2.270	2.280	2.290	2.300
3	3.674	3.708	3.743	3.778	3.813	3.848	3.883	3.918	3.954	3.990
4	5.446	5.524	5.604	5.684	5.766	5.848	5.931	6.016	6.101	6.187
5	7.589	7.740	7.893	8.048	8.207	8.368	8.533	8.700	8.870	9.043
6	10.183	10.442	10.708	10.980	11.259	11.544	11.837	12.136	12.442	12.756
7	13.321	13.740	14.171	14.615	15.073	15.546	16.032	16.534	17.051	17.583
8	17.119	17.762	18.430	19.123	19.842	20.588	21.361	22.163	22.995	23.858
9	21.714	22.670	23.669	24.712	25.802	26.940	28.129	29.369	30.664	32.015
10	27.274	28.657	30.113	31.643	33.253	34.945	36.723	38.593	40.556	42.619
11	34.001	35.962	38.039	40.238	42.566	45.031	47.639	50.398	53.318	56.405
12	42.142	44.874	47.788	50.895	54.208	57.739	61.501	65.510	69.780	74.327
13	51.991	55.746	59.779	64.110	68.760	73.751	79.107	84.853	91.016	97.625
14	63.909	69.010	74.528	80.496	86.949	93.926	101.465	109.612	118.411	127.913
15	78.330	85.192	92.669	100.815	109.687	119.347	129.861	141.303	153.750	167.286
16	95.780	104.935	114.983	126.011	138.109	151.377	165.924	181.868	199.337	218.472
17	116.894	129.020	142.430	157.253	173.636	191.735	211.723	233.791	258.145	285.014
18	142.441	158.405	176.188	195.994	218.045	242.585	269.888	300.252	334.007	371.518
19	173.354	194.254	217.712	244.033	273.556	306.658	343.758	385.323	431.870	483.973
20	210.758	237.989	268.785	303.601	342.945	387.389	437.573	494.213	558.112	630.165
21	256.018	291.347	331.606	377.465	429.681	489.110	556.717	633.593	720.964	820.215
22	310.781	356.443	408.875	469.056	538.101	617.278	708.031	811.999	931.044	1067.280
23	377.045	435.861	503.917	582.630	673.626	778.771	900.199	1040.358	1202.047	1388.464
24	457.225	532.750	620.817	723.461	843.033	982.251	1144.253	1332.659	1551.640	1806.003
25	554.242	650.955	764.605	898.092	1054.791	1238.636	1454.201	1706.803	2002.616	2348.803
30	1445.151	1767.081	2160.491	2640.916	3227.174	3942.026	4812.977	5873.231	7162.824	8729.985
40	9749.525	12936.535	17154.046	22728.803	30088.655	39792.982	52571.998	69377.460	91447.963	120392.883
50	65617.202	94525.279	135992.154	195372.644	280255.693	401374.471	573877.874	819103.077	1167041.323	1659760.743

APPENDIX D: SUM OF AN ANNUITY OF $1 FOR N PERIODS (Continued)

n	31%	32%	33%	34%	35%	36%	37%	38%	39%	40%
1	1.000	1.000	1.000	1.000	1.000	1.000	1.000	1.000	1.000	1.000
2	2.310	2.320	2.330	2.340	2.350	2.360	2.370	2.380	2.390	2.400
3	4.026	4.062	4.099	4.136	4.173	4.210	4.247	4.284	4.322	4.360
4	6.274	6.362	6.452	6.542	6.633	6.725	6.818	6.912	7.008	7.104
5	9.219	9.398	9.581	9.766	9.954	10.146	10.341	10.539	10.741	10.946
6	13.077	13.406	13.742	14.086	14.438	14.799	15.167	15.544	15.930	16.324
7	18.131	18.696	19.277	19.876	20.492	21.126	21.779	22.451	23.142	23.853
8	24.752	25.678	26.638	27.633	28.664	29.732	30.837	31.982	33.168	34.395
9	33.425	34.895	36.429	38.029	39.696	41.435	43.247	45.135	47.103	49.153
10	44.786	47.062	49.451	51.958	54.590	57.352	60.248	63.287	66.473	69.814
11	59.670	63.122	66.769	70.624	74.697	78.998	83.540	88.336	93.398	98.739
12	79.168	84.320	89.803	95.637	101.841	108.437	115.450	122.904	130.823	139.235
13	104.710	112.303	120.439	129.153	138.485	148.475	159.167	170.607	182.844	195.929
14	138.170	149.240	161.183	174.065	187.954	202.926	219.059	236.438	255.153	275.300
15	182.003	197.997	215.374	234.247	254.738	276.979	301.111	327.284	355.662	386.420
16	239.423	262.356	287.447	314.891	344.897	377.692	413.522	452.652	495.370	541.988
17	314.645	347.309	383.305	422.954	466.611	514.661	567.524	625.659	689.565	759.784
18	413.185	459.449	510.795	567.758	630.925	700.939	778.509	864.410	959.495	1064.697
19	542.272	607.472	680.358	761.796	852.748	954.277	1067.557	1193.886	1334.698	1491.576
20	711.376	802.863	905.876	1021.807	1152.210	1298.817	1463.553	1648.563	1856.230	2089.206
21	932.903	1060.779	1205.814	1370.221	1556.484	1767.391	2006.067	2276.016	2581.160	2925.889
22	1223.103	1401.229	1604.733	1837.096	2102.253	2404.651	2749.312	3141.902	3588.813	4097.245
23	1603.264	1850.622	2135.295	2462.709	2839.042	3271.326	3767.557	4336.825	4989.450	5737.142
24	2101.276	2443.821	2840.943	3301.030	3833.706	4450.003	5162.554	5985.819	6936.335	8032.999
25	2753.672	3226.844	3779.454	4424.380	5176.504	6053.004	7073.699	8261.430	9642.506	11247.199
30	10632.746	12940.859	15738.077	19124.859	23221.570	28172.276	34149.230	41358.175	50044.592	60501.081
40	158300.134	207874.272	272613.194	357033.889	466960.385	609890.482	795462.089	1036045.327	1347493.183	1750091.741
50	2356147.606	3338459.988	4721367.756	6664396.222	9389019.656	13202094.174	18527915.885	25951990.850	36280676.378	50622288.099

APPENDIX E: PRESENT VALUE OF AN ANNUITY OF $1 FOR N PERIODS

n	1%	2%	3%	4%	5%	6%	7%	8%	9%	10%
1	0.990	0.980	0.971	0.962	0.952	0.943	0.935	0.926	0.917	0.909
2	1.970	1.942	1.913	1.886	1.859	1.833	1.808	1.783	1.759	1.736
3	2.941	2.884	2.829	2.775	2.723	2.673	2.624	2.577	2.531	2.487
4	3.902	3.808	3.717	3.630	3.546	3.465	3.387	3.312	3.240	3.170
5	4.853	4.713	4.580	4.452	4.329	4.212	4.100	3.993	3.890	3.791
6	5.795	5.601	5.417	5.242	5.076	4.917	4.767	4.623	4.486	4.355
7	6.728	6.472	6.230	6.002	5.786	5.582	5.389	5.206	5.033	4.868
8	7.652	7.325	7.020	6.733	6.463	6.210	5.971	5.747	5.535	5.335
9	8.566	8.162	7.786	7.435	7.108	6.802	6.515	6.247	5.995	5.759
10	9.471	8.983	8.530	8.111	7.722	7.360	7.024	6.710	6.418	6.145
11	10.368	9.787	9.253	8.760	8.306	7.887	7.499	7.139	6.805	6.495
12	11.255	10.575	9.954	9.385	8.863	8.384	7.943	7.536	7.161	6.814
13	12.134	11.348	10.635	9.986	9.394	8.853	8.358	7.904	7.487	7.103
14	13.004	12.106	11.296	10.563	9.899	9.295	8.745	8.244	7.786	7.367
15	13.865	12.849	11.938	11.118	10.380	9.712	9.108	8.559	8.061	7.606
16	14.718	13.578	12.561	11.652	10.838	10.106	9.447	8.851	8.313	7.824
17	15.562	14.292	13.166	12.166	11.274	10.477	9.763	9.122	8.544	8.022
18	16.398	14.992	13.754	12.659	11.690	10.828	10.059	9.372	8.756	8.201
19	17.226	15.678	14.324	13.134	12.085	11.158	10.336	9.604	8.950	8.365
20	18.046	16.351	14.877	13.590	12.462	11.470	10.594	9.818	9.129	8.514
21	18.857	17.011	15.415	14.029	12.821	11.764	10.836	10.017	9.292	8.649
22	19.660	17.658	15.937	14.451	13.163	12.042	11.061	10.201	9.442	8.772
23	20.456	18.292	16.444	14.857	13.489	12.303	11.272	10.371	9.580	8.883
24	21.243	18.914	16.936	15.247	13.799	12.550	11.469	10.529	9.707	8.985
25	22.023	19.523	17.413	15.622	14.094	12.783	11.654	10.675	9.823	9.077
30	25.808	22.396	19.600	17.292	15.372	13.765	12.409	11.258	10.274	9.427
40	32.835	27.355	23.115	19.793	17.159	15.046	13.332	11.925	10.757	9.779
50	39.196	31.424	25.730	21.482	18.256	15.762	13.801	12.233	10.962	9.915

APPENDIX E: PRESENT VALUE OF AN ANNUITY OF $1 FOR N PERIODS (Cont.)

n	11%	12%	13%	14%	15%	16%	17%	18%	19%	20%
1	0.901	0.893	0.885	0.877	0.870	0.862	0.855	0.847	0.840	0.833
2	1.713	1.690	1.668	1.647	1.626	1.605	1.585	1.566	1.547	1.528
3	2.444	2.402	2.361	2.322	2.283	2.246	2.210	2.174	2.140	2.106
4	3.102	3.037	2.974	2.914	2.855	2.798	2.743	2.690	2.639	2.589
5	3.696	3.605	3.517	3.433	3.352	3.274	3.199	3.127	3.058	2.991
6	4.231	4.111	3.998	3.889	3.784	3.685	3.589	3.498	3.410	3.326
7	4.712	4.564	4.423	4.288	4.160	4.039	3.922	3.812	3.706	3.605
8	5.146	4.968	4.799	4.639	4.487	4.344	4.207	4.078	3.954	3.837
9	5.537	5.328	5.132	4.946	4.772	4.607	4.451	4.303	4.163	4.031
10	5.889	5.650	5.426	5.216	5.019	4.833	4.659	4.494	4.339	4.192
11	6.207	5.938	5.687	5.453	5.234	5.029	4.836	4.656	4.486	4.327
12	6.492	6.194	5.918	5.660	5.421	5.197	4.988	4.793	4.611	4.439
13	6.750	6.424	6.122	5.842	5.583	5.342	5.118	4.910	4.715	4.533
14	6.982	6.628	6.302	6.002	5.724	5.468	5.229	5.008	4.802	4.611
15	7.191	6.811	6.462	6.142	5.847	5.575	5.324	5.092	4.876	4.675
16	7.379	6.974	6.604	6.265	5.954	5.668	5.405	5.162	4.938	4.730
17	7.549	7.120	6.729	6.373	6.047	5.749	5.475	5.222	4.990	4.775
18	7.702	7.250	6.840	6.467	6.128	5.818	5.534	5.273	5.033	4.812
19	7.839	7.366	6.938	6.550	6.198	5.877	5.584	5.316	5.070	4.843
20	7.963	7.469	7.025	6.623	6.259	5.929	5.628	5.353	5.101	4.870
21	8.075	7.562	7.102	6.687	6.312	5.973	5.665	5.384	5.127	4.891
22	8.176	7.645	7.170	6.743	6.359	6.011	5.696	5.410	5.149	4.909
23	8.266	7.718	7.230	6.792	6.399	6.044	5.723	5.432	5.167	4.925
24	8.348	7.784	7.283	6.835	6.434	6.073	5.746	5.451	5.182	4.937
25	8.422	7.843	7.330	6.873	6.464	6.097	5.766	5.467	5.195	4.948
30	8.694	8.055	7.496	7.003	6.566	6.177	5.829	5.517	5.235	4.979
40	8.951	8.244	7.634	7.105	6.642	6.233	5.871	5.548	5.258	4.997
50	9.042	8.304	7.675	7.133	6.661	6.246	5.880	5.554	5.262	4.999

APPENDIX E: PRESENT VALUE OF AN ANNUITY OF $1 FOR N PERIODS (Cont.)

n	21%	22%	23%	24%	25%	26%	27%	28%	29%	30%
1	0.826	0.820	0.813	0.806	0.800	0.794	0.787	0.781	0.775	0.769
2	1.509	1.492	1.474	1.457	1.440	1.424	1.407	1.392	1.376	1.361
3	2.074	2.042	2.011	1.981	1.952	1.923	1.896	1.868	1.842	1.816
4	2.540	2.494	2.448	2.404	2.362	2.320	2.280	2.241	2.203	2.166
5	2.926	2.864	2.803	2.745	2.689	2.635	2.583	2.532	2.483	2.436
6	3.245	3.167	3.092	3.020	2.951	2.885	2.821	2.759	2.700	2.643
7	3.508	3.416	3.327	3.242	3.161	3.083	3.009	2.937	2.868	2.802
8	3.726	3.619	3.518	3.421	3.329	3.241	3.156	3.076	2.999	2.925
9	3.905	3.786	3.673	3.566	3.463	3.366	3.273	3.184	3.100	3.019
10	4.054	3.923	3.799	3.682	3.571	3.465	3.364	3.269	3.178	3.092
11	4.177	4.035	3.902	3.776	3.656	3.543	3.437	3.335	3.239	3.147
12	4.278	4.127	3.985	3.851	3.725	3.606	3.493	3.387	3.286	3.190
13	4.362	4.203	4.053	3.912	3.780	3.656	3.538	3.427	3.322	3.223
14	4.432	4.265	4.108	3.962	3.824	3.695	3.573	3.459	3.351	3.249
15	4.489	4.315	4.153	4.001	3.859	3.726	3.601	3.483	3.373	3.268
16	4.536	4.357	4.189	4.033	3.887	3.751	3.623	3.503	3.390	3.283
17	4.576	4.391	4.219	4.059	3.910	3.771	3.640	3.518	3.403	3.295
18	4.608	4.419	4.243	4.080	3.928	3.786	3.654	3.529	3.413	3.304
19	4.635	4.442	4.263	4.097	3.942	3.799	3.664	3.539	3.421	3.311
20	4.657	4.460	4.279	4.110	3.954	3.808	3.673	3.546	3.427	3.316
21	4.675	4.476	4.292	4.121	3.963	3.816	3.679	3.551	3.432	3.320
22	4.690	4.488	4.302	4.130	3.970	3.822	3.684	3.556	3.436	3.323
23	4.703	4.499	4.311	4.137	3.976	3.827	3.689	3.559	3.438	3.325
24	4.713	4.507	4.318	4.143	3.981	3.831	3.692	3.562	3.441	3.327
25	4.721	4.514	4.323	4.147	3.985	3.834	3.694	3.564	3.442	3.329
30	4.746	4.534	4.339	4.160	3.995	3.842	3.701	3.569	3.447	3.332
40	4.760	4.544	4.347	4.166	3.999	3.846	3.703	3.571	3.448	3.333
50	4.762	4.545	4.348	4.167	4.000	3.846	3.704	3.571	3.448	3.333

APPENDIX E: PRESENT VALUE OF AN ANNUITY OF $1 FOR N PERIODS (Cont.)

n	31%	32%	33%	34%	35%	36%	37%	38%	39%	40%
1	0.763	0.758	0.752	0.746	0.741	0.735	0.730	0.725	0.719	0.714
2	1.346	1.331	1.317	1.303	1.289	1.276	1.263	1.250	1.237	1.224
3	1.791	1.766	1.742	1.719	1.696	1.673	1.652	1.630	1.609	1.589
4	2.130	2.096	2.062	2.029	1.997	1.966	1.935	1.906	1.877	1.849
5	2.390	2.345	2.302	2.260	2.220	2.181	2.143	2.106	2.070	2.035
6	2.588	2.534	2.483	2.433	2.385	2.339	2.294	2.251	2.209	2.168
7	2.739	2.677	2.619	2.562	2.508	2.455	2.404	2.355	2.308	2.263
8	2.854	2.786	2.721	2.658	2.598	2.540	2.485	2.432	2.380	2.331
9	2.942	2.868	2.798	2.730	2.665	2.603	2.544	2.487	2.432	2.379
10	3.009	2.930	2.855	2.784	2.715	2.649	2.587	2.527	2.469	2.414
11	3.060	2.978	2.899	2.824	2.752	2.683	2.618	2.555	2.496	2.438
12	3.100	3.013	2.931	2.853	2.779	2.708	2.641	2.576	2.515	2.456
13	3.129	3.040	2.956	2.876	2.799	2.727	2.658	2.592	2.529	2.469
14	3.152	3.061	2.974	2.892	2.814	2.740	2.670	2.603	2.539	2.478
15	3.170	3.076	2.988	2.905	2.825	2.750	2.679	2.611	2.546	2.484
16	3.183	3.088	2.999	2.914	2.834	2.757	2.685	2.616	2.551	2.489
17	3.193	3.097	3.007	2.921	2.840	2.763	2.690	2.621	2.555	2.492
18	3.201	3.104	3.012	2.926	2.844	2.767	2.693	2.624	2.557	2.494
19	3.207	3.109	3.017	2.930	2.848	2.770	2.696	2.626	2.559	2.496
20	3.211	3.113	3.020	2.933	2.850	2.772	2.698	2.627	2.561	2.497
21	3.215	3.116	3.023	2.935	2.852	2.773	2.699	2.629	2.562	2.498
22	3.217	3.118	3.025	2.936	2.853	2.775	2.700	2.629	2.562	2.498
23	3.219	3.120	3.026	2.938	2.854	2.775	2.701	2.630	2.563	2.499
24	3.221	3.121	3.027	2.939	2.855	2.776	2.701	2.630	2.563	2.499
25	3.222	3.122	3.028	2.939	2.856	2.777	2.702	2.631	2.563	2.499
30	3.225	3.124	3.030	2.941	2.857	2.778	2.702	2.631	2.564	2.500
40	3.226	3.125	3.030	2.941	2.857	2.778	2.703	2.632	2.564	2.500
50	3.226	3.125	3.030	2.941	2.857	2.778	2.703	2.632	2.564	2.500